Indian Mounds of Wisconsin

Indian Mounds of Wisconsin

Robert A. Birmingham
and
Leslie E. Eisenberg

The University of Wisconsin Press

The University of Wisconsin Press
1930 Monroe Street
Madison, Wisconsin 53711

3 Henrietta Street
London WC2E 8LU, England

8   7   6

Printed in the United States of America

Library of Congress Cataloging-in-Publication Data
Birmingham, Robert A.
Indian mounds of Wisconsin / Robert A. Birmingham
and Leslie E. Eisenberg.
262 pp.   cm.
Includes bibliographical references and index.
ISBN 0-299-16870-0 (cloth)
ISBN 0-299-16874-3 (pbk.)
1. Mounds—Wisconsin.
2. Indians of North America—Wisconsin—Antiquities.
3. Earthworks (Archaeology)—Wisconsin.
4. Wisconsin—Antiquities.
I. Eisenberg, Leslie E.   II. Title.
E78.W8 B57   2000
977.5'01—dc21   00-008925

Contents

ILLUSTRATIONS   vii
TABLES   xi
PREFACE   xiii

1 The Mystery of the Mounds   3

2 Speculation, Excavation, Explanation: In Search
   of the Mound Builders   13

3 Wisconsin before the Mound Builders:
   The Paleo-Indian and Archaic Traditions   69

4 Early Burial Mound Builders: The Early and Middle
   Woodland Stages   82

5 Effigy Mound Builders: The Late Woodland Stage   100

6 Temple Mound Builders: The Mississippian Tradition   142

7 Mound Construction and Use in Later Times:
   Oneota, Northern Wisconsin, and the Historic Period   163

8 Indian Mounds in the Modern World   180

APPENDIX: Selected Mound Sites Open to the Public   193
NOTES   209
BIBLIOGRAPHY   227
INDEX   240

Illustrations

General distribution of mounds in Wisconsin 2
1.1 Indian mounds as part of the Wisconsin landscape 4
1.2 Increase A. Lapham, map of bird effigy and linear mounds 7
2.1 Ephraim G. Squire and Edgar H. Davis, map of earthworks
near Chillicothe, Ohio 19
2.2 Richard C. Taylor, map of effigy mounds near the
Blue Mounds 22
2.3 Increase A. Lapham 24
2.4 William Pidgeon, map of bizarre mound patterns 26
2.5 Theodore H. Lewis 28
2.6 Theodore H. Lewis, map of effigy mounds in
Richland County 29
2.7 Opening Indian mounds as a weekend activity 34
2.8 Double panther or water spirit effigy mound 40
2.9 Charles E. Brown, P. M. Gilmore, and William Ellery
Leonard at the Fox Bluff Mound Group 43
2.10 William C. McKern at the Schwert Mound 48
2.11 First mound near Madison cataloged as a burial site 63
2.12 Aerial photograph of soil shadow of a bird effigy mound 65
3.1 Paleo-Indians 70
3.2 Paleo-Indian spear points 71
3.3 Trade of chert for copper tools 72
3.4 Old Copper Complex weapons and tools 76
3.5 Native American scaffold "burial" 78
3.6 Red Ocher Complex ceremonial blades 80
4.1 Poverty Point site 83
4.2 Early and Middle Woodland mounds in Wisconsin 87

4.3	Early Woodland pot	89
4.4	Middle Woodland mound at the Outlet site	93
4.5	Plan and profile of the Nicholls Mound	94
4.6	Middle Woodland pot	97
4.7	Increase A. Lapham, map of enclosure in Milwaukee	98
5.1	Late Woodland pottery	105
5.2	Upperworld and lowerworld symbolism on Late Woodland pottery	106
5.3	Horned water spirit on Late Woodland pipe	108
5.4	Effigy mound region of Wisconsin and adjacent states	111
5.5	Aerial photograph of bird effigy mounds on grounds of Mendota State Hospital	112
5.6	Common effigy mound forms	114
5.7	Distribution of effigy mound forms	117
5.8	Human and bird-man effigy mounds	120
5.9	Lizard Mounds Group	123
5.10	Increase A. Lapham, map of mound group with intaglios	126
5.11	Woodward Shores Mound Group	130
5.12	Tollackson Mound Group	131
5.13	Theodore H. Lewis, map of effigy mound group with enclosures	135
5.14	Clam Lake Mound	137
5.15	Profile of the Clam Lake Mound	139
5.16	Pottery from Clam Lake Mound	140
6.1	Cahokia	144
6.2	Mississippian elite	146
6.3	Mississippian-related sites in Wisconsin	148
6.4	Gottschall Rockshelter paintings	149
6.5	Platform mounds at Trempealeau	151
6.6	Plan of the Diamond Bluff site	153
6.7	Increase A. Lapham, map of Aztalan	154
6.8	Modern conception of Aztalan	156
6.9	Southwestern platform mound at Aztalan	157
6.10	Conical mounds overlooking Aztalan	158
7.1	Oneota village in Wisconsin	166
7.2	Oneota population centers in Wisconsin	168
7.3	Oneota pottery	170
7.4	Increase A. Lapham, map of "turtle" effigy mound	176
7.5	Native American land cessions to United States	178

Illustrations

7.6	Ho-Chunk in the Wisconsin Dells	179
8.1	Panther or water spirit mound in Forest Hill Cemetery	182
8.2	Harry Whitehorse, *Let the Great Spirits Soar*	187
8.3	L. Brower Hatcher, artwork with effigy mound forms	188

Tables

2.1 Wisconsin archaeological chronology   55
5.1 Effigy mound forms in selected counties   115

Preface

This book was stimulated by growing public interest in Indian mounds. For more than a decade, rarely has a day passed when we at the State Historical Society did not respond to requests for background material on mound building and mound research in Wisconsin. Unfortunately, we found that there was no single source on these important and interesting topics to which we could refer the public. Consequently, a book was envisioned that would provide answers to many of the public's basic questions, while offering interesting and thought-provoking interpretations based on new evidence.

We would like to thank for their comments the two readers who reviewed the manuscript of *Indian Mounds of Wisconsin* for the University of Wisconsin Press. Appropriately, one of the reviewers is a member of the Ho-Chunk (Winnebago) Nation. We would also like to thank William Green, Iowa State Archaeologist, and Diane Holliday, Deputy Wisconsin State Archaeologist, for their thoughtful comments. Editor Irene Pavitt had the formidable task of readying the manuscript for publication. She corrected many errors and made many good suggestions. Most comments from all readers and reviewers were addressed in the book, but, naturally, we assume all responsibility for errors, omissions, or misinterpretations.

Original graphics and artwork for the book were created by Dick Dolan and Amelia Janes of Midwest Educational Graphics. In addition, we would like to thank the many organizations and institutions that granted permission to reproduce photographs and illustrations. We would also like to express our gratitude to Historic Madison, Inc., for permission to use the material entitled "Preservation: Charles E. Brown and the Wisconsin Archeological Society" (in chap. 2) from Robert Birmingham, "Charles E. Brown and the Mounds of Madison," *Historic Madison: A Journal of the Four Lake*

Region 13 (1996): 17–29; and to the Wisconsin Academy of Sciences, Arts and Letters for permission to use material scattered throughout chapters 5 and 6 on Late Woodland and the Mississippians and Aztalan from Robert Birmingham, "The Last Millennium: Wisconsin's First Farmers," *Wisconsin Academy Review* 46, no. 1 (winter 1999–2000): 4–8.

Amy Rosebrough and George Christiansen III, graduate students at the University of Wisconsin–Madison, compiled much information about the distribution of effigy mounds while working for the Office of the State Archaeologist and, since then, have provided many insights about the mounds and the ancient societies that constructed them.

Finally, we would like to thank all our many friends and colleagues in Wisconsin and elsewhere who, through the years, have formally or informally shared with us their thoughts, opinions, and research on the subject of mounds and related topics. We are especially indebted to James Stoltman, Anna Funmaker, David Benn, Robert Salzer, Robert Hall, David Overstreet, Lynne Goldstein, and those who work as regional archaeologists, Janet Speth, Robert Boszhardt, Robert Jeske, Thomas Willems, Jeff Behm, and Cindi Stiles. Likewise, we are appreciative of the perspectives and feelings expressed by Native American communities in Wisconsin, especially the intertribal Repatriation Committee, concerning mounds and mound research. A special thanks to Mary Braun who suggested this book.

A word should be said here about some conventions of terminology. There is much reference in this book to the Ho-Chunk, or Winnebago, people. Descendants of the original nation, which is indigenous to Wisconsin, who still live in Wisconsin are officially called the Ho-Chunk Nation. They use a shortened form of Ho-Chunk-gara, their name for themselves. Winnebago is a name that was used historically for the Ho-Chunk-gara by other Native Americans. It was adopted by Euro-Americans and is common in the literature. Descendants of the Ho-Chunk-gara living in Nebraska officially retain the name Winnebago and are a part of the Winnebago Tribe of Nebraska. To avoid confusion, we refer to all these people as Ho-Chunk, with the name Winnebago in parentheses at the start of each section, except when one or the other name is a part of a reference and quote.

In the same vein, we generally use the term "Native American" instead of "Indian" to refer to the indigenous people of North America. This is the wish of most of the people involved, although we realize that the word "Indian" is retained in many of the formal tribal names. One exception is the title of this book because the term "Indian mounds" is in common usage and is the most recognizable way to refer to the earthworks that are the topic of the book.

Preface

This book is dedicated to the memory of Charles E. Brown (1872–1946), director of the museum of the State Historical Society of Wisconsin, who, along with the Wisconsin Archeological Society, led the first efforts in Wisconsin to save the Indian mounds that are such a distinctive and haunting feature of the state.

Indian Mounds of Wisconsin

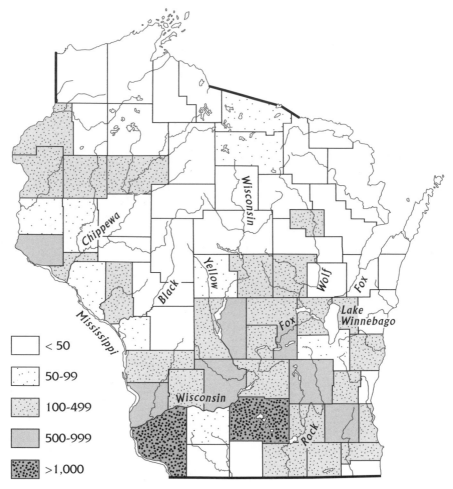

The general distribution of mounds and other earthworks in Wisconsin. (Map by Amelia Janes, Midwest Educational Graphics)

1

The Mystery of the Mounds

Indian mounds are a part of the Wisconsin landscape. When the first European and American explorers and settlers arrived in what would become the state of Wisconsin, between 15,000 and 20,000 of these earthworks could be found clustered along lakes, beside rivers, and on hilltops, often arranged in complex patterns that harmoniously, even artfully, blended with the natural topography. More Indian mounds were built in the territory now called Wisconsin than in any other equivalent area of land in midwestern North America. These ancient tumuli occurred almost everywhere in the state—more than 3,000 locations in all. They were especially abundant in the southern region, where they actually presented a major obstacle to nineteenth-century farmers as they struggled to clear land to plant crops. Since that time, most mounds in this area have disappeared under the plow.

Indian mounds are still a common sight despite their destruction over the past 150 years by agricultural practices, urban expansion, and looting (figure 1.1). Dozens of counties, towns, and villages have an "Indian Mound Park" or a similarly named green space. In Madison, for example, those living near the shores of the several lakes that surround the city are a short distance from at least one of the twenty-three mound locations preserved on public lands. Around the state, prominent mound clusters or groups can be viewed by visitors to High Cliff, Governor Nelson, Wyalusing, Nelson Dewey, Perrot, Aztalan, and many other state parks. Many more of these ancient earthworks survive in urban backyards, fields, and undeveloped woodlots in private hands. The records of the State Historical Society of Wisconsin indicate that as many as 4,000 mounds remain.

Figure 1.1. Indian mounds and other earthworks are still a part of the Wisconsin landscape, even though many, such as this group of large conical mounds near the Fox River being plowed in 1923, have been destroyed. (State Historical Society of Wisconsin, neg. no. WHi [X3] 51039)

They are protected by the Burial Sites Preservation Law, special state legislation passed in 1985 that prohibits any disturbance to the mounds and other burial sites without special permission.

Even so, with many mounds now gone, it is difficult to appreciate the wonder that they evoked in early travelers and settlers. In 1817, Stephen H. Long, army engineer and explorer, provided one of the earliest reactions (and an interesting interpretation) after visiting mound groups on the bluffs around Prairie du Chien:

[W]e had the occasion to be high[l]y gratified with a survey of curiosities that have baffled the ingenuity & penetration of the wisest to account for them. The curiosities alluded to are the remains of ancient works constructed probably for military purposes, which we found more numerous & extensive above the mouth of the Ouisconsin than any of which a description has been made public that have yet been discovered in the Western Country. They consist of ridges or parapets of earth and mounds variously disposed so as to conform to the nature of the ground they are intended to fortify. . . . At what period they were constructed and by what race of people, must in all probability remain a desideratum.[1]

Observers were particularly impressed by spectacular groupings of low effigy mounds, so-called because they appear to be in the shape of birds, other animals, human beings, or figures that are not easily decipherable. Such monumental concentrations of "emblematic mounds" are not found elsewhere in the world. Furthermore, the mounds did not appear to early observers to be the work of the indigenous peoples. These strange and often huge earthen sculptures easily conjured up images of mysterious gods that were worshiped during the course of long-forgotten rites and rituals.

In 1838, Richard C. Taylor drew public attention to the effigy mounds in Wisconsin with his maps and descriptions of the strange earthworks at Muscoda on the Wisconsin River, near small mountains called the Blue Mounds, along the shores of the Four Lakes (now the Madison area), and in other places. Familiar with the earthworks that settlers had discovered elsewhere in the Ohio and Mississippi River valleys, as well as with the great "barrows" of England and Europe, he nonetheless wrote of his astonishment to find these "singularly formed Indian Mounds," which in some areas formed a "species of *alto relievo*, of gigantic proportions."[2]

When he wrote the first book on the geography of Wisconsin, Increase Lapham found it necessary to refer to a class of earthworks "not found in any other country" that dominated much of the landscape.[3] Lapham, a land surveyor, became interested in Indian mounds as he laid out streets along the bluffs and rivers of the new community of Milwaukee in 1836. With support from the American Antiquarian Society, Lapham pursued his interest by researching and writing *The Antiquities of Wisconsin, as Surveyed and Described,* which was published by the Smithsonian Institution in 1855. This landmark book was the first attempt to systematically document the visible remnants of ancient civilizations in the state, particularly the sites of earthworks. Surprisingly, even with long popular interest in Indian mounds, it remains one of the few books ever published on the topic of the Indian mounds in Wisconsin intended for the general reader.

Lapham covered a variety of earthworks, all of which are referred to as "Indian mounds" in this book. In the mid-nineteenth century, when Lapham was writing his books, the identity of the builders of the North American mounds was so hotly debated that he only speculated about the origin of the earthworks. It is now known that the mounds in Wisconsin were constructed by various Native American societies in the relatively recent prehistoric past, from about 800 B.C. to A.D. 1200, although some evidence suggests that mounds continued to be built occasionally along the rivers and lakes of northern Wisconsin into the historic period.

Those acquainted with Indian mounds are most familiar with round and oval mounds, which are also known as conical mounds. This class was the earliest mound form to be made by Native Americans. Conical mounds almost always contain human burials, and thus early researchers frequently referred to them as "sepulcher mounds." The first such mounds appeared as early as 5,000 years ago in the southeastern United States, in areas now known as Arkansas, Louisiana, and Florida. Much later, people living in woodlands and parklands of the Midwest adopted the practice of building mounds. Whether the symbolic meaning of the mounds of the Midwest remained the same as that of the mounds of the Southeast is a matter of debate. At some locations in northern Wisconsin, single conical mounds grew in size as additional mass burials were periodically added over the years. A few of these mounds have attained diameters as large as sixty feet and heights of twenty feet. More commonly, mounds of this type were constructed in groups. Among the largest and most atypical of these distributions is along the swampy Cranberry Creek in a remote wildness of Juneau County, where more than 300 mounds have been counted. At the Diamond Bluff site in Pierce County, also known as the Mero Complex, 390 small conical mounds partially enclose a pair of 1,000-year-old villages.

The second class of earthwork, and the one most commonly associated with Wisconsin, is the effigy mound. The construction of effigy mounds appears to have coincided with an unsettled time of ideological and economic change, tribal movements, and warfare. The effigy mound people carefully designed at least 800 groups of effigy mounds in a broad band in the southern and west-central part of Wisconsin. The range of the so-called effigy mound culture spilled slightly into adjacent parts of Illinois, Iowa, and Minnesota. Wisconsin, however, is clearly the heartland for this activity. There is considerable evidence that the effigy mound people built their earthworks at the same locations where large conical mounds had been constructed hundreds of years earlier—a strong indication that the sacred character of a place continued to be recognized and shared over a long period of time, perhaps even by people from different cultural backgrounds.

Effigy mound groups frequently incorporated low conical burial mounds and curious long, narrow embankments, or "linear" mounds, commonly regarded as an obscure type of effigy (figure 1.2). Many of the effigy mound groups are arranged in complex and obviously nonrandom patterns that have stimulated some interesting interpretations over the years, including speculation that they functioned as devices to predict celestial events. Some effigy mound forms are spectacular, such as the great human-shaped mounds concentrated in the rugged southwestern part of the state and the long-tailed "panther" mounds found throughout the state, but especially in the east. Many effigies were and are gigantic, including the 700-foot-long linear mounds that once radiated from what is now downtown Monona and the

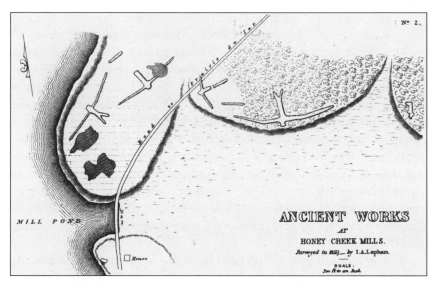

Figure 1.2. Huge effigy mounds and other earthworks, such as the bird and linear mounds depicted in this early map, awed early settlers and researchers. (From Increase A. Lapham, *The Antiquities of Wisconsin, as Surveyed and Described* [Washington, D.C.: Smithsonian Institution, 1855])

enormous bird with the arrow-straight 624-foot wingspan that still "flies" south across the grounds of Mendota State Hospital. The largest effigy mound possibly ever built in Wisconsin was discovered by mound researcher James Scherz near Muscoda in the early 1990s. A short distance from the Wisconsin River, ancient Native Americans built a phenomenal bird effigy with what appears to be a quarter-mile wingspan. Farming has obliterated the earthwork, but its soil shadow is still visible in aerial photographs.

Many believe that effigy mound groups are monumental expressions of an ancient belief system and that they functioned as ceremonial centers periodically used for social, religious, political, and economic activities. Most effigy mounds contain human burials, but some do not. They are among the most interesting and puzzling of the Indian mounds in Wisconsin.

Enclosures, the third class of earthwork commonly found in Wisconsin, consist of low, narrow ridges that form circles, squares, and rectangles. These earthworks sometimes occur alone and sometimes as part of conical or effigy mound groups, where they appear to have defined a sacred space. Although much smaller, Wisconsin enclosures are similar to the spectacular Hopewell enclosures and associated earthworks in the Ohio River valley. They also seem to have been constructed several hundred years later than those in the Ohio valley.

Finally, very large flat-topped "temple" mounds once served as platforms for special ceremonial structures. These truncated earthen pyramids are most at home far to the south of the present borders of Wisconsin, where they are associated with the spectacular Mississippian culture, which arose after A.D. 1000. More is known about these huge earthworks than about the other kinds of mounds both because extensive archaeological excavations have been undertaken at Mississippian sites, such as the ancient city of Cahokia in southern Illinois, and because Native American lords and their families still ruled from the tops of such structures in, for example, present-day Arkansas and Georgia when Spanish conquistadors first explored these areas in the sixteenth century. The presence of these unique mounds at a few special locations in Wisconsin, such as the famous village site of Aztalan in Jefferson County, provides clues to the movements of ancient people and ideas.

Indian mounds have always been shrouded in mystery: Who were the mound builders? When did they build the mounds and for what purposes? What do the effigies represent? What is the relationship of the mound builders to the modern Native American tribes? Lapham and his contemporaries asked these questions, and the search for the answers preoccupied subsequent generations of scholars and dilettantes. Several hundred articles and a half-dozen scholarly books have been written on the subject of the Indian mounds in Wisconsin. Several graduate-school theses and dissertations have examined aspects of mound construction, distribution, and history. Yet many questions remain unanswered. In regard to the effigy mounds, one prominent scholar testily concluded, "Thus, regarding the purpose of construction and which tribe or tribes built the mounds we are no further along than Lapham was in 1855."[4]

Such mystery inspires mythology and folklore. The earliest myth to emerge attributed the origin of the many earthworks in North America to a fantastic "Lost Race" that was inexplicably replaced by modern Native American tribes in the distant past. For many, the "Ten Lost Tribes of Israel" or unrecorded colonizers from one or another Old World civilization made up this mysterious people. This explanation gained a popular following during the early years of the American republic, before the beginning of efforts to learn about indigenous history, culture, and traditions being swept aside by the flood of white settlement. This great "Mound Builder Myth" dominated the debate about Indian mounds throughout much of the nineteenth century, until the maturing fields of archaeology and ethnology put it to rest by demonstrating that the mound builders were none other than the ancestors of modern Native Americans.

Some opinions are not easily dispelled, however. Variations of the myth of the Lost Race linger on and have a found a place in an era during which mysticism, revisionism, mistrust of traditional science, and even blatant ethnocentrism appear to be on the increase. Several Wisconsin-based periodicals have begun publishing alternative histories of pre-Columbian North America that attribute mound-building influences to a variety of Old World cultures as diverse as the Vikings, the Britons, the Hindus, and various Asians, as well as to knowledge obtained from Old World "secret lodges," such as the Freemasons.[5] The dubious premise of this "diffusionist" literature is that Native Americans in what is now the United States did not live in relative isolation until the time of the historically documented European incursions, but were frequently and routinely visited by people from the world over for thousands of years. These and other provocative notions have been especially embraced by mystically inclined New Age groups that have appropriated mounds, much as similar groups have "kidnapped" the pyramids of Egypt, the dolmens of the Celtic Druids, and Stonehenge.

Indeed, both the ubiquity of mounds in Wisconsin and the unanswered questions about them have guaranteed them a niche in popular Wisconsin folklore and legend. Large conical mounds are commonly explained as the mass graves of warriors killed in epic battles. And seemingly everyone has heard, at one time or another, that mounds mark the tombs of esteemed chiefs. In the city of McFarland, there is a story about a prominent local effigy mound group that supposedly contains a "horse" mound.[6] In such mounds, the story goes, local chiefs were buried "strapped to a live horse" so that the "spirit of the horse would carry the chief into another life." Nothing like that, of course, has ever been discovered, but the story is representative of the type of folklore that has been generated by modern people about Indian mounds.

The goal of this book is to clear up some of the mystery concerning the Indian mounds in Wisconsin. We attempt to do this not simply because of a scholarly motivation to correct misrepresentations, but because public interest in Indian mounds is at an all-time high. This phenomenon is generally traced to a broader interest in Native American culture and history that has grown dramatically in the United States over the past decade or so, reflected in the steadily increasing number of books, films, television programs, school courses, and artistic themes that focus on Native American culture. In Wisconsin, the Indian mound is the most visible legacy of a Native American past. Madison, which mound researcher Charles E. Brown called "mound city," so closely identifies with this legacy that images of effigy mounds are now incorporated into the floor of the new exposition center and into outdoor public art.

Public interest in the Indian mounds in Wisconsin can also be specifically traced to state legislation passed in 1985, the Burial Sites Preservation Law, that defines mounds as human burial places and thereby protects them from disturbance and destruction. The passage of this law immediately led to a number of highly publicized controversies as developers attempted to build on or around existing mound groups. By the same token, the publicity surrounding the effort to protect Indian mounds also focused attention on many private landowners who have been conscientious stewards of mounds on their property, providing them with a renewed sense of pride.

For contemporary Native Americans, mounds are physical links to the ancestors and the land, and they are an important symbol of cultural continuity and persistence in the face of change and competing cultural values. Indeed, the social functions of mounds in these regards may not have changed over time. Many Wisconsin tribes have become fiercely protective of remaining mounds found throughout the state.

The approach in this book is anthropological, interpreting the mysterious mounds from the viewpoints of the various societies that created them. In essence, it provides the social or cultural context from which customs, such as mound building, become understandable. For this perspective, it is necessary to trace the evolution of Native American societies in Wisconsin and to reconstruct their social, political, religious, and economic worlds. We are especially interested in the "worldview" and belief systems of these ancient people because mound construction, as it is now understood, has more to do with the symbolic relationships of people with the spirit worlds than with the practical need to dispose of the dead.

This task is not easy. An ancient belief system cannot be "dug up" and described; this is one reason that explanations for ancient mound building are elusive. Furthermore, archaeologists do not have ancient Native American texts, such as the Aztec codices, to instruct them in the mound builders' own words. Instead, they must deduce and infer aspects of belief systems both from physical "clues" left behind by the ancients and from the beliefs, traditions, and practices of their descendants.

To accomplish this goal, we assemble a vast body of information collected in the past about Wisconsin Native Americans and mounds by archaeologists, ethnohistorians, ethnologists, and physical anthropologists. To this we add some new insights, often controversial, derived from recent discoveries, new interpretations, and fresh perspectives. Some of the information is from recently discovered settlements of the effigy mound people that offer the first comprehensive picture of the social and economic life of these previously unknown people.

Where possible, we include the rich oral traditions of, coupled with opinions expressed by, the descendants of the mound builders—modern Native Americans. Although this perspective is still often conspicuously absent in considerations of Native American history, it was not always overlooked. For example, when confronted with questions about effigy mounds during the first decades of the twentieth century, Charles E. Brown and his colleagues went directly to the Ho-Chunk (Winnebago), whom they considered to be the direct descendants of the mound builders. These researchers collected invaluable information from various knowledgeable individuals on mounds and other aspects of Native American culture and history. But later scholars dismissed or ignored some of this material. Nevertheless, even the names for effigy mounds that are commonly used today were obtained from the Ho-Chunk at that time.

For a modern anthropological consideration of mounds and Native American belief systems, we draw heavily on the fine work of Robert Hall, who has long argued for the necessity of using Native American cognitive frameworks, along with physical evidence, to interpret North American prehistory. We are inspired by his warning that if American archaeology is to achieve its goal of understanding the past, it must go beyond interpretations based solely on economics and technology and recognize the magical and religious dimensions that underlie all human society: "Archaeology seeks to explain the inner workings of cultures in which even baked clay pots were animated with particular spirits. But, until as archaeologists we develop more than a little empathy for the prehistoric Indians we presume to understand, prehistory may never be more than what it has become, the soulless artifact of a dehumanized science."[7]

Some further comments on the use of Native American traditions and oral history are in order. First, much of the information of this type has been published and consists of material originally collected by non-Indians who undoubtedly, although unconsciously perhaps, infused the accounts with their own bias. Therefore, we interpret and use this information with a critical eye. Second, we know from first-hand experience that additional information and insight lies in the considerable traditional knowledge of tribal elders. They and other "traditional" people, however, are understandably reluctant to share this intimate knowledge. "You have already taken too much from us" is the sentiment that we have heard voiced. Consequently, we have made no effort to acquire additional stories and traditions to include in this book. A book about mounds from a purely Native American perspective and based solely on Native American knowledge and tradition is waiting to be written. We hope our effort here will serve as a catalyst.

Despite all that archaeologists, anthropologists, and ethnologists have learned about the mounds of the Midwest in the past 150 years, since Increase Lapham made the first systematic study of the earthworks of Wisconsin, the mounds continue to be a mystery because perceptions and interpretations about them continually change—molded and limited by the social and scientific climates of the times.

2

Speculation, Excavation, Explanation

In Search of the Mound Builders

Who built the mounds? This is the question still most frequently asked about Indian mounds. Today, the question most often concerns the identity of the specific Native American people among the Ho-Chunk (Winnebago), Menominee, Potawatomi, Chippewa, and other modern tribes that live or lived in the Wisconsin mound district. As ludicrous as it may now seem, when Euro-American settlers asked the question in the eighteenth and nineteenth centuries, most did not believe that Native Americans were responsible.

WHO BUILT THE MOUNDS?

Immigrants to the New World found mounds and other mysterious earthworks just about everywhere they went in the eastern part of North America. In the South, they encountered abandoned communities in which were large flat-topped pyramids of earth reminiscent of the massive stone structures described as having been built by the Aztecs of Mexico. In the Ohio River valley, they were astounded to come across colossal earthen embankments, ramparts, and ditches in complex geometric forms as well as groups of conical mounds. Throughout the upper Mississippi River drainage in the Midwest, the new people discovered other earthen mounds, including those sculpted into the shapes of giant birds and other animals.

But most Americans had never actually witnessed the natives build

13

mounds and, as a reflection of the prejudice of the day, seriously doubted that such "savages," in the midst of being displaced, starved, and killed, could organize the labor to achieve the purpose. Consequently, the colonial residents of the eastern seaboard and later settlers of midwestern lands hotly debated the origin of the mounds and elaborate earthen structures. They filled newspapers, books, magazines, and scholarly journals of the day with their theories, fueling the imagination of an American public hungry for information about their new home. On one side of the debate was a small cadre of scholars and scientifically inclined individuals—including politician-philosopher Albert Gallatin, founder of the American Ethnological Society of New York, and Wisconsin's own Increase A. Lapham—who made the seemingly logical connection between the native inhabitants of North America and the ancient earthen structures. On the other, much larger, side were those people, many of them also well educated, who argued that the mounds were the products of a mysterious and distinctly non-Indian (that is, civilized) "race" that had disappeared before both Native Americans and Euro-Americans came to occupy the North American continent. During the nineteenth century, interest in the question of the identity of the mysterious mound builders became so great that it precipitated investigations and publications by a new government agency, the Smithsonian Institution, and stimulated the growth of North American archaeology into a discrete and scientifically based field of inquiry.

THE MYTH OF THE "LOST RACE"

Why was a "Lost Race" evoked to account for the mounds, and why was such wild speculation so universally accepted? The answers to these questions lie not only in the obvious lack of specific information concerning Native American cultural history, but in the worldview of Europeans and their American descendants that limited all observations and interpretations to rigidly held religious and Eurocentric beliefs. Historian Robert Silverberg, in *Mound Builders of Ancient America,* and archaeologists Gordon R. Willey and Jeremy A. Sabloff, in *A History of American Archaeology,* cite a number of specific factors that contributed to the development of the myth of a Lost Race as the builders of the mounds. [1]

The Myth before the Nineteenth Century

Before the mid-nineteenth century, there was an absence of not only reliable information about the cultural history of the New World, but also a scientific framework in which to collect and evaluate such information. Much of what was known was derived from the accounts of explorers who had been less interested in the history and culture of the natives they had encountered than in gold, God, and glory and from the musings of "armchair explorers" who wrote books based on second-hand information and literary fantasy. Scientific reasoning, with its emphasis on the accumulation and analysis of objective and empirical data, had not yet fully emerged. Even basic concepts, such as that of an ancient and ever-changing natural world, would have to await the acceptance of the geology of Sir Charles Lyell and the biology of Charles Darwin. Knowledge about the world and its history was not as much formed and tested by accumulated data as it was molded by Christian religious views. Conflicts that arose between observations and dogma were settled or rationalized in the context of church teachings and the Bible. Until the construction of a scientific and empirical foundation in the later part of the nineteen century, "theological explanations remained the accepted means of reconstructing events of the past."[2]

For a long time during the period of New World exploration, Europeans had trouble fitting their discoveries, especially the existence of other peoples, into this religiously based worldview. For example, it took a papal edict, or bull, in 1537 to settle the issue of whether the inhabitants of the New World were even human.[3] Having officially established the humanity of Native Americans, the question then necessarily turned to the origin of this exotic people. Since, for Christian Europe, all humans were descended from Adam and Eve through Noah and his family, the Native American genealogy should be traceable through biblical writings. From this premise, one popular eighteenth- and nineteenth-century explanation for the existence of Native Americans was that they were none other than the descendants of the Ten Lost Tribes of Israel, a concept adhered to by the Mormon church, founded during the height of the debate about the Lost Race.

Intellectuals of the day applied reason to the problem. The eighteenth century was the time of the Enlightenment, a philosophical movement characterized by the belief in the power of human reason that facilitated enormous innovations in social, political, and even religious thought. Thomas Jefferson and many of his well-educated colonial contemporaries were men of this age who applied their prodigious intellectual skills to the questions about the origins of North American Indians and the identity of the builders of the mysterious earthworks found throughout the eastern United States. As a young man, Jefferson even opened a burial mound and made the kind of meticulous observations that would not characterize archaeological investigations for another century. For this reason, some consider Jefferson the first American archaeologist. In true scientific fashion, he cautiously concluded that more data were needed to determine the origin of the mounds.[4]

A second factor that contributed to the speculation about a Lost Race was the need of the emerging American nation to create a heroic and romantic past for itself, but one that could accommodate and justify the elimination of native people. It is hardly a coincidence that at the height of the popularity of the Lost Race explanation in the nineteenth century, Native Americans were being displaced and exterminated by the westward advance of American society. By denying these people an elaborate and colorful history, it was easier to perceive them as interloping savages, undeserving of the land they occupied. The acceptance of Native Americans as the builders of the sometimes huge and wonderful earthworks would also make them an architectural people, a hallmark of civilization that Euro-Americans reserved for themselves.[5] Silverberg goes so far as to state that "the controversy over the origin of the mounds was not merely an abstract scholarly debate, but had its roots in the great nineteenth century campaign of extermination waged against the American Indian."[6]

This "campaign of extermination" obviously precluded the collection of information about mounds and other cultural customs and beliefs from Native Americans themselves. In large parts of the colonized East, there was nobody left to ask. There were some exceptions, but they did not settle matters. In 1819, for example, John Heckewelder, a Moravian missionary to a group of converted and transplanted Delaware, or Leni-Lenape, living in Ohio in the late eighteenth century, published an account of Leni-Lenape beliefs and traditions that gave one explanation for the existence of the monumental Ohio earthworks.[7] Heckewelder recounted a story of warfare between the Leni-Lenape and the Ohio mound builders, who, according to the account, were called the Tallegewi or Alligewi and were described as having been remarkably large in physical stature. Despite the construction of the fabulous earthen fortifications, the Tallegewi lost the war. They subsequently buried their dead warriors in earthen mounds and fled southward. This story was used far into the nineteenth century to bolster arguments by both sides in the mound builder debate. Those who believed that mounds had been built by Indians identified the Cherokee as the Alligewi, based on traditions collected from the Cherokee that they had once lived along the Ohio River. However, believers in a different race of mound builders, including the Reverend Stephen Peet, a Wisconsin antiquarian and mound researcher, pointed to the large size of the Tallegewi as evidence that the builders of the Ohio earthworks and other mounds had been a people different from the "Red Indians."[8]

A third factor contributing to the popularity of the myth of the Lost

Race was the prevailing view that indigenous culture was simple and static: if Native Americans did not now construct earthworks, there is no reason to suppose they ever did. Significantly, eyewitness accounts of mound-building Native American cultures in the South, dating to the early years of New World exploration, were either not known or conveniently ignored. A Spanish *entrada* in the sixteenth century dutifully chronicled a mound-building civilization even as it destroyed it. In 1539, the lost and miserable expedition led by Hernando de Soto rampaged through what is now the southeastern United States, encountering a variety of people now known as the Natchez, Creek, and Choctaw who built and lived on large earthen platform mounds.[9] Some years later, French explorers and colonists in the same area further described and even illustrated burial-mound-building ceremonies.[10]

These accounts describe a complex agricultural civilization referred to as the Mississippian, which maintained an elaborate social system of chiefs and commoners, buried their rulers in earthen mounds, and used huge earthen platform structures as bases for chiefly residences and civic and ceremonial buildings. By the time of major white settlement in the late eighteenth and the nineteenth centuries, however, the various Mississippian nations had been decimated by disease and warfare and the mound centers had been abandoned. This process had started even before de Soto's time: he described looting a town depopulated by disease.[11] In the early nineteenth century, the remnants of these populations were forced into western regions as part of the federal policy to remove Native Americans from lands needed for settlement. The nature of their elaborate culture, including their architecture, was conveniently forgotten.

The Myth in the Nineteenth Century

Candidates for the mound builders were diverse and imaginative. Among them were such Old World peoples as the Phoenicians, Hebrews, Greeks, Romans, Persians, Hindus, Vikings, Welsh, and Danes, or such colorful Mesoamerican civilizations as the Aztecs. Wherever there could be found a reference to heaping up dirt to make earthworks, there was also a group that, through migration, could have been the Lost Race mound builders of North America. Mythical civilizations, such as that of Atlantis, were also evoked. But what had happened to these wondrous people? According to Silverberg, "The answer was obvious: they had been exterminated at some past date by the despicable, treacherous, ignorant red-skinned savages who even now were causing so much trouble for the Christian settlers of the New World."[12]

The public interest in earthworks and these provocative explanations for their origin led to the proliferation of detailed surveys and crude excavations by a generation of "antiquarians"—self-trained archaeologists whose interest in antiquities went beyond the mere collection of ancient objects d'art. Among them were land surveyors, natural scientists, newspapermen, ministers, doctors, and other learned and curious people who especially took an interest in the spectacular earthworks district of the Ohio River valley. As accounts of these explorations were published throughout the nineteenth century, there steadily accumulated a body of empirical knowledge about mounds and Native American antiquities in general, even if the conclusions that accompanied the reports were fanciful and erroneous. Caleb Atwater, an Ohio postmaster, was one such antiquarian. He produced some of the earliest drawings and maps of the huge Ohio valley earthworks in 1820.[13] Like others, Atwater was nevertheless constrained in his interpretations by prevailing prejudices and stereotypes, so his conclusions did not follow from his observations. He thought it most likely that Hindus of India had been responsible for the construction of the earthworks of Ohio.

Another watershed study, the first real archaeology book published in the United States, derived from the work of Ephraim G. Squier, a newspaperman, and Edgar H. Davis, a physician, both of Chillicothe, Ohio. Chillicothe lies in the heart of the Ohio earthwork country and offered easy access for the men to study these monuments. Supported by Albert Gallatin's newly organized American Ethnological Society, Squire and Davis made detailed maps of earthworks and mounds (figure 2.1), excavated some, and brought together the work of other researchers, including the initial reports on the effigy mound district in what is now Wisconsin. Lacking the finances to publish the voluminous work, the American Ethnological Society turned to the Smithsonian Institution. The Smithsonian had been established in 1846 with a large amount of money willed to the United States by James Smithson, an Englishman, for the purpose of creating an institution that would increase and diffuse knowledge. The first publication of the Smithsonian became Squire and Davis's *Ancient Monuments of the Mississippi Valley.*[14]

This book contributed to the mound builder debate in two ways. First, it anticipated modern scientific methodology by both classifying the earthworks, albeit crudely (for example, Works of Defense, Mounds of Sacrifice, Mounds of Sepulcher), and forming testable hypotheses about the uses and purposes of the mounds.[15] Second, it engaged the Smithsonian, and thus the United States government, in the debate. Even though Squire and Davis quite clearly sought to be objective in their investigations, they could not intellectually extricate themselves from the power of the myth of the Lost

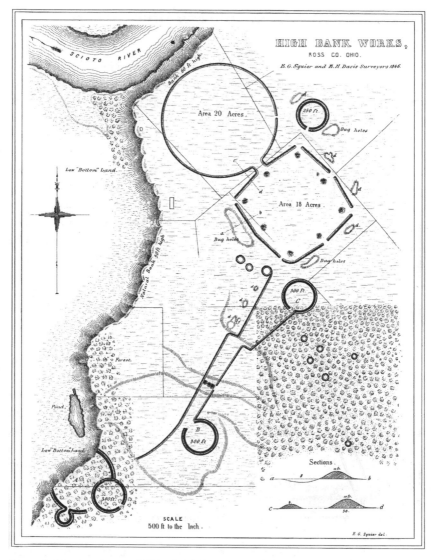

Figure 2.1 Earthworks near Chillicothe, Ohio. (From Ephraim G. Squire and Edgar H. Davis, *Ancient Monuments of the Mississippi Valley* [Washington, D.C.: Smithsonian Institution, 1848])

Race and the negative stereotypes of Indians. They concluded that the native peoples of North America had been incapable of building the elaborate earthworks and speculated instead that mound builders from Mexico were the likely architects. But the Smithsonian continued to press the matter throughout the nineteenth century and in the last decade of that century finally settled the debate.

Wisconsin and the Myth of the Mound Builders

The Lost Race idea in its many versions had become the most popular explanation for the existence of mounds in North America just as the mounds in Wisconsin were brought to public attention in the late 1830s, during the first great wave of white settlement in the territory. The influx of settlers was made possible by the removal of much of the native population.

Until this time, the southernmost part of Wisconsin's mound district was occupied largely by the Ho-Chunk (Winnebago) and Potawatomi. The Ho-Chunk are a Siouan-speaking tribe, indigenous to Wisconsin, that in the nineteenth century maintained villages throughout southern Wisconsin from Lake Winnebago to the Mississippi River. The Algonquian-speaking Potawatomi, a tribe related to the more northerly Chippewa, apparently had migrated to Wisconsin from Michigan in the seventeenth century and, in the early nineteenth century, lived in villages throughout eastern Wisconsin.

Before the 1830s, the white population was comparatively small. Several fur-trading communities had developed at such places as Green Bay, La Pointe, and Prairie du Chien. In the 1820s, lead miners had begun to trickle into the southwestern part of the territory, establishing a number of small mining communities, often causing friction with the resident Native Americans. Following the infamous Black Hawk War of 1832 and other frontier conflicts, there began a popular call for the removal of the troublesome Native American population from Wisconsin's agriculturally rich southern region. Through treaties and coercion, most of the Ho-Chunk and Potawatomi eventually moved to reservations in the "Indian Country" of Nebraska and Kansas. Two other Wisconsin residents, the Menominee and Chippewa, lived in less desirable areas and retained reservations in the state by treaties with the United States.

By the 1840s, the white population had grown to more than 30,000 people.[16] Small groups of refugee Ho-Chunk and Potawatomi continued to live on the fringes of white settlements, shifting residence as the frontier expanded.[17] These were people who defiantly refused to go to the western reservations or quietly walked back to Wisconsin from them. The existence of these "stray bands" and "lost tribes" was not formally recognized by the federal government until much later.

The first public reports of mounds in Wisconsin were made by settlers, surveyors partitioning lands for settlement, naturalists assessing the resources of the newly opened land, and various travelers who happened to notice, or deliberately went to see, the odd mounds situated along the Indian trails and waterways. In 1836, Increase A. Lapham, a young surveyor and engineer originally from Ohio, wrote to a Milwaukee newspaper about a large, long-tailed, "lizard"-shaped mound that he had encountered near Waukesha.[18] At about the same time, Judge Nathaniel Hyer published in several newspapers notes on and a map of the ruins of an ancient town with huge flat-topped mounds along the Crawfish River in what is now Jefferson County.[19] As a reflection of the beliefs of the day, Hyer suggested that the town was of Aztec origin and called it Aztalan, a name still used for Wisconsin's premier archaeological site.

Richard C. Taylor first drew national attention to the now famous effigy mounds of Wisconsin. Traveling "in the society of some scientific friends," he examined effigy mounds in present-day Iowa and Dane Counties and obtained information from elsewhere in the territory. In 1838, he published an article containing his observations (figure 2.2). Taylor, like many others who would follow him in Wisconsin, advanced a variation of the Lost Race idea that narrowed the argument: he accepted the notion that Native Americans had constructed the mounds, but argued that these ancient mound builders could not be related to the modern tribes of the region, based on both the familiar premise that these people were intellectually inferior to the ancient mound builders and his conviction that they, whom he called "degenerate" and "slothful," had only recently come to occupy the mound territory in what had been a long succession of tribal displacements in historic times: "But to a far different race, assuredly, and to a far distant period, must we look when seeking to trace the authors of these singular mounds, and the earthworks of such various forms, which are spread over the North American continent, from Lake Superior to Mexico. But who were they who left almost imperishable memorials on the soil, attesting to the superiority of their race?"[20]

Based on their beliefs, he and others also continued to reject the possibility that local Native Americans could have any knowledge about or insight on the mounds, although many observers did report that various tribes, including those "disaffected" people, occasionally excavated new graves into previously existing mounds. The belief that Native Americans had no traditions that involved the mounds and the continuing stereotype of Native Americans as "savages" would continue to block potentially fruitful cross-cultural dialogues on this and other matters for a very long time.

At the same time, Taylor provided an insight that drew a powerful link between the social structure of contemporaneous Indians and the effigy mounds. Although he claimed no "positive evidence," he noted a correspondence between the different mound shapes, birds and animals, and the

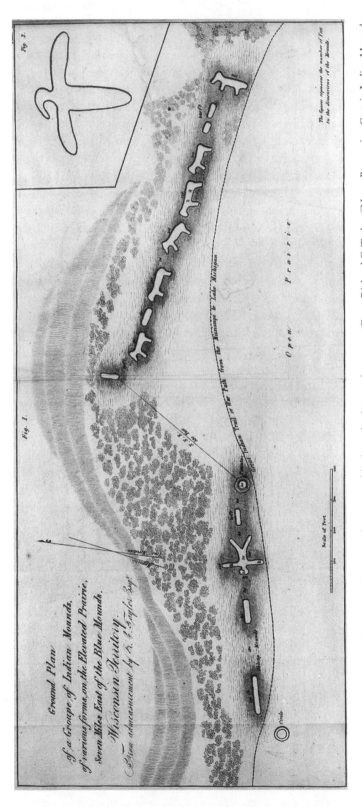

Figure 2.2. Group of effigy mounds near the Blue Mounds as mapped in the early nineteenth century. (From Richard C. Taylor, "Notes Respecting Certain Indian Mounds and Earthworks in the Form of Animal Effigies," *American Journal of Science and Art* 34 [1838])

totems or clans described for many Native American tribes in some published ethnological accounts. Might not these shapes represent the "respec-
tive tribes or branches" of the people found buried in the mounds?[21]

In rapid succession, other travelers described and mapped mounds and
offered their theories about their origin. But it was Increase Lapham, later
to become Wisconsin's preeminent natural scientist, who was the first to
comprehend and document the truly phenomenal nature of the Wisconsin
mound district (figure 2.3). Intrigued by the mounds he had encountered in
Milwaukee and sponsored by the American Antiquarian Society, he spent
several years mapping and examining mound groups and other ancient
places, such as Aztalan, throughout the southern part of the state. The
Smithsonian Institution published the results of Lapham's research in 1855,
seven years after Wisconsin became a state.[22] The book, *The Antiquities of
Wisconsin, as Surveyed and Described,* is still a remarkable source of detailed
maps of mounds that have long since disappeared and an important historical document of nineteenth-century mound research.

Lapham saw links between the mound builders and the modern Native Americans in the types of artifacts recovered from the mounds, such as
pipes and pottery. In general, his research convinced him that the "mound
builders of Wisconsin were none other than the ancestors of the present
tribes of Indians."[23] He considered any other theories to be "far fetched." But
Lapham also did not believe that the modern indigenous peoples of the region, whom he considered "little advanced in civilization," were mound
builders, although he left open that possibility. As to what had happened to
the Native American mound builders of the past, Lapham was not certain.
Perhaps they had been driven off or had migrated to another area and were
living in some remote western region. Or perhaps they had simply been
overrun by a stronger tribe with different customs. Lapham, however, anticipated the development of later theories of cultural evolution by pointing
out that while dramatic changes in customs and institutions have occurred
throughout history among the many cultures in the world, these changes
were not necessarily accompanied by the replacement of indigenous people
with others:

The inhabitants of Egypt have ceased to build pyramids and sphinxes; the Greeks
have ceased to erect temples: and yet, we have reason to believe that their descendants occupy the same country. Is it more strange that the ancestors of the present
Indians should have erected mounds of earth, that the aboriginals of any country
should have had habits different from their posterity? We need not, therefore[,] look
to Mexico, or any other country, for the descendants of the mound-builders. We
probably see them in the present red race of the same or adjacent regions.[24]

23

Figure 2.3. Increase A. Lapham, natural scientist and antiquarian, wrote the first book on the mounds in Wisconsin: *The Antiquities of Wisconsin, as Surveyed and Described*. He served as the president of the State Historical Society of Wisconsin from 1862 to 1871. (State Historical Society of Wisconsin, neg. no. WHi [X3] 17916)

One of the most interesting and bizarre contributions to the Lost Race debate involving Wisconsin mounds was a fabulously popular book written by William Pidgeon: *Traditions of De-coo-dah and Antiquarian Researches*, subtitled, after the fashion of the day, *Comprising Extensive Explorations, Surveys, and Excavations of the Wonderful and Mysterious Earthen Remains of the*

Mound-Builders in America; the Traditions of the Last Prophet of the Elk Nation Relative to Their Origin and Use; and the Evidences of an Ancient Population More Numerous Than the Present Aborigines.[25] The book is fantasy on an epic scale, but Pidgeon was a compelling writer and used a device known to modern writers of pseudoscientific literature: he wove just enough fact into his fiction to appear credible. The first part of the book is a collection of concocted evidence that purports to demonstrate pre-Columbian visits by just about all the usual Lost Race suspects, including Egyptians, Greeks, Romans, and Persians. Even Alexander the Great makes an appearance in the form of an alleged stone with his name on it found in Brazil. The greatest appeal is in the second part of the book, where Pidgeon claimed to provide a perspective that had been missing in most other discussions of mounds: the history and traditions of the mound builders *as told by themselves.*

Pidgeon acquired an interest in Native American monuments in his native Virginia. He claimed to have traveled to South America to examine mounds there. In 1829, he became a trader in Ohio, where he visited the spectacular tumuli and earthworks of that region. In the late 1830s, he went to the upper Mississippi River valley, where, among other places, he visited Muscoda on the Wisconsin River. At Muscoda, he found "relics of many an ancient mound, varying much in size and form; some representing redoubts, or fortifications, others presenting forms of gigantic men, beasts, birds, and reptiles, among which may be the eagle, the otter, the serpent, the alligator, and others pertaining to the deer, elk, and buffalo species."[26] At least some of the mounds that Pidgeon observed there were probably part of a spectacular cluster of mound groups located in Eagle Township on the northern side of the Wisconsin River that was documented by later researchers.

Pidgeon ended up at Prairie du Chien on the Mississippi River. There he engaged in some mound digging and made the acquaintance of local Native American people who shared their language with him. According to his account, he had the extraordinary good fortune to be introduced to an old man named De-coo-dah, who was the very last member of the "Elk Nation," the ancient people who had built the mounds. As luck would also have it, De-coo-dah just happened to be descended from the very same family entrusted with the sacred traditions of the nation. The old man became Pidgeon's teacher, and for several years they lived together on an island in the Mississippi River where De-coo-dah revealed the secrets of the mounds and their builders.

From this rambling and frequently incoherent narrative, we learn that the Elk Nation, the mound builders, were descended from an indeterminate, non-Indian race who had intermarried with the Native Americans and

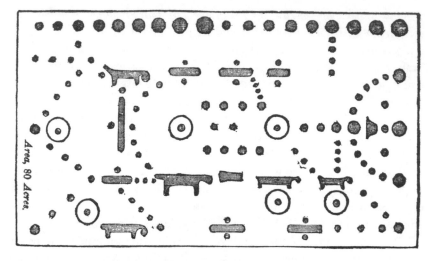

Figure 2.4. Bizarre mound patterns reportedly found in Wisconsin. (From William Pidgeon, *Traditions of De-coo-dah and Antiquarian Researches* [New York: Thayer, Bridgman, and Fanning, 1853])

then vanished before the appearance of Columbus. In giving us a history of the Elk Nation, Pidgeon crafted an epic story of ancient kingdoms, great wars and alliances, assassinations, and internal conflicts that reduce the great civilization to small bands that no longer built earthen monuments. On the last page of his book, Pidgeon brought in a flood of biblical proportions to hasten their extinction.

We also learn that effigy mounds, recorded in hieroglyph form, document this dramatic history. According to Pidgeon, in the guise of De-coo-dah, some mounds were built during national festivals of the Elk Nation, while others commemorate important events, such as the union, extinction, or migration of affiliated tribes. There were matrimonial mounds, sacrificial mounds, and mounds that told the story of dynasties and battles. Accompanying the fanciful narrative are equally fanciful illustrations of mound groups in oddly geometric patterns (figure 2.4).

In a harsh critique, Silverberg characterized *Traditions of De-coo-dah* as a "crazy masterpiece of pseudoscience," the epitome of the grand era of humbug typified by Pidgeon's contemporary P. T. Barnum.[27] The Smithsonian Institution had come to the same conclusion and refused to publish Pidgeon's manuscript after he offered it. But as a commercial publication, the book became a big hit with the public and eventually gained some respectability even among a few uncritical scholars. A later mound surveyor, Theodore H. Lewis, a fellow believer in a Lost Race, located some of the mounds that Pidgeon had discussed and illustrated, and talked to some of the people who had known Pidgeon. It may not come as a surprise to learn that he found little resemblance between Pidgeon's descriptions and reality: "The result of my research in this respect is to convince me that the Elk Nation and its last prophet De-coo-dah are modern myths, which have never had any objective existence."[28]

Mound researchers of a more serious vein continued to publish maps and discuss theories about the origin of the Wisconsin mounds throughout the later part of the nineteenth century. Stephen Peet, a minister from the Beloit area, contributed to the effort by starting, in 1878, the *American Antiquarian,* a journal "designed to be a medium of correspondence between Archaeologists, Ethnologists and other scientific gentlemen." In it, he published a number of studies of the mounds penned by people with antiquarian interests. A collection of these articles later appeared in *Prehistoric America,* a two-volume work by Peet.[29] Peet published maps and descriptions of a number of mound groups he had personally observed throughout the state, but unlike Lapham and some of the other researchers, he was not a trained surveyor and seems to have had little patience for details. Consequently, his maps are quite imaginative.

Of far greater value today are the maps of thousands of mounds made by Theodore H. Lewis, a Minnesota land surveyor of remarkable skill and ability who worked in Wisconsin and adjacent areas of the upper Mississippi River drainage, from Canada to Missouri, during the years 1881 to 1894 (figure 2.5).[30] Lewis's project, the Northwestern Archaeological Survey, was organized and financed by Alfred J. Hill, a wealthy St. Paul businessman who shared with Lewis an intense interest in the ancient earthworks. That both men were also believers in a Lost Race did not prevent the production of some of the most accurate surveys of mound groups ever made in the midwestern United States. So meticulous are they that some are being used as base maps to reconstruct, on paper, complex mound arrangements that once existed in several parts of the state.

The Northwestern Archaeological Survey was interrupted by Hill's death, but not before 13,000 mounds in eighteen states and one Canadian province had been recorded and meticulously mapped. Among them were more than 900 effigy mounds, most in Wisconsin (figure 2.6). During the course of the project, Lewis is said to have covered 54,000 miles—10,000 on foot.[31] In Wisconsin, Lewis worked chiefly along the Mississippi River and in the southwestern part of the state. The results of the survey were never published, but the many volumes of maps and notebooks generated by Lewis were diligently archived at the Minnesota Historical Society. Some of this information was used to help reconstruct the prehistory of Min-

Figure 2.5. Theodore H. Lewis made detailed maps of hundreds of mound groups in the upper Midwest in the late nineteenth century, many of which have been destroyed. (Photograph courtesy of the Goodhue County Historical Society, Red Wing, Minnesota)

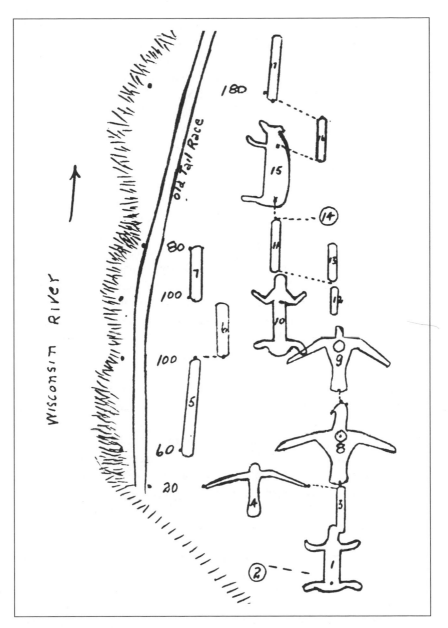

Figure 2.6. This example of a map drawn by Theodore Lewis in 1886 shows an effigy mound group on the Wisconsin River in Richland County. (From Theodore H. Lewis, field notebook 25, Northwestern Archaeological Survey, Notebooks and Related Documents, Minnesota Historical Society, St. Paul; used with permission of the Minnesota Historical Society)

nesota, but the excellent material on Wisconsin was inexplicably ignored by most researchers until quite recently. Today, the records are considered to be one of the best resources for maps and descriptions of mounds in Wisconsin, especially those that have been destroyed since Lewis's visits, and are routinely consulted by the state's Burial Sites Preservation Program, the Office of the State Archaeologist, and a variety of researchers, including members of Wisconsin's Native American communities.

MOUNDS AND THE DEVELOPMENT OF AMERICAN ARCHAEOLOGY

Research in the Nineteenth Century

During the late nineteenth century, research on the histories and cultures of Native American tribes became increasingly well organized on a national level. This was influenced in great part by a general trend begun in Europe toward a scientific formulation of human history brought about by discoveries of fossils of prehistoric humans, the publication of Charles Darwin's *On the Origin of Species by Means of Natural Selection,* and the emergence of the science of geology, all of which challenged prevailing theological dogma.

In the United States, attitudes toward Native Americans also began to shift. The perception that Indians were simple savages, stimulated by the concept of Manifest Destiny, was being gradually replaced in some scholarly quarters with the view that Native American cultures were sufficiently rich to deserve thorough documentation before they vanished. In 1878, John Wesley Powell, a Civil War hero and western explorer, wrote a report to the Department of the Interior claiming that it was ignorance of Native American culture that was responsible for the "inconceivable mismanagement in our management of the Indians" and for the "blunders we have made and the wrongs we have inflicted upon the Indians." He further wrote:

The field of research is speedily narrowing because of the rapid change in the American population now in progress: all habits, customs, and opinions are fading away; even languages are disappearing; and in a very few years it will be impossible to study our North American Indians in their primitive condition, except from recorded history. For this reason ethnologic studies in America should be pushed with the utmost vigor.[32]

Powell, like similar well-intended voices of the time, sounds condescending to Native Americans in his appraisal of the situation. His concern seems as much for the impending loss of the objects of study as for the plight of the people themselves. This attitude continued to characterize some

American anthropological research well into the twentieth century—understandably creating resentment from Native American communities. But this attitude helps explain a great nineteenth-century American paradox: at the height of the bitter fighting between the federal government and the western tribes, Congress appropriated money for the systematic study of the very cultures the government was systematically destroying. In 1879, it created the Bureau of Ethnology within the Smithsonian Institution, to be headed by Powell. Whatever the motivations for its creation, the results of the ethnographic work of the bureau, published as annual reports, are still used and cited widely by those engaged in Native American cultural research. Furthermore, the formation of the Bureau of Ethnology provided a number of critics (largely ignored at the time) of government efforts to force surviving Native Americans into the mainstream American culture. Finally, the bureau also gave encouragement and employment to a generation of formally trained anthropologists who at long last went to the Native Americans themselves to inquire about their beliefs and traditions about the mounds.

As the controversy about the identity of the mound builders continued to escalate, Congress appropriated money in 1881 for the creation of the Division of Mound Exploration within the Bureau of Ethnology. Cyrus Thomas, an entomologist and botanist from Illinois, was selected to head the division. His primary directive was finally to answer the question: Who built the mounds? For the next ten years, division personnel systematically examined mounds and collected information from throughout the North American mound district to answer the question. Archaeologists today look at the project as the prototype for modern archaeological research: clearly stated research questions, a research program designed to collect data to answer the questions, an analysis of the data, and the preparation of summary report.[33] Thomas's huge concluding work, simply called *Report on the Mound Explorations of the Bureau of Ethnology,* marks the formal birth of American archaeology.[34]

While the identity of the mound builders was the primary focus of the research, Thomas also sought to collect detailed information about the mounds and their construction. To accomplish this large task, he developed a two-tiered sampling strategy. On one level, he attempted to determine the geographic distribution of mounds throughout the eastern United States by defining eight archaeological districts that contained mounds: Appalachian, Arkansas, Central or Tennessee, Dakotan, Gulf, Huron-Iroquois, Illinois, and Ohio. Wisconsin was subsumed in the Dakotan District. On the second level, he examined examples of the different mound types or classes found within the districts.

Most of the Smithsonian's work in Wisconsin took place in counties adjacent to the Mississippi River, such as Grant, Crawford, and Vernon, although mounds in Dane, Barron, and Sheboygan Counties were also examined. Maps of selected mound groups were made, and measurements of individual mounds were taken. Dozens of the mounds in Wisconsin were opened and their contents and structural evidence described and illustrated. Along the Mississippi River, Thomas excavated and studied large, round "burial mounds" as well as groups of effigies. In some of the conical mounds, he found numerous burials, often represented as bundles of disarticulated bones in the mounds themselves or beneath the mounds in a central pit. Occasionally, burials were encased in stone vaults. Associated with the burials in a number of these mounds were copper ornaments, spears, knife blades made from obsidian from the western United States, and perforated bear-tooth pendants—distinctive items that one day would culturally link the ancient mound builders of the upper Mississippi River valley to the Hopewell builders of the spectacular Ohio earthworks.

While working in Grant County, Thomas's assistants took time to look into the problem of the alleged elephant-shaped mound, which had become embroiled in a side controversy that concerned the authenticity of artifacts reportedly recovered from some mounds and other sites near Davenport, Iowa. The artifacts were slate tablets elaborately inscribed with the characters of an unknown language and several stone effigy pipes carved in the form of elephants. All had been found by the same man. Taken at face value, these objects would support the case for Old World contacts in North America. A Smithsonian map of the mound, which had been continually plowed, simply shows an animal with a large head, and the surveyors concluded that previous reports of a long trunk probably had been based on a shifting line of sand. The general shape of the mound is well within the variation of forms common to the Mississippi River bluff area called bear effigies. Furthermore, Thomas concluded that the tablets and pipes found near Davenport were badly conceived hoaxes, a view supported by modern research.[35]

For Thomas and the Bureau of Ethnology, there was no question about the real identity of the mound builders. Beginning as a believer in a Lost Race, Thomas was won over to the other side by several lines of evidence, all of which he presented in a lengthy conclusion to his book. This information included historical accounts of Native American mound building, especially in the South, and Native American oral traditions of mound building, although they are from second- and third-hand sources. Drawing on evidence from his extensive excavations, Thomas offered a series of proofs derived from the similarity of types of burials found in many mounds to observed burial customs of contemporary Native Americans. He also made the link between the mound-building people and more recent tribes by reporting the discovery, in some mounds, of objects introduced to Indians by Europeans after the time of Columbus.

Thomas's research and excavations were not precise by any means, and his report is far from perfect. Moreover, in his enthusiasm to embrace Indians as mound builders, he also uncritically accepted a number of uncollaborated historical accounts of mound building. For example, he reported as fact the legend that a great burial mound on the shore of Lake Butte des Morts in Wisconsin had been built by the Fox to bury victims of a war with the French.[36] While the war actually occurred, the mound in question was almost certainly constructed two thousand years earlier.[37] This and other similar errors led him to the generalization that the mounds had been built by modern and familiar tribes, or at least their immediate ancestors. He failed to recognize, and at the time could not have known, that most of the mounds he studied were very old. Nevertheless, he made the important observation, supported by compelling evidence in the form of differing customs, constructions, and artifacts, that the various earthworks could not have been constructed by a single "race" or group of Native Americans, but by various Native American "tribes and peoples." It would be up to later researchers to establish that some of these different tribes and peoples were also separated in time.

Cyrus Thomas's monumental work was well received by the nation, and the myth of the Lost Race was indeed finally laid to rest. It can be argued, however, that the wide acceptance of the work by the Smithsonian's Division of Mound Exploration was not due to just the compelling nature of Thomas's evidence, but to the social climate of the late nineteenth century. As R. Clark Mallam pointed out, had Thomas presented the same evidence a little earlier—during the height of the Indian Wars, say—it may have been ignored.[38] But by the time of the publication of the report in 1894, the Indian Wars in the West had been concluded—unhappily for Native Americans—and the Euro-American conquest of North America had been completed. The idea that Native Americans were something other than simple savages no longer posed an uncomfortable challenge to American sensibilities and the promise of Manifest Destiny. Native Americans could now be accepted as historical and sophisticated peoples with ancient and visible links to the land because, to white America, it simply did not matter any more.

The resolution of the Lost Race debate had come at a high cost. Thousands of mounds had disappeared under the shovels and picks of mound diggers searching for artifacts and bones. It certainly can be argued that the westward expansion of the American frontier would have led to the destruction of many of these mounds in any case. Nevertheless, the remains of

Figure 2.7. Opening Indian mounds was a popular Sunday-afternoon activity during the late nineteenth century. (State Historical Society of Wisconsin, neg. no. WHi [X3] 51037)

thousands of Native American people had been disinterred as a direct result of the debate over the Lost Race. Only a fraction of the remains ended up neatly cataloged on the shelves of museums, such as the Smithsonian, allowing the descendants of those buried to claim their bones today. To these can be added the countless mounds and graves looted by curiosity seekers and relic hunters excited by the more scholarly debates and discoveries (figure 2.7).

The obsession with Indian mounds in the nineteenth century also set the trajectory of the emerging field of archaeology in the United States. The excavation of mounds in places like Wisconsin would continue to be a focal point of archaeological research well into the twentieth century, firmly associating archaeology in the view of the general public with Indian graves and in the opinion of Native Americans with "grave robbing." Ironically, 100 years after the first American archaeologists and anthropologists fought the ethnocentric impulses of a nation by trying to reconstruct a Native American history for the land, their successors would become the very symbols of that ethnocentricity because of a disregard for Native American beliefs about the treatment of the dead.

Research in the Early Twentieth Century

During the first half of the twentieth century, mound research in Wisconsin took three different but occasionally intersecting paths. The first path, unfortunately short-lived, was ethnological. For practically the first time, both amateur and professional anthropologists seriously considered Native American beliefs, traditions, and opinions about the mounds and went directly to Native Americans for insights about mound origins and meaning. An archaeological and scientific path was taken by the Public Museum of the City of Milwaukee and similar institutions and led to the detailed and controlled archaeological excavation of mounds and other Native American sites. This great period of mound excavation lasted until the 1950s and would help identify and define the several different prehistoric cultures responsible for building mounds. The third path was wider, being both humanistic and anthropological. Drawing on a vast pool of amateurs and other interested members of the public, Charles E. Brown and the Wisconsin Archeological Society attempted to study, publish, and preserve all facets of Native American culture and history—archaeological sites, antiquities, ritual practices and beliefs, customs, stories, and legends. This approach led to the first statewide inventory of mounds and other Native American sites in Wisconsin and to the first coordinated mound-preservation movement.

Ethnology: The Ho-Chunk as Mound Builders

Cyrus Thomas and the Smithsonian Institution had demolished the Lost Race explanation for the erection of mounds in North America, but one of the "proofs" had directly linked mound building with modern Native American tribes. Since the antiquity of most mound types had been surmised but not firmly established, the next question in Wisconsin logically focused on which of the modern tribes were the mound builders. Of particular interest was the identity of the mysterious effigy mound people. Among the likely candidates were the three tribes that were believed to have ancient roots in Wisconsin: the Santee Sioux, or Dakota, who had been driven from the state in early historic times by the westward movement of the Chippewa; the Menominee; and the Ho-Chunk (Winnebago).

For many, the Dakota were most likely the builders of many of the large conical mounds found scattered throughout their former territory in northern Wisconsin. Working on the reservation in northeastern Wisconsin that the Menominee had retained by treaty in 1852, ethnologist Walter Hoffman reported in 1896 that the nearby Chippewa believed that the mounds in the area had been built by the Dakota before they were pushed westward. These may or may not be the people involved in a story recorded by Samuel Barrett and Alanson Skinner of the Public Museum several decades later.[39] The story relates how the mound builders were vanquished by an eastern people called the Kine'ma nikin, who brought with them guns and magical powers. The story is incomplete and the Menominee revere the mounds as ancestral graves. But for the origin of the ubiquitous effigy mounds of southern Wisconsin, attention in the early twentieth century turned to the Ho-Chunk.

A connection between the Ho-Chunk and mounds had been made by Euro-Americans as early as the mid-nineteenth century, when the first annual report of the newly founded State Historical Society of Wisconsin reprinted a highly romanticized "legend," first published in 1829 by the *Buffalo* (New York) *Journal*. The legend, supposedly obtained from a Ho-Chunk chief, identified certain Wisconsin mounds as the graves of great Ho-Chunk chiefs who had died in battles with Sauk and Fox.[40] Thomas used this reference in establishing his proofs for the Native American authorship of mounds. In 1907, George A. West, a lawyer in Racine and later an officer of the Public Museum, published a lengthy review of the question of the identity of the mound builders in the newly established journal *Wisconsin Archeologist*.[41] After delivering a literary coup de grâce to the Lost Race notion, which was still in its death throes, he reasserted an interpretation, first presented by Richard Taylor in 1838 and growing in popularity, that the effigy mounds represented Ho-Chunk clan symbols. As one piece of evidence that the Ho-Chunk had built mounds, West described a ceremony observed among the Ho-Chunk at a reservation in Nebraska during which small ritual mounds were made. West predicted that the hypothesis of the Ho-Chunk as builders of the effigy mounds "will be accepted as undisputed fact, within the next generation."[42]

In 1911, Arlow B. Stout wrote an assessment of the nature and distribution of mounds in Wisconsin based on surveys, including his own around Lake Koshkonong and in the Four Lakes region around Madison. He also stressed the probable relationship of effigies to Ho-Chunk clans.[43] In another article published about the same time, he told of his own surprise to learn, first hand, that, contrary to frequent earlier reports, Native Americans did have traditions and beliefs about the construction of the mounds.[44] Visiting a Ho-Chunk family camped in the Wisconsin Dells—the descendants of the Ho-Chunk who had stayed in Wisconsin—he inquired about their beliefs about mounds. A member of the band told him not only that the Ho-Chunk had constructed the mounds, both conical and effigies, but that the elders identified some long-tailed effigy forms, commonly called lizards or panthers, as representations of a prominent Ho-Chunk spirit being, a mysterious creature that lived in the water and came out at night. From this, Stout made the inference that unidentified effigy mounds, including linear mounds frequently associated with the effigies, may represent "spirit animals."

Charles E. Brown, the new director of the museum of the State Historical Society of Wisconsin, took up the argument for a connection between the Ho-Chunk and the effigy mounds in an article published in 1911.[45] He described his visit with two Ho-Chunk men, Oliver La Mere and John Rave, who were descended from the Ho-Chunk who had been removed from Wisconsin to Nebraska in the early nineteenth century and who had been working for Paul Radin, an anthropologist with the Bureau of Ethnology. La Mere, who served as Radin's interpreter, also traced his ancestry on his father's side to prominent Wisconsin fur traders. Brown reported that both men were well versed in Ho-Chunk traditions and beliefs.

Escorting the men to effigy mound groups in the Madison area, Brown elicited their views about the meaning of the various mound forms. La Mere and Rave told Brown, as they also had advised Radin, that the Ho-Chunk believed that the various animals represented both important spirit beings and clan symbols. Rave, for example, quickly identified a huge cross-shaped mound as the symbol of Earth-Maker, who is the creator of the world and human beings in Ho-Chunk cosmology and whose symbol appears on many types of ritual paraphernalia.

Brown acknowledged that some of the information provided by the men appeared to be conjecture. For example, linear mounds were said to be foundations for longhouses or fortifications, an explanation that Brown doubted on the basis of archaeological work. Nevertheless, he recognized the potential for Ho-Chunk and other Native American belief systems to provide insights on effigy mounds in Wisconsin and advised researchers that "in this section of the country at least ethnological science may greatly assist in our archaeological history."[46]

More than anybody else, Paul Radin is identified with the theory of the connection between the Ho-Chunk and the builders of the effigy mounds. Trained in Germany and the United States, Radin was employed by the Bureau of Ethnology to collect cultural information among the Ho-Chunk. From the data he gathered primarily from the Nebraska Ho-Chunk between 1908 and 1913, he wrote both an article addressing the relationship of the Ho-Chunk to the effigy mounds and a monumental work: *The Winnebago Tribe*.[47] In these studies, Radin "demonstrated beyond any doubt that the Effigy Mounds are the work of the Winnebago alone"—at least to his own satisfaction. To support his case, Radin offered four principal arguments. First, he contended that central Algonquian tribes (for example, the Chippewa, Menominee, Potawatomi, Sauk, and Fox) had been intruders into Siouan territory and that ethnographic evidence on burial customs indicated that they had not built the mounds. By the process of elimination, that left the Siouan-speaking Ho-Chunk, since the other Siouan tribe, the Dakota, had left the area in the early years of the historic period. Second, he matched the known distribution of effigy mounds with the territory of the nineteenth-century Ho-Chunk. Third, he noted the close correspondence between types of effigy mounds and Ho-Chunk clan symbols and cited oral traditions to support this association. Finally, he rejected the notion, then becoming popular in archaeological circles, that the mounds were necessarily of great age, again citing information obtained from Ho-Chunk people that their ancestors had built mounds in relatively recent times.

Based largely on Radin's work, the argument for the Ho-Chunk as the builders of the effigy mounds became widely accepted by both scholars and the public during the first quarter of the twentieth century. Here and there throughout Wisconsin can still be found historical markers, dating to that time, that assert this to be fact. This conclusion was seriously challenged after the late 1920s, when archaeologists who used the archaeological evidence of the time began to argue that the mounds had not been built in the recent past and therefore could not be associated with the historic Ho-Chunk and that the effigy mound builders were not even the prehistoric ancestors of the modern Ho-Chunk.

Radin's views, and the uncritical use of ethnographic data to interpret the past in general, came under increasingly harsh scrutiny as time went on. Radin was and still is criticized by some for accepting as fact the views of a few carefully selected people, especially since some of his sources had abandoned traditional belief systems.[48] In 1928, William C. McKern even suggested that Radin's personal interpretations directly influenced Ho-Chunk oral tradition:

On paper, Radin's argument looks good. One thing is certain; Radin thoroughly convinced many of the Winnebago that their ancestors built the mounds. Since his sojourn in their midst, they have talked the matter over at length and are now quite proud of these, the supposed products of their forebears. However, when it comes to the matter of explaining their purpose and use, a great confusion of ideas, much at war with each other, and all smacking of rationalization, are contributed. Some are entirely possible; others quite implausible. Not a few actually quote Radin as an authority.[49]

Two observations may bear on the strength of Ho-Chunk traditions regarding the mounds. First, according to Nancy Lurie, a renowned expert on Ho-Chunk culture and history, while there are no reliable first-hand accounts of Ho-Chunk building mounds, most contemporary Ho-Chunk certainly believe they did.[50] Second, while the antiquity of Indian mounds is firmly established by modern techniques, some archaeologists interpret archaeological evidence not available to McKern and others in the first half of the twentieth century to argue that the Ho-Chunk are among a number of related Native American peoples who could indeed rightfully place effigy mound people in their family trees, although in the very distant past.

As archaeology became more rigorously "scientific" during the twentieth century, it became cautious about accepting bodies of information that could not be objectively verified. This ultimately, and unfortunately, resulted in the dismissal of ancient ideologies as unknowable, and the consideration of Native American traditions and belief systems as not useful except when they fit "archaeological facts." By the second half of the twentieth century, the use of Native American beliefs and traditions to form ideas about the past had again fallen into disfavor.

Preservation: Charles E. Brown and the Wisconsin Archeological Society

Excited by the research on mounds and the ever-growing literature generated by the emerging field of archaeology, popular interest in Native American antiquities was quite high in the late nineteenth century. Large collections of artifacts and information on archaeological sites grew in the hands of well-educated amateur archaeologists and antiquarians, among them doctors, lawyers, judges, professors, and farmers. Although the "opening of mounds" had become a popular Sunday-afternoon social activity, many of these enthusiasts sought to find a more productive outlet for their interest

Figure 2.8. Under the leadership of Charles E. Brown, the Wisconsin Archeological Society documented many unusual mounds that have since been destroyed. This double panther or water spirit effigy mound near Lake Winnebago in Calumet County was photographed in 1915. (State Historical Society of Wisconsin, neg. no. WHi [X3] 51102)

and hobby. In addition, many were becoming increasingly disturbed by the disappearance of Native American sites, especially the mounds, as a result of farming, road building, urban expansion, and looting.

This interest and concern gave birth to the Wisconsin Archeological Society in 1899 as an organization of amateur archaeologists dedicated to "advancing the study and preservation of Wisconsin Indian Antiquities." It was established first as a special section of the Wisconsin Natural History Survey in 1899 and then was reorganized as a separate society in 1903. A founding father and long-standing guiding force was Charles E. Brown, who also served for forty years as both organizational secretary and editor of the *Wisconsin Archeologist,* the society's publication.

A Milwaukee native, Brown acquired an early interest in natural history and Native American culture from his father, a civil engineer who collected geologic specimens and Indian relics, and from his own visits to the Public Museum. Self-educated in anthropology, he joined the staff of the museum in 1900 and later in the decade moved to Madison, where he became the first director of the museum of the State Historical Society of Wisconsin, a post he held until his retirement in 1944.[51]

As secretary of and editor for the Wisconsin Archeological Society, Brown developed and maintained the "Records of Wisconsin Antiquities," an inventory of state archaeological sites that has since evolved into an ever-expanding computer database and map library kept by the Office of the State Archaeologist at the State Historical Society (figure 2.8). He communicated with thousands of individuals throughout the state to obtain information about the distribution of sites, especially mounds, and this correspondence fills fifty-three boxes in the archives of the State Historical Society.

Alarmed by the destruction of mounds throughout Wisconsin, Brown urged the Wisconsin Archeological Society to make the preservation of mounds its first priority. He further helped the society formulate an elaborate strategy to preserve mounds and, in doing so, created Wisconsin's first historic-preservation movement. This strategy would be familiar to modern preservationists: systematic surveys to identify important sites, protective legislation, public acquisition and stewardship, partnerships with influential people and organizations, landmarking, fund-raising, and, above all, relentless promotion and public education.

One of the first projects undertaken by the Wisconsin Archeological Society was the preservation of three large conical mounds, now the centerpiece of Cutler Park in downtown Waukesha. In 1906, a special committee working with the Sauk County Historical Society raised money to purchase the famous Man Mound near Baraboo, thereby saving it from being turned into cropland.[52] A county park now preserves this truly unique landmark.

Collaborating with the Landmarks Committee of the Federated Women's Clubs of Wisconsin, the Daughters of the American Revolution, local historical societies, and other public-service organizations, the Wisconsin Archeological Society placed historical markers and commemorative plaques on mound groups throughout the state as a means of calling public attention to the importance of these ancient structures. In 1912, it formed the Mounds Preservation Committee, a standing committee that actively worked to save mounds from destruction through acquisition by public agencies or the society. By the 1920s, the committee was able to boast that 500 mounds had been preserved largely by its efforts. Virtually all of them are extant. In 1920, the society formed Save Aztalan, a movement that eventually led to the public ownership of the premier archaeological and mound site in Wisconsin.

Throughout its early years, the Wisconsin Archeological Society encouraged and organized mapping expeditions undertaken by volunteers and published the results of these extensive studies in the *Wisconsin Archeologist*. Although written by amateurs, many of these reports stand as models of professional research reports. As is the information compiled by Increase A. Lapham and Theodore H. Lewis, these records are all the more valuable because of the great loss of the mounds to agriculture and development.

In 1911, a delegation from the Wisconsin Archeological Society, headed by Brown, successfully lobbied the Wisconsin legislature to pass a law to protect antiquities on public lands—Wisconsin's first historic-preservation law. At the same time, the legislature made an annual appropriation of $1,500 to the State Historical Society for the purpose of conducting a statewide inventory of archaeological sites, particularly mounds.[53] The work was carried out by volunteers under Brown's direction. The money provided by the state covered only their travel expenses. Funding for the project lasted for only two years, but during 1911 and 1912 as many as ten crews fanned out across the state to record the location of mounds and other sites, hundreds of which were inventoried and mapped. Public funding for such a worthy enterprise was not to become available again in Wisconsin until the 1970s.

Brown became personally committed to the preservation of the many mound groups found along the shores of the Four Lakes region surrounding Madison. Greatly concerned that the monuments in the Four Lakes area were doomed by rapid city and lakeshore development, Brown led a lifelong local campaign to save or at least document as many mounds as he personally could. From his base at the State Historical Society and between his tasks as museum director, he launched a number of mound surveys that built on the work of Arlow B. Stout, then a student at the University of Wisconsin. Brown was assisted by a number of volunteers recruited from the vast academic and professional community in the Madison area. One of Brown's companions in his own mapping expeditions was William Ellery Leonard, a writer and poet of national reputation and great eccentricity who read a lengthy poem at the annual field assembly of the Wisconsin Archeological Society in Madison in 1910 (figure 2.9). It, in part, spoke to the purpose of studying the mounds:

> Why should we leave our figuring for gold
> To figure out a vanished world of old?—
> Except that thus in human nature lurks,
> Except that thus in human nature works
> Some sense of common comradery and kin
> With human life, wherever it has been,
> And in the use of such a sense we find
> Enlargement of our human heart and mind.[54]

Leonard later developed a literal vision of a "locomotive god" and a case of severe agoraphobia. In his autobiography, *The Locomotive God,* Leonard

Figure 2.9. Charles Brown (*right*) led efforts to map and preserve mounds between 1908 and 1944. Assisting him at the Fox Bluff Mound Group were the Reverend P. M. Gilmore (*left*) and William Ellery Leonard (*center*). (State Historical Society of Wisconsin, neg. no. WHi [X3] 50302)

made the spooky revelation that it had been during the course of a mound survey with Brown near Lake Mendota that he suddenly received both his vision and his debilitating sickness.[55]

Brown worked vigorously to gain public ownership of mound groups, the only way at the time that could provide even the promise of preservation. He cajoled and badgered public officials into protecting mounds in their jurisdictions. Brown later worked closely with the University of Wisconsin when it acquired land for an arboretum on which he had identified three mound groups. He served on the arboretum's advisory committee and personally supervised the restoration of mounds that had been damaged by looting.

A large part of Brown's success was the result of his enthusiastic attention to public education. In addition to his many scholarly articles, he wrote a number of pamphlets, brochures, and feature articles for the general public. He was a popular speaker on the lecture circuit and, between 1923 and 1935, gave numerous lectures on WHA, the nation's first public-radio station. Each summer during the 1920s and 1930s, Brown offered the popular "Lake Mendota Historical Excursion" for university students and professors and for other interested residents of Madison. Using a motorized launch, he led "pilgrimages" to historical and archaeological sites along the lake, including a half dozen mound groups.[56]

Brown was a tireless and innovative organizer who rarely missed an opportunity to promote mound preservation. In 1914, the Madison Board of Commerce asked him to arrange a reception and entertainment for the Society of American Indians, a national organization of "progressive and patriotic" Native Americans that had selected Madison for its annual congress. Brown seized the opportunity to draw public attention to his efforts to save a small effigy mound group overlooking Lake Wingra from urban expansion by arranging a well-publicized dedication ceremony at the mounds attended by representatives of thirteen tribes from throughout the United States.[57] During the 1930s, Brown took advantage of public-works programs by using laborers to repair and restore vandalized mounds on the University of Wisconsin campus.

The interests of both Brown and the Wisconsin Archeological Society went beyond the preservation of mounds as memorials to past civilizations. As an organization of archaeologists, amateur and professional, the society was driven by a quest to learn about Wisconsin's past. Mounds were preserved because they were important repositories of information that could and should be carefully excavated someday. Accordingly, Brown and members of the society excavated mounds when the situation presented itself, although usually when the mounds faced imminent destruction and could not be saved. In Brown's time, however, the knowledge that came from this work was limited to determining how the mounds had been constructed and learning what they contained. These were the days before radiocarbon dating and before the 12,000-year sequence of prehistoric Native American cultures had been ordered from stratigraphic layers in caves and rockshelters in southwestern Wisconsin. Therefore, the results of these digs were difficult to interpret. Nevertheless, valuable information, artifacts, and even the very bones of the mound builders themselves would have been lost in many cases had it not been for Brown and the Wisconsin Archeological Society.

Another direction in Brown's own mound research stemmed from his interest in Native American traditions, stories, and folklore and from his firm conviction that the Ho-Chunk had constructed the effigy mounds in

Wisconsin. He cultivated close ties with Native Americans from whom he gathered stories, beliefs, and oral history. He gained a profound respect for these people and, in return, became so highly regarded that he was reportedly adopted into several tribes. Brown's special relationship with Native Americans had begun shortly after he moved to Madison and while he was living in what was then the outskirts of town. One winter day, a Ho-Chunk man, Joseph White, came to his door and asked for food. His family was camped in the woods and had run short of supplies. Brown obliged and returned with White to the wigwam in the woods, striking up a friendship with the family that lasted for many years. Brown returned frequently to the camps of the Ho-Chunk, which were seasonally maintained in the Madison area as late as 1925.[58]

Through the years, Brown expanded his friendships with and ties to Native Americans. Among the many Native American guests to his home were Oliver La Mere; John Blackhawk from Black River Falls, a descendant of Chief Winneshiek; and Albert Yellow Thunder from the Wisconsin Dells, a grandson of Yellow Thunder, a noted Ho-Chunk war chief. From these and other friends, Brown collected Ho-Chunk stories and traditions, some of which pertained to effigy mounds. Although it still cannot be demonstrated with absolute certainty that the builders of the effigy mounds were ancestral to the Ho-Chunk, the perspectives that Brown obtained during this period add immeasurably to an understanding of the underlying belief systems of ancient Native American societies.

The mound-preservation effort spearheaded by Brown and the Wisconsin Archeological Society lasted into the 1940s, but the Great Depression and World War II had diminished public interest. The legacy of the effort is visible throughout the state. Just a few of the many mounds and mound groups that owe their existence to the activities of the Wisconsin Archeological Society can be found in Aztalan State Park near Lake Mills, Cutler Park in Waukesha, Indian Mound Park near Chetek, Lake Park in Milwaukee, Man Mound Park near Baraboo, Mound Cemetery in Racine, Myrick Park in La Crosse, State Fair Park in West Allis, Wyalusing State Park near Prairie du Chien, and many other places. As a tribute to Brown's own persistence, the Madison area alone has more than twenty-three different locations where mound groups can be visited by the public.

Excavation:
The Development of Wisconsin Archaeology

In the nineteenth century, archaeology emerged in the United States as a branch of the broader field of anthropology devoted to the scientific study of the past. Through empirical observation, archaeologists established that mounds and other earthworks were the products of Native American societies. Furthermore, they introduced the idea that variations in the archaeological record could be explained by the fact that ancient North America had been populated by differing Native American cultures. As yet, however, no general or local sequence of Native American societies had been worked out, except in the most rudimentary fashion. Even the age of prehistoric cultures could only be guessed at, except in the southwestern United States, where they could occasionally be directly dated by examination of tree-ring sequences in preserved timbers.

The establishment of a chronology of prehistoric cultures in Wisconsin and elsewhere in North America became the primary goal of archaeological research in the first half of the twentieth century. Interestingly, the ultimate source of critical information would not come from the mounds, but from the camps, villages, and rockshelters where the relationships among superimposed layers of the past could be more easily studied. But since the whole emphasis of preceding archaeological research had been mounds, mounds remained the most visible and intriguing sources of information on ancient societies for researchers in the early decades of the twentieth century.

Samuel Barrett, one of the first professional American archaeologists, having been awarded one of the first doctorates in anthropology in the United States, joined the Public Museum of the City of Milwaukee in 1909. In 1917, he led excavations of a mound group in the state, at the Kratz Creek Mound Group at Lake Buffalo in Marquette County. The work at Kratz Creek was the initial step in a plan conceived by Barrett to investigate the prehistory of Wisconsin by conducting a series of controlled excavations at "typical mound groups and other archaeological remains" throughout the state.

The Kratz Creek Mound Group consisted of fifty-one conical, linear, and effigy mounds, thirty-six of which were excavated by Barrett. The results of the investigation were published in the *Bulletin of the Public Museum of the City of Milwaukee*,[59] a series that published the findings of mound researchers for the next several decades. Barrett's work was different from previous mound explorations in that many mounds of a single group were examined. This allowed comparisons to be made among mounds. Barrett also broke from nineteenth-century excavation methods by paying close attention to the internal structuring and layering of mound soils. He concluded that two different cultures may have been involved in constructing mounds based on differences in soil layers and bone preservation and on comparison with material from the surface collected from village sites in the vicinity. In addition, Barrett discovered that some effigy mounds had been made by first digging "intaglios," or negative images, of mound forms. The intaglios had been filled in and the mound constructed above. The dead had been buried in mounds in three ways: as cremations, flexed "in the flesh," and as bundles of bones cleaned of flesh. Barrett also reported evidence that mounds were not simply cemeteries. The remains of ceremonial activities were found in the form of stone "altars," "sacrificial" items, evidence of fire, and, most interesting, what Barrett termed "sacred soils"—layers of different colored soils that had not originated on the site. On the floor of one mound, a circle of bright red sand neatly surrounded several bundles of human bones. Barrett speculated that these features and soils had ritual meaning to the Native Americans.

Barrett moved the research on mounds conducted by the museum to the Menominee reservation in 1919 and then began an ambitious archaeological excavation at Aztalan, the famous site that contained large flat-topped "temple mounds" and remnants of a great clay-covered wall that enclosed the town. The results of this major work, which still makes fascinating reading, were published as "Ancient Aztalan."[60] On the basis of what he found, Barrett rejected the old notion that the site was somehow related to the Aztecs and instead compared it with similar but larger sites in southern Illinois and the southeastern United States. The culture that had lived at Aztalan was called Middle Mississippian by archaeologists because of its location in the middle part of the Mississippi River drainage basin.

Also working at the Menominee reservation, heading the research on mounds, was Alanson Skinner, a trained ethnologist. He was assisted in the excavations by John Satterlee, a member of the Menominee tribe who also served as an interpreter for ethnological research. Skinner's research was enthusiastically supported by the superintendent of the reservation—his father-in-law—but the digging of Native American graves was not appreciated by other people on the reservation. Some years after the completion of the project, Charles Brown visited the reservation to inspect some Indian mounds and learned that Skinner's work had upset many who had warned that disturbing the dead was dangerous business. As if to confirm their fears, Skinner's wife had died between field seasons, and a short time after he finished the excavations, Skinner himself was killed in an automobile accident. Some on the reservation interpreted these tragedies as punishment by angry spirits.[61]

Sadly, but with some notable exceptions, disregard for Native American concerns about disturbing graves continued throughout much of the twentieth century in Wisconsin and the United States. For the archaeologists involved, it was a matter of the primacy of science over the religious sensibilities of a rather small group of people. For Native Americans, the disinterment of their ancestors was sacrilege and a continuing insult. Accordingly, tensions between archaeologists and Native Americans escalated during the heyday of mound excavation.

Figure 2.10. Visitors look on as William C. McKern (*back to camera*) and his crew from the Public Museum of the City of Milwaukee excavate the Schwert Mound on the Mississippi River in Trempealeau County. (Photograph used with permission of the Milwaukee Public Museum, neg. 406890)

William C. McKern joined the staff of the Public Museum in 1925 and, in the words of a historian of Wisconsin archaeology, "moved Wisconsin to the forefront of scientific archaeology."[62] In order to gain a better understanding of the prehistoric societies that had inhabited the state, McKern, along with Barrett, devised a strategy to sample archaeological sites along an imaginary east–west line that bisected the state, cutting across many river systems and ecological zones. Again, mounds tended to be the focus of attention, although some villages and campsites were also examined. During the 1920s and 1930s, McKern excavated more than a dozen mound groups throughout Wisconsin (figure 2.10). Information resulting from this work led to a rudimentary classification of prehistoric cultures that once lived in the region.

During this time, McKern directly challenged Paul Radin's hypothesis about the relationship of the Ho-Chunk to the effigy mounds by establishing that the burials made in effigy mounds at the time of their construction contained no articles of European manufacture.[63] This argued for prehistoric rather than historic dating. He went on to reject all of Radin's arguments for the Ho-Chunk as the builders of the mounds, contending that they did not fit the facts. What seems to have been at the center of the disagreement was the increasing conflict between ethnological and archaeological information as a means to reconstruct events. In 1930, McKern wrote:

When ethnological findings are in drastic conflict with known archaeological facts, I do not hesitate to insist that the ethnological data must give way. For example[,] when living Indian informants positively state that certain linear mounds were built to serve primarily as defensive earthworks, or as game drives, and the archaeologist finds that the same mounds contain burials, placed at the time of construction and therefore planned features of the mounds, the Indian definition must give way.[64]

But more than anything else, it was McKern's pioneering research on prehistoric pottery styles that led him to eliminate the Ho-Chunk from contention as the effigy mound builders. His inspection of pottery sherds from some habitation sites in areas that had been occupied historically by the Ho-Chunk, along with (ironically) some of Radin's ethnographic evidence on pottery making, convinced McKern that the Ho-Chunk had made a distinctive form of thin-walled pottery from clay mixed with crushed clamshell and decorated with incised geometric patterns. This type of pottery he called Upper Mississippian. In contrast, the mounds he excavated yielded a different type of pottery, tempered with crushed rock and decorated with cord impressions, that he believed was associated with Algonquian-speaking peoples, such as the Menominee and Potawatomi. This type of pottery, which he called Lake Michigan Ware, came to be referred to as Woodland pottery. According to McKern, therefore, the Siouan-speaking Ho-Chunk could not have been the builders of the effigy mounds.

McKern's viewpoints and classifications dominated archaeological thought in Wisconsin during 1930s and 1940s, although research at the time was still hampered by the dearth of archaeological data from habitation sites. As the relationships between Woodland and Upper Mississippian peoples were studied in the last quarter of the twentieth century, one hypothesis would emerge that would credit *both* McKern and Radin for having been right in some respects: the Upper Mississippian people did emerge as the Ho-Chunk (as well as several other related tribes) in the historic period, but the Woodland effigy mound people were, in turn, the ancestors of the Upper Mississippians.

Although McKern did not believe that the Ho-Chunk had built the effigy mounds, he did believe that mound building in Wisconsin had persisted into the early part of historic times by Woodland people in northern Wisconsin. He cited as evidence large conical mounds that he thought had been built by the Dakota. The excavation of one of these mounds, the Spencer Lake Mound in Burnett County, involved McKern in a controversy that dogged him for the rest of his career and clouded interpretations of mound building in Wisconsin during historic times. The controversy involved what Robert Ritzenthaler dubbed "The Riddle of the Spencer Lake Horse Skull."[65]

In the mid-1930s, McKern's exploration of mounds took him to Burnett County in northwestern Wisconsin, where, assisted by student archaeologists from a number of institutions, he excavated two mounds from the Spencer Lake and Clam Lake Mound Groups. Both were large conical mounds that had been built in stages, apparently over a period of time. McKern was convinced that both were fairly recent because of well-preserved remains, such as birch bark, but especially because of the discovery, in the Spencer Lake Mound, of a piece of wood that appeared to have steel ax marks—*and a horse skull!* The skull, reportedly that of a mustang, was found about four feet from bundles of human bones, but in the same layer. McKern originally reported the discovery of the skull as solid evidence that a local historic tribe, the Dakota, had built the mounds, since the presence of horse bones would obviously date the mound to after European contact. Announcements of the discovery caused quite a stir in archaeological circles, since the proverbial smoking gun that linked mounds to a historic tribe had been found.

Three decades later, as the final report of the excavations of the mounds in northwestern Wisconsin was being finalized by the Public Museum, a professor of geology startled museum staff with the news that the horse skull had been a "plant." With a great deal of embarrassment, he related that, as teenagers in 1928, he and a friend had dug into the Spencer Lake Mound and, before filling in the hole, had thought it would be amusing to bury the skull of a horse they had found in a nearby field in order to confound future diggers. When the results of the investigations in Burnett County were published in 1963 by the Public Museum, reference to the discovery of the skull had been removed. When a knowledgeable reviewer questioned the omission, Ritzenthaler published the story without naming the prankster, along with an anonymous apology for the trouble the plant had caused.

McKern countered that the mound he had excavated could not have been the mound in which the skull had been planted because the horse skull recovered by his team had been found in deposits unequivocally undisturbed since they were originally made by Native Americans during the burial ceremony. This was supported by his field assistants, who themselves had gone on to become highly respected archaeologists. To help resolve the riddle, organic material recovered by McKern from the Spencer Lake Mound, and then stored by the Public Museum, was dated in 1964 using the revolutionary new technique of radiocarbon dating. The dates cast doubt on the authenticity of the skull; samples from various parts of the mound dated its construction to between A.D. 500 and 700—many centuries before Europeans brought modern horses to North America.[66] McKern, though, never gave up his contention that the horse skull had been found in mound strata undisturbed by recent digging and that its presence dated the burial to the historic period.[67] Because of this, the case of the horse skull in the Spencer Lake Mound remains a riddle.

This controversy aside, McKern made tremendous contributions to mound research during his career. By the early 1940s, he had acquired sufficient information to develop the first classification of prehistoric cultures for Wisconsin.[68] This classification was defined on the basis of similarities and differences in artifact styles, as well as differing mortuary customs. What McKern termed the Mississippian Pattern was divided into the Middle Mississippian, as represented by Aztalan, and the Upper Mississippian or Oneota, which McKern believed to be ancestral to the Ho-Chunk and Ioway. The Woodland Pattern included the ancient effigy mound people and two other cultures that he linked to the Dakota and Menominee. The classification included two other cultural phenomena in Wisconsin: Hopewellian, a variant of the famous Hopewell mound builders of Illinois and Ohio, and what McKern termed the Old Copper Industry (now known as the Old Copper Complex) because of the extensive use of copper tools and ornaments. Without proper dating techniques, McKern was unable to date these cultures or clarify their relationships to one another. Furthermore, because few villages and campsites had been explored, the lifestyles of these various peoples were unknown. Both of these topics occupied scholars for the next several decades, changing the course of archaeological research on the mound builders and shifting attention from tombs to the places where people had lived.

THE EFFIGY MOUND TRADITION

Defining the Tradition

The accumulated information collected by William McKern and his colleagues from their excavations of effigy mounds was summarized by Chandler Rowe in his book *The Effigy Mound Culture*.[69]

Rowe focused on the Raisbeck Mound Group in Grant County, presenting previously unpublished information that was derived from excavations conducted in 1932 by McKern, but he used for comparison more than 400 mounds excavated to date, 6 of which he had dug himself. The purpose of his work was to define the effigy mound phenomenon by providing a comprehensive list of cultural characteristics, such as artifacts, methods of mound construction, basic effigy mound forms, and burial customs. Rowe did one other interesting thing. Since the possible connection between effigy mounds and historic tribes, particularly the Ho-Chunk (Winnebago), was still being debated, he sought to put the matter to the test by comparing his list of identifiable effigy mound forms with lists of clans drawn from ethnographic accounts of the Menominee, Chippewa, Sioux, Fox, Sauk, Ho-Chunk, and Prairie Potawatomi—all tribes that had, at one time or another, lived in Wisconsin. Assuming that the mounds represented clan totems, he reasoned that any tribe whose totem animals resembled the shapes of the mounds might be a candidate for the effigy mound builders. Rowe could not find a good match and, on this basis, confirmed McKern's earlier views that the Ho-Chunk (or any of the others, for that matter) could not have built the mounds. Rowe went beyond this conclusion to suggest that even the clan-totem theory itself should be dismissed as an explanation for effigy mound forms.

Actually, Rowe may have been on the right track by examining the social systems of midwestern tribes for clues to the effigy mounds, but he was limited by a lack of knowledge about belief systems that underlie Native American social patterns. Had he consulted information on the meaning of certain mound forms gathered by Charles E. Brown, Arlow B. Stout, and others from the Ho-Chunk earlier in the century, he might have reached different conclusions.

Nonetheless, Rowe's study brought together an impressive amount of information on the customs and material culture of the effigy mound builders, even though he could not absolutely anchor it in time. This would await the general application of a technical advance that was in the making as Rowe completed his research—radiocarbon dating.

Dating the Tradition

Until the 1950s, the dating of mounds and other ancient Native American sites was a matter of educated guesswork. But in 1949, Willard Libby, a Chicago chemist, developed a process that revolutionized the field of archaeology. Aside from the basic recognition, in the nineteenth century, of stratigraphic relations of soil layers, there is probably no greater advance in the development of archaeology than radiocarbon dating, a technique for determining the time that has passed since organisms, both plant and animal, died. The principles of the technique are relatively simple. All organisms absorb radioactive carbon from the atmosphere. When an organism dies, absorption stops and the carbon decays at a rate that can be measured by special laboratory apparatus. Experience has shown that charcoal is the best substance for radiocarbon dating, but almost any organic material, including bone, can be used. Dates are given by radiocarbon labs in calendar years and are accompanied by a statistical standard deviation. Thus the radiocarbon date of 1200 ± 100 B.C. means that there is a high probability that an organism died between 1300 and 1100 B.C.

Among the first applications of radiocarbon dating in Wisconsin were samples from two mound groups: the Kolterman effigy mound site in Dodge County (A.D. 770 ± 250) and the Wakanda Park site in Menominee (A.D. 1200 ± 200). The dates supported the view that the mounds in Wisconsin are indeed very old.[70]

William Hurley wanted to determine the span of the effigy mound culture when he began what might go down in history as the last major mound excavation in Wisconsin. In 1965 and 1966, while still a student, Hurley dug a total of fifty-six mounds and adjacent camps associated with the Sanders and Bigelow effigy mound sites near Stevens Point in central Wisconsin.[71] The sites are on the northern edge of the effigy mound region. Hurley combined radiocarbon dates taken from charcoal found in the mounds and living areas with data derived from other archaeological sites in Wisconsin to define the effigy mound culture as a tradition that persisted for 1,300 years—from about A.D. 300 to the historic period. He also defined a series of pottery styles characteristic of the effigy mound people that are commonly found in mounds and habitation areas.

Perhaps as a way of avoiding the pratfalls suffered by early researchers, he used little ethnographic information in his account of the effigy mound people and provided no historical evidence, despite arguing for the persistence of the effigy mound people in northern Wisconsin when the Europeans came on the scene. And he refused to identify his candidates for the historical mound builders, although he made broad hints in the direction of the Dakota.

Some of Hurley's conclusions were eventually superseded by the work of other archaeologists who argued that he had defined the effigy mound culture much too broadly and had included evidence from sites of other cultures that probably had little to do with effigy mounds. For example, he associated with the effigy mound culture some artifacts that later research linked to earlier or otherwise different peoples. Furthermore, his argument that the effigy mound people persisted into the historic period in northern Wisconsin could not be supported with evidence. Hurley's series of radiocarbon dates from the mounds at the Bigelow and Sanders sites are between A.D. 600 and 1200, a time range that most now agree brackets the effigy mound tradition.

The radiocarbon dates from the Bigelow and Sanders sites provided Hurley with a valuable observation in regard to the construction of effigy mound groups that set the stage for later interpretations: single mound groups had been constructed over a long period of time—perhaps even hundreds of years. The theory that would emerge from this fact is that effigy groups functioned as long-lived ceremonial centers for specific bands or tribes.

FROM THE MOUNDS TO THE CAMPS

By the late 1950s and well before William Hurley undertook his project, it was becoming increasingly clear that mound excavation alone, as a way to reconstruct the past, was approaching a dead end. Certainly there was, and still remains, a great interest in and need to refine the dating of the various mound-building cultures, but little new information was being found about the people who had built the mounds. Archaeological research had revealed much about the way they had been treated in death, but little about their day-to-day lives: housing, food resources, or the many technical and economic changes that had taken place over millennia. These data could be valuable clues that could help explain the origins and context of mound building.

Aided by advances in technology and methods and fueled by the growth of anthropology departments at universities that provided eager student researchers, archaeology in Wisconsin during the 1950s and 1960s increasingly looked to the places where people had lived for clues about the past. As it did, the era of mound digging slowly came to an end. A few mounds were excavated after the 1960s, but primarily to save the remains and other physical data from imminent destruction.

A great part of the new information about the ancient societies of Wisconsin came first from inside caves and beneath rocky overhangs in the deep valleys of southwestern Wisconsin. Generation after generation of Native Americans had used these rocky places as base camps from which to hunt

Table 2.1. Wisconsin archaeological chronology

Tradition	Stage
Paleo-Indian	
Early	10,000–8000 B.C.
Late	8000–6000/5000 B.C.
Archaic	
Early	8000–4000 B.C.
Middle	6000–1200 B.C.
Late	1200–100 B.C.
Woodland	
Early	500 B.C.–A.D. 100
Middle	100 B.C.–A.D. 500
Late	Late A.D. 500–1200 (historic period in northern Wisconsin)
Middle Mississippian	A.D. 1000–1200
Upper Mississippian (Oneota)	A.D. 1000–historic period

Source: Robert A. Birmingham, Carol I. Mason, and James B. Stoltman, eds., "Wisconsin Archaeology" [special issue], *Wisconsin Archeologist* 78, nos. 1–2 (1997).

Note: Some dates overlap because some traditions or stages lasted longer or started earlier in some areas. In addition, some traditions or stages are partially contemporaneous, such as Oneota, Late Woodland, and Middle Mississippian.

deer that gathered in the valleys during the winter. The living debris cast aside by each of these seasonal occupants became sealed by sand, soil, and disintegrating roofs of the shelters, encapsulating a cultural record. One recently discovered cave, Gottschall Rockshelter, was found to have at least sixteen feet of alternating cultural and natural deposits. Such places are books on prehistoric Wisconsin that can be read by a careful archaeologist, layer by layer, ever deeper into the past. One such archaeologist was Warren Wittry, who, as a graduate student, carefully pealed back the layers of time in a number of rockshelter sites in southwestern Wisconsin.[72] Assisted by the judicious use of radiocarbon dating, Wittry was able to develop the first chronological sequence for the region.

Others of this generation of archaeologists explored village sites occupied by many different prehistoric cultures, producing additional data on changing artifact styles and lifeways in the past. These sites also provided radiocarbon dates that helped place the different Native American cultures in relation to one another. Combining all this information with discoveries made elsewhere in North America, archaeologists by the 1970s were able to construct the general succession of prehistoric Wisconsin cultures extending back over 10,000 years, expanding and filling in the frameworks and sequences developed by McKern and Wittry. The modern archaeological sequence, which is constantly being refined, is presented in table 2.1.

THE TIMES THEY ARE A-CHANGIN'

Cultural Ecology

During the 1960s, dramatic change not only swept across American society, but influenced the study of human cultures itself. Broadly reflecting insights gained by ecology, the study of the relationships of organisms to their environment, the emphasis in anthropology turned to the relationship of culture and the environment. Using ecological and systems models, culture came to be regarded as a complex system of interconnected subsystems broadly adapted to specific natural and social environments. Culture was viewed as the *way* that humans make such adaptations. This new view of culture was stimulated by the earlier writings of anthropologist Julian Steward, who had noticed that societies living in similar environments in different parts of the world had developed many similar characteristics.[73] He and others reasoned that as the environment changed, so did cultural adaptations, leading to "cultural evolution." Thus it is cultural evolution that accounts for similarities and differences among different societies, both past and present.

The concept of cultural evolution was introduced in the nineteenth century to explain cultural variation. At that time, cultural change was perceived as proceeding in one direction: all societies could be expected to go through similar stages of development. At the bottom level was "savagery." At the top was "civilization," a level that, not surprisingly, resembled the societies of Europe and North America. The nature of this model made it difficult for scholars to accept the mound builders as ancestral to the modern tribes. How could a society like that of the mound builders, obviously advanced well along the line of social evolution, have led to what were perceived as the much simpler Native American societies of the historic period? For obvious reasons, this ethnocentric approach to cultural evolution was soon abandoned. The new view of cultural evolution was multidirectional, acknowledging that societies could develop in any number of ways, depending on their adaptations.

In Wisconsin, as elsewhere, cultural ecology stimulated research into the ways that the different prehistoric societies had adapted to their environments. Since the economic subsystem of culture is the one that directly interacts with the environment, research tended to emphasize economic issues, such as how the ancient peoples made a living (subsistence) and where they lived on the landscape in relation to a variety of critical natural resources (settlement patterns). Archaeologists also began to collaborate with such scientists as climatologists, palynologists (pollen analysts), and geologists whose expertise helped reconstruct changes in prehistoric environments and landscapes.

This ecological approach also provided insights into the purpose of mound construction by ancient Native American cultures. In the late 1970s, R. Clark Mallam analyzed the location of effigy mounds in Iowa and showed that their distribution coincided with a biological province consisting of prairie, parkland, and forest that included the richest areas of seasonally recurring plant and animal resources for a people that lived off the land.[74] From this, he suggested that the mound groups were much more than simple cemeteries; rather, they were important ceremonial centers that drew together related families that shared proscribed territories, perhaps seasonally, for a variety of economic, social, and religious activities. The mound groups and the many rituals that were practiced at these sacred places, including burial ceremonies, served to bond people together into bands or tribes.

The 1960s and 1970s witnessed other great advances in archaeological theory, methods, and technology. The field of archaeology became even more scientifically oriented, using "harder" sciences as models. It introduced new approaches, such as hypothesis testing, mathematical modeling, and statistical analysis. This trend added even more rigor to archaeological studies, but, oddly, continued the trend of distancing archaeology from the people it studied.

Archaeology also became more specialized. Beginning in the 1970s, archaeologists began to develop specialties, including the identification and analysis of animal- or plant-food remains and the study of certain artifact classes, such as stone tools. Among the specializations that gained prominence during this time is human osteology, the study of human bones. The analysis of human remains was only occasionally done in the past to describe the age and sex of an individual, to note strange pathologies and examples of violent death, or to make very broad generalizations about a population. In his summary of the effigy mound tradition, Chandler Rowe wrote that all that was known from the numerous skeletal remains recovered from effigy mounds was that the effigy mound people were long-headed and did not practice cradle-board deformation.[75] Up to this point, very few of the hundreds of skeletons recovered during the several major excavations of mounds had been closely examined.

As people trained in osteology became available, however, discoveries of human remains at North American archaeological sites almost always led to study at one level or another. This, in turn, has resulted in new insights into ancient disease vectors (tuberculosis may have been present among the effigy mound people), diet and nutrition, life expectancies, and genetic relationships among different cultures. Indeed, modern advances in DNA testing have the potential to help answer the question of the relationship of modern tribes to specific prehistoric ancestors, including the mound builders. Many Native Americans, however, object to the scientific examination and testing of Native American skeletons, and consequently such studies are currently mired in controversy.

Cultural Resource Management

A national ecology movement and deep public concern about environmental degradation led in the 1960s to important legislation to protect the environment. The environmental movement also generated public interest in the preservation of the "cultural environment." Noting the rapid destruction of historic and archaeological sites in the country, Congress passed the landmark National Historic Preservation Act of 1966, which instructed federal agencies to help manage the nation's "cultural resources" by ensuring that their actions—such as funding, licensing, and building—did not destroy significant historic or archaeological sites. The measure of "significance" would be whether a property, whether a Victorian-era building or a Native American burial mound, would be eligible for listing on the National Register of Historic Places.

The National Historic Preservation Act also set up State Historic Preservation Offices, which would be responsible for coordinating with federal agencies on matters of preservation and for conducting inventories of significant historic and archaeological sites. The primary way this was accomplished in Wisconsin was through grants given to communities, universities, and historic-preservation organizations. Some years later, the Wisconsin legislature also passed a series of measures designed to protect important historic and prehistoric sites during other publicly regulated projects that modified the landscape.

To help organize the collection of information for preservation purposes, the State Historical Society of Wisconsin instituted a regional archaeology program that designated cooperating institutions to research an area of the state. A significant part of the research concerned mounds. In the 1980s, for example, the Department of Anthropology at the University of Wisconsin–Milwaukee conducted the first modern inventory of mounds in a nine-county area comprising southeastern Wisconsin, while the Burnett County Historical Society compiled data on mounds in the northwestern part of the state.[76]

It is impossible to overestimate the impact of cultural research management on archaeologists' understanding of Wisconsin's past. Thousands of development projects, from the building of roads to the construction of sewer systems, have been first studied for their potential impacts on archaeological sites. If impacts could not be avoided, teams of archaeologists carefully excavated the sites in order to preserve the information that they contained. Thousands of ancient sites were found and documented. Spectacular archaeological discoveries were made that literally forced the rewriting of texts. Among them are a village of longhouses near La Crosse that provided a snapshot of life in Wisconsin as Columbus stepped ashore in the Caribbean and several villages in other areas where the effigy mound people may have lived. As a result of cultural resource management, more archaeological work was conducted in the past few decades than in the preceding 150 years. More information has been collected than can presently be assimilated, guaranteeing dramatic changes in the interpretation of the archaeological record in the future.

Cultural resource management has also presented increasing opportunities for collaboration between Native Americans and archaeologists, especially in regard to the preservation of Indian mounds and other burial places. A number of federal historic-preservation grants administered by the Historic Preservation Division of the State Historical Society went to Native American tribes, such as the Chippewa and Ho-Chunk (Winnebago), to locate cemeteries and mounds so they could be preserved for the future.[77] The Dane County parks department used these federal grants to inventory and map mounds in Dane County, assisted by Larry Johns, a surveyor of Native American ancestry who has dedicated himself to the preservation of Indian mounds in Wisconsin.[78] Consequently, this area has some of best mound data in the state.

Growing concern for Native American cultural sensibilities has promoted "in place" preservation of mounds and other Native American cemeteries rather than removal during the course of development. Exceptions to this policy, however, increasingly have involved the participation of Native Americans. In 1977, road construction threatened six mounds in the Rehbain I Mound Group near the Kickapoo River in Richland County. Lacking alternative routes for the road, the Department of Transportation contracted with the State Historical Society to excavate the mounds. In consultation with the Great Lakes Intertribal Council, the six mounds were later reconstructed nearby and all human remains reinterred.[79] Two mounds in the Bade Mound Group in Grant County were excavated under similar circumstances in 1980.[80] The mounds were rebuilt elsewhere on the site, and the human remains were reburied three years later under the supervision of Ho-Chunk religious leaders. Continuing dialogue on the matter of the unearthing and disposition of human remains has been mandated by the Native American Graves Protection and Repatriation Act, which requires consultation with appropriate Indian tribes on the removal of graves on federal land and, if requested, the return to Native American tribes of human remains and other sacred items recovered in the past by federal projects.

While general federal and state historic-preservation legislation helps preserve ancient Native American sites, it is Wisconsin's unique Burial Sites Preservation Law, passed in 1985, that has promoted the second great mound-preservation effort in the twentieth century. The law differs from other legislation in that it applies to all activities affecting burial places on both public and private land. The National Historic Preservation Act and equivalent state legislation can be brought into play only when governmental actions are involved. The Burial Sites Preservation Law was enacted when, in the early 1980s, Native Americans and archaeologists discovered that their objections alone could not block a housing project from being built on top of an eighteenth-century Chippewa cemetery. Significantly, however, the first site to be formally preserved under the law was a panther effigy mound on Lake Monona. Since then, hundreds of burial places, both Native American and Euro-American, have been saved from destruction, including a considerable number of Indian mounds.

The Lost Race Found Again?

Social changes stemming from the social upheavals of the 1960s and early 1970s promised for many a new age, one that would be harmonious, environmentally conscious, and tolerant of many lifeways and belief systems. Racism came under attack and was exposed in many areas of life, including established histories that excluded whole classes of people or distorted their contributions to the grand sweep of human history. Out of that era came some very positive social changes in American society and ideology, including an emphasis on social justice, a respect for the environment, and the rewriting of histories to include, for example, the roles played by Native Americans. Native Americans themselves reasserted their status as sovereign nations, claiming long-denied rights under treaties and demanding respect for their cultures, beliefs, and traditions.

But the era also produced a mistrust of science, the apparent cause of some modern problems, and many turned instead to mysticism, religious movements, and alternative realities associated with paranormal and psychic phenomena. It also spawned alternative histories written by people skeptical of mainstream science and history and excited by the flirtation with mythology, mysticism, and even notions of extraterrestrial contacts. Old books on the lost continent of Atlantis and mythical places became popular once again. Starting in 1968, Erich von Däniken, a Dutch restaurateur, published a number of best-sellers that attributed the existence of many ancient monuments in the world to visits by beings from other planets. And in 1976, Barry Fell published *America B.C.*, which, much to the chagrin of archaeologists and Native Americans, reopened the Lost Race debate.[81]

Fell, a former marine biologist, presented the idea, elaborated in several subsequent books, that there had been continual transoceanic migrations from the Old World to the New for thousands of years. The mark of these ancient visitors, Phoenicians and Celts, among others, is allegedly seen throughout North America in the form of settlements, ancient writing on rocks, and the works, customs, and even languages of the resident Native Americans, who took up certain Old World cultural characteristics through the process of diffusion. Diffusion is a cultural process by which ideas and customs spread from people to people, and the concept was commonly used in the past to explain the existence of similar characteristics in different cultures. Serious scholars who have examined Fell's work have pointed to numerous errors, fallacies, and misrepresentations.[82] He accepted as fact hoaxes that were debunked long ago, and he "read" as ancient writing nonrandom scratches on rocks that could have been produced in a number of less glamorous ways. Virtually all the evidence for ancient Old World contacts is presented without critical examination. Nevertheless, Fell's books attracted a huge readership and have produced a new generation of diffusionists, who are searching for evidence of Old World imprints on ancient Native American culture.

The popularity of Fell's version of diffusionism can be viewed as part of a general late-twentieth-century trend in which many myths of pseudoscience (UFOs, for example) are gaining respect, as reflected in tabloids, magazines, books, and popular television programs. The trend was so worrisome to noted astronomer and popular science writer Carl Sagan that he devoted one of his last books to the phenomenon.[83] In his passionate argument for a rigorous scientific perspective, Sagan warned that a people that cannot distinguish among mythology, pseudoscience, and real scientific evidence stand to lose control over their basic freedoms.

The reasons for this disturbing antiscientific trend are undoubtedly numerous and complex. Probably, like the resurgence of religious fundamentalism, they are based on the need to believe in simple truths and explanations in a world that is becoming more technologically complex and less understandable. With regard to diffusionism, there is also no little amount of ethnocentrism involved, as was the case with the Lost Race advocates of the nineteenth century. The resurgence of ethnocentric worldviews at the end of the twentieth century is a disturbing matter that deserves great study in itself.

Diffusion is a real cultural process that is indeed responsible for change now and in the past as peoples of differing cultural backgrounds come into contact. It is only one of several processes responsible for change. Furthermore, there is solid empirical evidence for a European presence in the New World before the time of Columbus in the form of Viking settlements on the coast of Newfoundland in the tenth century.[84] However, there is absolutely no evidence for the type of continual and extensive contact that Fell championed and no reason to believe that the development of Native American customs were influenced by others.

Curiously, as with the Lost Race debate of the nineteenth century, diffusionist beliefs in the late twentieth century have helped refocus public interest on Wisconsin's mounds and have even stimulated advances in mound research, specifically in the areas of mapping and documentation. In the 1980s, James Scherz, a professor of civil engineering, brought together his interest in ancient engineering principals and his belief in pre-Columbian contacts between peoples of the Old and New Worlds, forming the Ancient Earthworks Society. The stated objectives of the organization are to make precise maps of the arrangements of mounds from which angles, alignments, and "sacred" geometric patterns can be better studied and to promote the preservation of mounds.

Over the past several decades, Scherz and a cadre of students and volunteers have mapped and analyzed dozens of mound groups in Wisconsin (figure 2.11). One of them is at the famous Lizard Mound County Park, where, Scherz has argued, Native Americans once used mound alignments to observe the solstices and equinoxes as well as other astronomical phenomena. However, he also sees encoded in the mound arrangements at the park and elsewhere the knowledge of sacred geometry and units of measure commonly found in the Old World, where, he believes, it was carefully protected and handed down by secret societies, such as the Freemasons.

Much of this Old World influence on mounds Scherz sees as coming from the East. While surveying the Lizard Mounds site, he was informed by a local Native American mentor that "in the days when the mounds were built there was contact with people across the sea including those from India, where much of our harmony of proportion and mathematics would seem to have had at least one very important root."[85] "If his stories are true," Scherz wrote, "one would expect that there would be Old World canons of measure in the layout of the mounds. They indeed can be found here." Scherz has offered other insights that would have delighted Lost Race advocates Ephraim G. Squier and Edgar H. Davis 175 years ago: "[T]here is

Figure 2.11. This mound near Madison was the first to be cataloged as a burial site, saving it from development. (Photograph by Robert Birmingham)

other geometrical data, art styles, and writings by Hindu scholars (books not generally available to the American public) which are consistent with what our Indian teacher at Lizard Mound told us (i.e that ancient influences from the area of the Old World near the country we now call India once reached the shores of the Americas)."[86]

At the same time, Scherz, like his nineteenth-century civil engineer predecessor Theodore H. Lewis, can be credited with the production of some of the best maps of mound groups ever made. His skills in mapping mounds are widely recognized and have on occasion been used by both professional archaeologists and Native Americans involved in preservation projects. He also can be credited with bringing the important work of Lewis to the attention of contemporary scholars. During one project, careful study of aerial photography led Scherz to discover the largest effigy mound ever built in Wisconsin, a bird mound with a 1,300-foot wingspan (figure 2.12).

The recent work of diffusionists in Wisconsin has inspired the publication of a slick, public-oriented magazine called the *Ancient American,* which publishes primarily what it regards as evidence of ancient transoceanic contacts between the Old World and North America. The articles on Indian mounds read like many similar popular articles published in the nineteenth century, attributing influences and inspirations from Europe, the Middle East, Asia, and other places. Implicit in these and other articles is the notion that any sophisticated technologies, architecture, or ideas found in Native American societies must have come from contacts with the Old World.

Many archaeologists and other scholars, as well as some Native Americans, consider the claims of these new diffusionists to be highly dubious and simple recapitulations of the nineteenth-century myth of the Lost Race, which attempted to divest Native Americans of their unique place in the world by creating a new history filled with Europeans and others. Writers for the Wisconsin-based Native American newspaper *News from Indian Country* accused those involved with the *Ancient American* of "slandering our past, so that their future might be enriched at the expense of others."[87]

WHY WERE THE MOUNDS BUILT?
RESEARCH IN THE LATE TWENTIETH CENTURY

In growing frustration with the inability of archaeology to explain the meaning and purpose of the mounds, William Hurley concluded an essay on the effigy mound tradition by suggesting that knowledge had not progressed since the days of Increase A. Lapham.[88] But even as he wrote these words, changes in the way that mounds were being studied were again under way.

In reaction to archaeology's emphasis on statistics and objects rather than people and ideas, and the use of models of cultural change that left out ideology as an important component, some anthropologically trained archaeologists began arguing in the 1970s that if archaeologists were ever really to understand ancient people and cultures, they had to try to view the world as they did, not through a lens of modern culture. They also resurrected the perspective that clues to the ancient worldview can be readily

Figure 2.12. Aerial photograph of a soil shadow of a huge bird effigy mound that has been plowed (*lower arrow*). Also evident are the soil shadows of other destroyed mounds, including a conical mound with an approximate 200-foot diameter, a linear mound, and another bird or human effigy (*upper arrows*). (United States Department of Agriculture photograph, April 13, 1968. Catalogue no. WQ 1 JJ 131, Department of Geography Map Library, University of Wisconsin–Madison)

found in the belief systems of Native Americans. In other words, as Charles E. Brown observed in 1911, "ethnological science may greatly assist in our archaeological history."

Perhaps the opening shot in this revolution focusing on "cultural meanings" was fired in 1976 by Robert Hall in the pages of the national journal *American Antiquity*. In his article, Hall returned archaeology to the study of Native American beliefs to help explain, in part, mysterious circular ditches and earthen enclosures found in the Ohio River valley and elsewhere. He referred to the widely held belief among Native Americans that the geometry of the circle can confound ghosts and other supernatural forces. The red sand ring that Samuel Barrett found in a mound in the Kratz Creek Mound Group could well express this concept. Hall suggested that the inclusion of such features in monumental earthen construction in the past was just a more conspicuous way of symbolizing this concept than was used in more recent times. His point is that archaeologists have "to think in Native American categories and to proceed deductively in this frame of reference." The alternative, he fears, is that "prehistory may never be more than what it has become, the soulless artifact of a dehumanized science." [89]

In other articles and in a book provocatively called *Archaeology of the Soul*, Hall has explored other aspects of mound symbolism from the perspective of Native American belief systems.[90] His premise is always that the dramatic period of mound building could not have come and gone without having left clues in surviving Native American traditions that archaeologists can use to reconstruct ancient ideologies. For example, he pointed out that such things commonly found in mounds as mucky soils and other offerings from watery environments are used as symbols for renewal of the earth and rebirth of the soul by many Native American tribes and that these symbolic objects can be found in more modern rituals and ceremonies among many tribes.

Using ethnographic information, Hall even reopened the debate about the connection of the Ho-Chunk (Winnebago) to effigy mounds by taking Chandler Rowe to task for his faulty analysis of the relationship of effigy mound forms to clan symbols.[91] Hall pointed out that Rowe ignored some vital pieces of information contained in Native American belief systems that had been presented by Arlow B. Stout, Charles Brown, and Paul Radin almost a half century earlier—notably, that one of the most common mound forms, that of the long-tailed panther, is equivalent to the "water spirits" found in the belief systems and clans of the Ho-Chunk and other tribes. Furthermore, Rowe failed to see the rather common-sense connection between the thunder clans found in many tribes and the spirit beings called thunderbirds, who make the thunder and are easily recognized among common effigy mound forms. Although Hall has not argued that the Ho-Chunk built the effigy mounds, he has argued that Rowe failed to prove that they did not.

In perhaps the most dramatic example of the strength of oral traditions and their potential to illuminate the past, Hall used Ho-Chunk stories carefully recorded by Radin to "read" the famous Gottschall Rockshelter paintings. The faded paintings were found by a child in the 1980s on the wall of a cave on the family farm and were documented by Robert Salzer.[92] Among the paintings are opposing human beings, some much larger than others, as well as depictions of a turtle and a falcon or hawk. Hall was able to relate these figures to the story of Red Horn, a legendary culture hero to the Ho-Chunk and Ioway. In one of the stories, Red Horn battles with a race of giants assisted by his friends Turtle and Thunderbird. This example attests to the strength of oral traditions: the Red Horn stories were recorded by Radin from the Ho-Chunk in the early part of the twentieth century, while the Gottschall paintings and the story they tell are, at the very least, many hundreds of years old.

There are other contributors to the study of the meaning of mounds in the Midwest. Analyzing the symbolism from pit features, ash and rock layers, earthen fills, scattered human bones, and other offerings found in effigy mound groups in Iowa, David Benn, Arthur Bettis, and R. Clark Mallam discerned major differences in the beliefs of the effigy mound people and the mound builders who proceeded them and further suggested that these dissimilarities were clues to different changing social arrangements and economic practices.[93] From the physical remains of ancient ceremonial practices, they inferred that the ideological concerns of the effigy mound people were directed at maintaining balance and harmony between human beings and the natural world through spiritual forces.

This new approach, which focuses on cultural meanings as inferred from both archaeological evidence and Native American traditions and beliefs, is not without its critics and for many good reasons. Many researchers point out that it is impossible to crawl inside the heads of ancient people and that attempts to do so can lead to erroneous interpretations of the past. As William McKern and others argued many years ago, archaeology can ultimately describe only what people did; it is not within its capacity to attribute ideological motivations. Likewise, some archaeologists are deeply concerned about the uncritical use of oral traditions and "mythic history" as sources for credible information. Ronald Mason, representing an empirical school of thought, has warned that well-meaning considerations of Native American traditional knowledge only jeopardize the intellectual integrity of the field of archaeology. Citing such potential problems as alterations in the transmission of information from generation to generation, inaccurate translations, recorder bias, and reliance on only a few unrepresentative interviewees, Mason states:

Who knows how much recorded as "oral literature," "legend," or "mythology" is genuinely aboriginal and not adulterated by culture contact? Not sharing a common historiographic tradition with Europeans, Indian views of the past and the nature of history are not simply additional "data" like radiocarbon dates or pollen spectra, that can be plugged into a scientific exploration of the past. These distinct patterns of thought call for more rigorous testing than they have received before we build too much upon them.[94]

Nevertheless, the serious consideration of such "distinct patterns of thought" and the reintegration of Native American ideology into archaeological studies has proved to be an interesting and exciting direction in the search for the mound builders. It gives researchers much to think about regarding the meaning and purpose of the mounds and adds a much-needed human dimension to the story of the mound builders. This story keeps changing. But as it does, it is becoming progressively clearer, steadily building on information acquired over 150 years of mound research.

3

Wisconsin before the Mound Builders

The Paleo-Indian and Archaic Traditions

The story of the mound builders began when the first humans migrated into what is the state of Wisconsin. When and where the first people appeared in the Western Hemisphere are interesting issues that are currently a focus of great debate and discussion in archaeological circles. Most archaeologists would agree, however, that the first Americans trekked from Asia across the narrow Bering Strait, which separates modern Alaska from Siberia. The discovery of a 13,000-year-old village, Monte Verde, at the southern tip of South America established the fact that people have been in the Western Hemisphere for a very long time—much longer than originally supposed.[1] The Native Americans themselves have a variety of origin stories involving supernatural forces and spirit animals. Many traditional people believe that their ancestors have lived in the Americas since time began.

THE PALEO-INDIAN TRADITION IN WISCONSIN

The dates of the arrival of humans in Wisconsin are relatively easy to approximate because before 12,000 to 13,000 years ago much of the land was covered by mountainous glaciers that effectively prevented human settlement. As the ice age ended, the glaciers slowly melted and people colonized the area (figure 3.1). These early people, called Paleo-Indians by archaeologists, moved in an environment that had been shaped and influenced by gla-

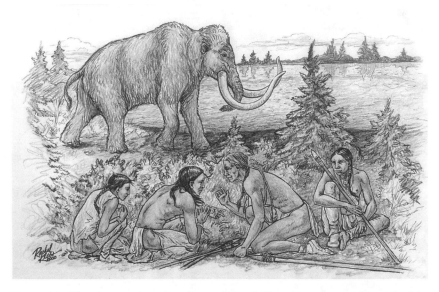

Figure 3.1. The first people, referred to as Paleo-Indians by archaeologists, arrived in Wisconsin 12,000 years ago. (Drawing by Rachel Klees; used with permission of the Kenosha Public Museum)

ciers.[2] Torrents of water and dirt from the melting ice fronts formed huge river channels, great and cold glacial lakes, and vast outwash plains of sand and gravel. In many areas, the landscape had been dramatically sculpted by glaciers, leaving behind hills—drumlins, moraines, and kames—and deep kettles, created by huge blocks of detached ice, that would later became the familiar lakes of the state. During this time of great and rapid environmental change, the vegetation and wildlife were very different from the plants and animals in present-day Wisconsin. Nearer to the wasting glacial front was tundra, the great frozen and barren ground. Farther away were muskeg swamps and forests of spruce and fir. In some of these areas, large lumbering mammoth and mastodon browsed. Caribou herds undoubtedly migrated seasonally northward and southward over thousands of square miles, and moose, elk, and bison could be found in some places. Many smaller animals, such as birds, rabbits, and aquatic life, also shared the Paleo-Indian world.

Paleo-Indians are known in Wisconsin from dozens of scattered locations where their distinctive stone spear points have been found (figure 3.2). The earliest of these implements were fashioned with channels or flutes so they could be easily hafted to wooden shafts. Later Paleo-Indian spear

Figure 3.2. Paleo-Indian spear points from the Skare site, near Madison, Wisconsin. The three points on the right are fluted and date to the early Paleo-Indian stage, around 11,000 years ago. The two on the far right are made from Hixton Silicified Sandstone. The three points on the left date to the late Paleo-Indian stage. (Photograph by Robert Granflaten; used with permission of the State Historical Society of Wisconsin)

points are larger, beautifully made lanceolate styles. Both of these Paleo-Indian styles found in Wisconsin are remarkably similar to those found throughout North America, indicating that the techniques for making tools were widely shared.

The Paleo-Indian population was very small, and these people's camp- or habitation sites are rarely found. Furthermore, because of the extreme age of Paleo-Indian sites, day-to-day items of a more perishable nature are rarely preserved. Thus there remain few clues from which to reconstruct Paleo-Indian lifestyles. A series of newly discovered "bone beds" in Kenosha County offer evidence that Wisconsin's first people butchered mammoths for food.[3] Whether they systematically hunted these huge beasts or simply scavenged dead or dying mammoths is yet to be learned.

The little physical evidence that is extant suggests that the Paleo-Indians traveled great distances in small family groups in order to make a living off a comparatively sparse and barren landscape, erecting temporary shelters at many different locations. Every so often, perhaps annually, these small groups would gather to undertake communal hunts and to exchange goods and news. Such meetings also would have been important for people to

71

Figure 3.3. Widespread trading systems developed in eastern North America after 3000 B.C. One valued trade item was chert, for making stone tools, here being traded for copper tools. (Drawing by Phoebe Hefko; used with permission of the State Historical Society of Wisconsin)

find spouses outside the family. One such gathering place may have been the Skare site, near Madison.[4] Now located on the Yahara River, 11,000 years ago this site was on a peninsula in a huge glacial lake. Many Paleo-Indian fluted points and hundreds of other stone tools characteristic of Paleo-Indians have been discovered on the surface of plowed fields over the years by amateur and professional archaeologists—many more artifacts than have been recovered from any other known Paleo-Indian site in Wisconsin.

Among the resources exchanged when Paleo-Indian families met were special types of stone used to make spear points, knives, and other tools. One kind of stone was chert, which occurs in some abundance throughout southern Wisconsin and elsewhere in the Midwest. Certain high-quality and colorful cherts were preferred, though, and they seem to have been traded or carried long distances from their sources (figure 3.3). A second raw material heavily used and exchanged in Wisconsin by Paleo-Indians was Hixton Silicified Sandstone, a grainy yellowish to reddish stone that occurs mainly in Jackson County in and around a large natural outcropping called Silver Mound. The Paleo-Indians may have believed that Hixton and the variously colored cherts were imbued with special magical or supernatural characteristics, thus explaining their wide distribution. Significantly, Hixton Silicified Sandstone continued to play an important role, unknown now, in the belief systems of midwestern Native Americans for 10,000 years, as indicated by its continual use as a trade item.

The Paleo-Indians, like all human beings, undoubtedly had a rich and elaborate spiritual life. Like that of later Native Americans, the world of the Paleo-Indians probably was shared with a number of spirit beings, deities, and supernatural forces. And like those of their descendants, the spirits and deities of the Paleo-Indians were surely inspired by the animal life around them: birds, aquatic life, and mammals, including the huge mastodon and mammoth. The Paleo-Indians undoubtedly believed in some sort of afterlife, and they engaged in special ceremonies upon the death of a member of the group. The oldest human burial in Wisconsin is that of a single individual who was cremated approximately 9,000 years ago and buried in a pit in Brown County. The burial pit, called the Renier site, included a number of heat-shattered spear points meant to accompany the individual to the afterlife.[5] Many of these points were made from Hixton Silicified Sandstone. Cremation is a custom shared by many people of the world, past and present, and has many different meanings. For the highly mobile Paleo-Indians, the cremation of a corpse may have been a convenient way to transport the remains over long distances to the desired place of burial. Whatever the reason, there is evidence that the custom of ritual burning was widespread. At three other locations in northern Wisconsin, clusters of burned spear points similar to those found at Renier have been recovered. Human bone was not found with these artifacts, but archaeologists suspect that it had long ago disintegrated.[6]

THE ARCHAIC TRADITION:
TERRITORIES, TRADE, AND CEMETERIES

Over the next 5,000 years, climatic change continued to alter the landscape of Wisconsin. The climate warmed, and the North American glacial environment retreated northward, into present-day Canada. This was accompanied not only by the mass extinction of many animals adapted to cold weather, such as the mammoth and mastodon, but also by the proliferation of other, more easily hunted species, such as moose, elk, and, especially, deer. Deciduous forests and grasslands replaced the relatively unproductive spruce forests, providing a variety of edible plants and supporting abundant game. Rapidly running and frigid glacial discharge was replaced by rivers and streams that offered abundant aquatic life, including many species of fish and mussels. The many lakes and wetlands left in the wake of the glaciers also provided habitat for fish, waterfowl, and aquatic mammals. By about 5000 B.C., the essentially modern distribution of plants and animals had been established in Wisconsin, although climatic fluctuations would sometimes affect the distribution even into recent times.

Native Americans adapted to these resource-rich environments by developing new hunting and gathering strategies and by introducing a number of technological innovations: axes for clearing land and chopping wood, stone implements for grinding and processing plant foods, specialized gear for fishing, and a long wooden spear thrower for increasing the effectiveness of hunting. This long period of adjustment has been called the Archaic period or tradition.[7]

As is the time of the Paleo-Indians, the first part of the Archaic period is shrouded in mystery, again due to the very low population density and the small number of artifacts that have been preserved. These early people, like the Paleo-Indians, are known primarily from their distinctive spear points and knives. It is believed that early Archaic people lived much like their Paleo-Indian ancestors, ranging widely over the landscape.

There is better evidence for the latter half of the Archaic, when the increasing availability of seasonally recurring food resources promoted tremendous growth in population and important changes in economic strategies. It no longer was necessary to travel vast distances to find food. By scheduling food-collecting activities to coincide with the maximum availability of the food—such as spawning fish, herding animals, seeding plants, and migrating birds—families and bands were able to use much smaller territories. A typical year in the life of Archaic people in south-central Wisconsin may have found them, in summer, on lakeshores and river floodplains, where many different plant and animal foods, including fish, could be found; in autumn, near oak–hickory groves, where protein-rich nuts and acorns could be gathered; and in winter, under rock overhangs in sheltered valleys, where deer could be hunted in large quantities. As a consequence of shrinking band territories, clear regional cultural differences among peoples began to emerge after about 3,000 years ago, as indicated by differing subsistence strategies, artifact styles, and other customs.

A tendency to stay in one area for longer periods of time stimulated other important social and economic changes. One was the experimentation with plant cultivation, which led to the domestication of certain wild plant species that provided starchy seeds for consumption. Among them were marsh elder, chenopodium or goosefoot, and sunflower. Native Americans began to control their food sources by planting and encouraging the growth of these plants near major camps rather than gathering wild seeds over large areas. Although these local plants never became a major part of the diet, they were a significant and reliable supplement. Most important, the cultivation of these plants predisposed people in the Midwest to adopt the plants that had been domesticated elsewhere—squash from the Gulf coast, corn and beans from Mexico—that would much later revolutionize Native American life.

Another important development was the expansion of trade. Not all band territories were comparable in the types of resources they supplied that were needed for daily life, including food, stone for tools, and animal skins for clothing. Furthermore, it can be expected that local shortages in critical resources, such as food, occurred from time to time. Without a mechanism for evening out these disparities, the potential for conflict, even warfare, was very real. Formal trade relationships among neighboring bands helped reduce conflict by guaranteeing a flow of critical resources. To keep trade networks open and continually running, special items of great symbolic value were exchanged. The ceremonial exchange of such items facilitated the trade of more commonplace items when they were needed.

One of the first of these symbolic items traded extensively in Wisconsin and adjacent areas was copper acquired from northern Michigan and Isle Royale in Lake Superior. Exchanged as raw material or finished items, copper appears in many forms as tools, weapons, and personal ornaments. The use of copper was so common during the Archaic that archaeologists once referred to the phenomenon as the Old Copper Culture. In recognition that the use and trade of copper probably involved people of different cultural backgrounds, it is now known as the Old Copper Complex (figure 3.4), the word "complex" referring to a cluster of shared rituals.[8] Over time, other exotic goods were exchanged that ultimately linked much of eastern North America in one vast trade network. Trade items found at Archaic sites in Wis-

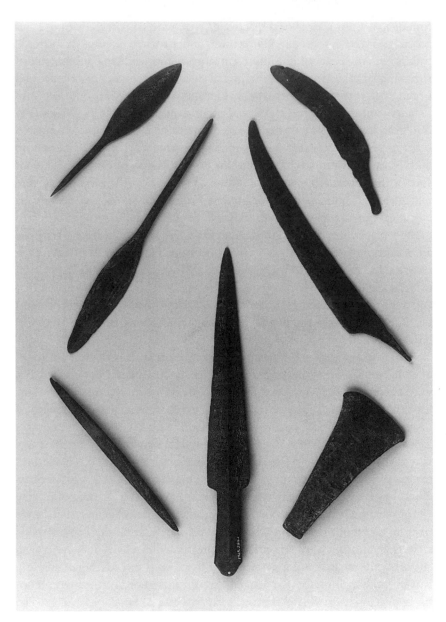

Figure 3.4. Old Copper Complex weapons and tools, including spear points and knives. (Photograph by Andy Kraushaar; used with permission of the State Historical Society of Wisconsin)

consin include seashells from the Atlantic Ocean, blue-gray hornstone chert from Indiana, and obsidian, or volcanic glass, from the Yellowstone area of Wyoming. Unlike the earlier copper objects, however, these items seem to have become status symbols for certain families and individuals in new, more complex social arrangements.

A third trend that grew from the development of smaller, fixed territories was the elaboration of rituals related to the burial of the dead and the selection of places within these territories as permanent symbols of the rights of the social group to the land and its resources. Cemeteries become territorial markers in which social groups staked their claim to a place in the world by virtue of links to the ancestors buried there.

The earliest cemeteries recorded in Wisconsin appear during the Archaic period, or between about 4000 and 1500 B.C., and are assigned to the Old Copper Complex. One of them is the Osceola site, on the Mississippi River in Grant County, in which 500 people were buried in a single mass grave, or ossuary.[9] Grave offerings were few at this site, but became more common in later Old Copper Complex sites. At Osceola, individuals were interred as bundles of bones, as cremations, and as bodies placed "in the flesh" or in a prone or an extended position before they decomposed. Most of the people in the ossuary are represented by bone bundles, and this somewhat grisly form of "secondary burial" or "reburial" continued to be common practice throughout North America right up to the time of European contact. After death, the body was left out on a scaffold or sometimes even buried in the ground until it decomposed (figure 3.5). At an appointed time, the bones of all those who had died during a certain interval were gathered, carefully scraped clean, and buried together in one place in the midst of great ceremony.

A similar ritual was recorded with a fair amount of disgust in the seventeenth century by Jesuit missionaries living among the Huron of the eastern Great Lakes region.[10] Their descriptions of the "Feast of the Dead" celebrated by the Huron provide an insight into what might have happened at Archaic cemeteries thousands of years ago. The Feast of the Dead lasted for several days, but was conducted only every eight to twelve years by a host village, perhaps when the location of the village was about to be moved. The purpose of the ceremony was to rebury in a common grave all those who had died in years past. Relatives disinterred their kin, cleaned the bones, and hung the robe-covered bone bundles on poles surrounding the large pit. After a time, all the bone bundles, along with grave offerings, were placed in the pit so that the spirits of friends and relatives could be together. The grave was then covered over. The Feast of the Dead was more than a mortuary ritual. It reinforced the common identity of the Huron and even helped create

Figure 3.5. Many Native American tribes temporarily placed the dead on scaffolds until the bodies decomposed, eventually gathering and burying the bones. (From Henry Rowe School-craft, *The Indian Tribes of the United States* [Philadelphia: Lippincott, 1884])

alliances with others. Feasts and other social activities accompanied the re-burial, and neighboring villagers were invited to participate in ceremonies and festivities. In a version of the ceremony, later documented for the western Great Lakes, several tribes formed important political and economic alliances by participating in this mortuary ritual.[11]

CEMETERIES INTO MOUNDS

Cemeteries created toward the end of the Archaic suggest that some important social changes were taking place in Native American societies at that time. At the Riverside site, on the Menominee River at the Michigan–Wisconsin border, archaeologists discovered in the 1950s a number of small ossuaries that contained the remains of sixty-five people, mostly in the form of cremations and bone bundles and frequently covered with thick layers of a red powder called red ocher.[12] Red ocher is made from grinding hematite, an iron ore, and was used as a pigment in mortuary ceremonies in North America for many thousands of years. The widespread use of red ocher in midwestern burials between 1200 and 500 B.C. has led archaeologists to classify the burial sites as part of the Red Ocher Complex (figure 3.6).[13] Another attribute associated with this elaborate ceremonial complex is the burial of certain people with exotic and beautiful objects obtained through long-distance trade, including ceremonial chipped-stone blades, seashell ornaments, and obsidian blocks. The use of more readily available copper decreased and was now largely restricted to the manufacture of such ornaments as beads. One explanation for this pattern is that the people buried with these precious materials occupied a higher social status than others. Perhaps these high-status positions were linked to trade. The fact that men, women, and even children were buried with these exotic items may mean that social status extended to the whole family, not just individuals.

All the Old Copper Complex and Red Ocher Complex cemeteries of the Archaic are located on prominent knolls or hills that easily could have functioned as visible territorial markers for the people who created the cemeteries. As archaeologist and writer Brian Fagan observed, it is only one short step from the use of natural eminences to the construction of more visible markers in the form of mounds of dirt placed over the cemeteries.[14] Conspicuous mortuary structures containing the bones of honored ancestors would have been particularly important if ancestral territories and resources were being contested. There is good evidence that sporadic warfare was erupting between bands or tribes. Several Red Ocher Complex cemeteries included the remains of individuals killed by spears or by other violent means. In 1978, the construction of a building in Elm Grove, near Milwaukee, unearthed a Red Ocher ossuary pit that contained the haphazardly arranged skeletons of seven adult men and a child, all of whom probably had died in a single battle or attack.[15] Spear points were embedded in the bones, and some bodies were partially dismembered and scalped.

Figure 3.6. Red Ocher Complex ceremonial blades. (Photograph from Katherine P. Stevenson et al., "The Woodland Tradition," *The Wisconsin Archeologist* 78, nos. 1–2 [1997]; used with permission of the Wisconsin Archeological Society)

Sometime just before 500 B.C., Native Americans began to build the first burial mounds on the Wisconsin landscape. The construction of these mounds reflects the elaboration of rituals surrounding death and the desire to create visual and symbolic links among human beings, the land, and the supernatural world.

4

Early Burial Mound Builders

The Early and Middle Woodland Stages

Until recently, the construction of burial mounds, along with the introduction of pottery vessels after about 1000 B.C., was used to mark the beginning the Woodland period or tradition in eastern North America. It is now clear that the custom of mound building is much older and the result of social and economic changes already under way during the Archaic.

THE FIRST EARTHWORKS IN NORTH AMERICA

Mound building seems to have begun independently in several regions of North America. Along the Atlantic coast in Labrador, a complex maritime culture of caribou and sea-mammal hunters had begun to bury their kin, covered with red ocher, in low earthen and rock mounds by 5600 B.C. Near the Gulf of Mexico, larger earthen burial mounds excavated in such places as Louisiana and Florida have recently been radiocarbon dated to between 4000 and 2000 B.C.[1] The mound-building tradition in Louisiana eventually led to the construction of the imposing Poverty Point site on the Bayou Macon in the Mississippi River valley about 100 miles below the mouth of the Arkansas River (figure 4.1). Poverty Point is considered to be the first major civic, ceremonial, and trade center in North America. Around 1200 B.C., ancient Native Americans built huge concentric earthen embankments that enclosed a large plaza.[2] Immediately to the west of the complex is a mound in the shape of a hawk that is 710 feet long and more than 70 feet high. Bird

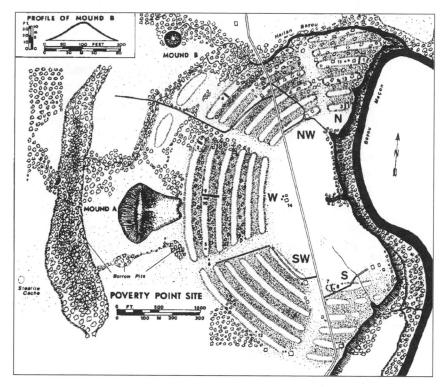

Figure 4.1. The Poverty Point site, on the Bayou Macon in Louisiana, is the remains of the major earthen ceremonial center in North America. (Drawing by Clarence H. Webb, *Geoscience and Man* 17 [1982]; used with permission of Louisiana State University, Baton Rouge)

imagery, representing the "upperworld" in the cosmology of Native Americans, carries through to the modern day, appearing in such forms as thunderbirds. As we shall see, birds of various sorts, particularly raptors, played a prominent role in the artwork and belief systems of Woodland and Mississippian peoples in the Midwest.

ADENA

After 1000 B.C., the custom of building burial mounds spread to the bands and tribes living in the Ohio River valley, where it marks the beginning of the Early Woodland stage or period and the great Adena Complex.[3] Like the Old Copper and Red Ocher Complexes in Wisconsin and adjacent regions, Adena was not one culture, but a cluster of rituals shared by a number of different peoples. One ritual was the erection of large conical mounds over burial pits or chambers dug into the ground that frequently contained the remains of a single person. In later Adena Complex mounds, these elaborate chambers were lined with logs and lay beneath the floors of pole-and-thatch grave shelters that were burned to the ground before the mounds were constructed. Mounds grew in size through time by the addition of more burials and earth. One Adena mound in Moundsville, West Virginia, was more than sixty-seven feet high. Near the burial mounds, the Adena people built large earthen enclosures that possibly served as sacred spaces for conducting ceremonies related to the burials.

The burial of relatively few people in pits below the mounds reflects the growing complexity of Native American societies in eastern North America in which differences in social status were becoming evident. This trend continued throughout the eight centuries of Adena life and beyond. Simultaneously, long-distance trade networks grew more elaborate, and important people buried in the mounds are often accompanied by symbolic items of great prestige value acquired from distant places: seashells, sheets of mica from North Carolina, pipestone from Ohio, blue-gray hornstone chert from Indiana, lead (for white pigment) from southwestern Wisconsin or northern Illinois, and copper from around Lake Superior.

HOPEWELL

Around 200 B.C., Adena climaxed with the development of the phenomenal cultural complex in the Ohio River and lower Illinois River valleys called Hopewell.[4] Archaeologists date Hopewell in these areas to between 200 B.C. and A.D. 400 and assign it to the Middle Woodland stage or period. During this time, trade networks continued to expand, moving around great quantities of exotic items and raw materials and ultimately linking together much of North America east of the Rocky Mountains. This vast ceremonial trade network and its associated rituals has sometimes been called the Hopewell Interaction Sphere.

During Hopewell times, the construction of earthworks in Ohio reached awe-inspiring dimensions. Massive geometric earthworks—squares, circles, and octagons—covered vast tracts of land, sometimes hundreds of acres. Large, wide "sacred roads" seem to have connected some of these ceremonial areas. These spectacular structures required sophisticated engineering and architectural skills and thus were the special focus of the adherents of the myth of the Lost Race in the nineteenth century. The scale and engineering complexity of Hopewell earthworks still excite the imagination.

Hopewell earthworks often enclose clusters of large burial mounds. As do those of the Adena Complex, the mounds frequently cover the elaborate log-lined crypts of important people. The burial chambers appear to have functioned as repositories for the dead for quite some time before being covered by mounds. Typically, one or sometimes several individuals were placed in a subterranean crypt not long after death, and the crypt was roofed over. As other deaths occurred in the family or clan, the bones of the decomposed bodies that had been interred earlier were moved to one side in carefully arranged bundles and the newly dead were placed in the center of the chamber. Some of the burials were in the form of cremations. Eventually, the crypt was covered by a mound—undoubtedly with great ceremony—and some burials were occasionally added to the mound at later times. Other Hopewell mounds covered the burned remains of charnel houses. These were large aboveground wood-and-thatch crypts in which members of a family or clan were placed after death, either "in the flesh" or as cremations, and that sheltered a variety of rituals attending burial ceremonies. At some point, possibly when it was full, the structure was ritually burned and a mound was built over the spot to mark its location.

Offerings of great prestige value accompanied people buried in Hopewell mounds. Beautifully crafted ornaments and objects of copper, mica, slate, fine chert, obsidian, and silver were typically placed in these special burials, as were exquisitely crafted pottery vessels with intricate designs. Also usually included were stone platform pipes, sometimes carved in the form of beautiful animal effigies. Smoking had become an important part of ritual life, and tobacco, a plant originally domesticated in Mexico, was grown for ceremonial purposes.

In Ohio and southern Illinois, subsistence was based on plentiful natural resources and small gardens of domesticated local plants that were enhanced by small amounts of corn and squash. The complexity of Hopewell burial customs and the elaborate nature of their earthworks have led some archaeologists to believe that some Hopewell societies had arranged themselves into social aggregates called chiefdoms. Like bands and tribes, chiefdoms are integrated by networks of kinship relations, but unlike these simpler forms of social organization, chiefdoms are hierarchical. Social power is concentrated in certain families or clans that control the distribution of food and resources to the rest of the population. Other archaeologists see Hopewell as simply a series of interacting, largely egalitarian, kin-based societies with little centralized social or political control.

Whatever the case, the fabulous items in Hopewell burials probably do not represent personal wealth. Leaders in most types of Native American societies demonstrated their wisdom and power by giving away wealth, not acquiring it for themselves. Aside from personal ornaments, the grave offerings probably represent contributions made to the burial by others in respect for the status of the deceased.

It is clear that the construction of burial mounds and associated earth-works played an important role in Hopewell societies. They functioned as ceremonial centers for small nearby settlements and helped reinforce the identity of the social group as a whole. Perhaps as with the Feast of the Dead conducted by the Huron, neighboring tribes and chiefdoms were invited to bring gifts and grave offerings and to participate in ceremonies, thus help-ing to reinforce or create alliances. The exchange of gifts during these peri-odic burial rituals was probably one of the many ways that the vast Hopewell trade network moved goods around eastern North America. Certainly, the burial of important people in prominent structures with symbols of prestige not only emphasized the status of the chiefly families, but also created a con-tinuing demand for exotic goods that kept the trade networks operating.

The construction of mounds in Hopewell times also reflected spiritual concerns. Robert Hall has observed that many Middle Woodland mounds, including some in Wisconsin, contained offerings that are symbols of or metaphors for rebirth, world renewal, and fertility in many Native Ameri-can belief systems. They include layers or pockets of white sands, mucky soils, puddled clays, and clamshells.[5] For the Woodland mound builders, the most important aspect of the ceremonial of mound burials may have been that it provided an opportunity to associate the death of prominent people with the rebirth and renewal of the world and all its living things. This con-cept was clearly present as the first mounds were being built in Wisconsin.

THE EARLY WOODLAND STAGE: THE BURIAL MOUNDS

The onset of mound building in Wisconsin is usually associated with the Early Woodland stage or period, dated in Wisconsin to between 500 B.C. and A.D. 100, but the first burial mounds in Wisconsin actually appeared a little before that time, during the transition from the Archaic period about 800 B.C. The first mounds seem to have been a direct outgrowth of the elab-orate burial ceremonialism of the Red Ocher Complex. The construction of burial mounds in Wisconsin began around the same time that Adena was flourishing farther east, and these Wisconsin sites have much in common with this more elaborate complex. Ideas, not just precious items, were being shared. Only a few mound groups have been identified for the Late Archaic and Early Woodland stages in Wisconsin, although it is suspected that many more have not yet been identified (figure 4.2).

Life in Wisconsin during the Early Woodland period appears to have been much like that during the Late Archaic. Long-distance trade networks continued to flourish. Bands or tribes occupied defined territories, shifting locations occasionally to take full advantage of nature's bounty. Several ex-

Figure 4.2. The distribution of some prominent Early and Middle Woodland mounds in Wisconsin. (Map by Amelia Janes, Midwest Educational Graphics)

amples of Early Woodland camps have been found at various places in the state, and they provide insights into how Native Americans adapted to different environments.[6] At the Bachman site, near Sheboygan, archaeologists found the seeds of domesticated sumpweed at a deer-hunting camp, the first evidence of cultivation in the state. The Beach site, on Lake Waubesa near Madison, was a warm-weather camp from which Early Woodland people collected a wide variety of foods, including fish, mammals, waterfowl, plant seeds, nuts, and acorns. On the Mississippi River floodplain, a late-summer camp called the Mill Pond site produced evidence of intensive clam gathering as well as fishing and hunting of riverside animals. The same people also may have been growing sunflower and squash. As for the Archaic, no housing structures have yet been found representing this period.

One major technological innovation during Early Woodland times was the development of ceramic containers, pottery, used for storing and cooking food. Of all the artifact classes that archaeologists study, pottery is the most useful because different societies made pottery in different ways and decorated the pots with distinctive designs. Even within one group or culture, ceramic characteristics and decorations changed over time. Once a ceramic type is dated by radiocarbon or other means, the discovery of similar sherds can reveal much about where specific cultures lived and with whom they interacted.

The appearance of pottery, after about 500 B.C., is related to the tendency of Native American groups to spend longer periods of time at one place. For obvious reasons, the use of easily broken and unwieldy clay pots for storing and cooking is of questionable value to a highly mobile society. In earlier times, skins, baskets made from woven grasses or bark, and bark containers were commonly used. As people increasingly settled down in relatively long-lasting camps, however, the advantages of hard-walled, comparatively leak-proof containers for cooking and storage became more apparent.

Woodland pottery in Wisconsin was made with local clays mixed with crushed rock. As was the case with most Native American groups, the potters were probably women. The surfaces of clay pots made in Woodland times were first roughened or marked with cords or fabrics. Decorations were then stamped, impressed, incised, or trailed on this surface. Although there is much individual variation, the decorative motifs found on pottery were not based on the fanciful whim of the potters or selected for purely aesthetic reasons. Pottery designs appear to have included symbols that represented the underlying structure of the people's belief systems. David Benn, who has specialized in the study of design symbolism on Woodland pottery, suggests that chevrons found on Woodland pots are bird symbols that denote the "upperworld" in Native American cosmology, while other designs, such as some arrangements of parallel lines, represent the "lowerworld," which includes earth and water (figure 4.3).[7] Many Native American cultural traditions in North America conceptualize the earth itself as lying between the upperworld, which contains the sun, the moon, and celestial birds, and the watery underworld, which is inhabited by various powerful water spirits and monsters.[8] In many instances, the upperworld and lowerworld are viewed in direct opposition to each other, but are depicted together in symbols in order to conceptualize harmony. Variations on this upperworld/lowerworld theme appear in decorations on pottery made in the

Figure 4.3. Early Woodland pot decorated with chevron and linear designs, possibly denoting the upperworld and the lowerworld. (Photograph from Katherine P. Stevenson et al., "The Woodland Tradition," *The Wisconsin Archaeologist* 78, nos. 1–2 [1997]; used with permission of the Wisconsin Archeological Society)

Midwest throughout the rest of the prehistoric period. Such symbolism provides invaluable clues to ideology and possibly even the social divisions of ancient cultures and assists in the interpretation of the meaning of other customs, such as mound building.

In Illinois and Iowa, the first burial mound sites are directly linked to the Red Ocher Complex, and this seems to be the case in Wisconsin. One example in Wisconsin is the Henschel site, which once included three large conical mounds arranged around a spring on a hill overlooking the huge Sheboygan Marsh in Sheboygan County. To the east of the conical mounds was a linear mound and a group of "panther" effigy mounds, all of which were built during a later period. The Sheboygan Marsh provided an extraordinary abundance of food resources—waterfowl, fish, mammals, and a wide variety of plants—to the people who used the Henschel mounds. It must have been a place where Native Americans gathered frequently, and thus was a logical location for periodic ceremonial activities. The construction of the Henschel mounds around a spring is also significant because springs issue life-giving water and are the sources of special earth, fine sands, and muck, all of which are associated with concepts of rebirth and fertility in many Native American belief systems. Springs are believed to be entrances to the watery underworld, the residence of the great and powerful water spirits. For probably all these reasons, many mound groups were constructed on or near "sacred" springs throughout the entire period of mound building.

Like those of many other mounds in Wisconsin, the aboveground portions of the three conical mounds at the Henschel site were leveled by farming. However, a map made in 1920 by Alphonse Gerend, a Sheboygan dentist, preserved the locations of the mounds.[9] The largest of the three, which was about eight feet high, reportedly had been excavated in the 1870s by a local mound digger. The startling discovery made the local newspapers, and a version of the story found its way into Cyrus Thomas's report for the Bureau of Ethnology.[10] Evidently, the digger had found a large boulder vault or enclosure within which many skeletons were arranged around a large conch shell. More than a century later, in the 1990s, heavy machinery inadvertently exposed part of a burial pit that had been beneath another of the leveled mounds. This portion of the chamber also contained a concentration of large rocks, possibly a cairn or vault, and an unknown number of burials covered with red ocher, reminiscent of burials of the Red Ocher Complex. Grave offerings included copper and conch-shell beads as well as knifes or spear points similar in style to those made by the Adena people in Ohio and made of hornstone from Indiana. This part of the chamber was covered by a layer of black soil. Charcoal from the pit dates the funerary activities to about 600 B.C., a date consistent with the last phases of the Red Ocher Complex in Wisconsin.[11]

A second Early Woodland mound group, this one near Cedarburg, also consisted of just three conical mounds. The Hilgen Spring Mound Group overlooks Cedar Creek, a tributary of the Milwaukee River and, as its name implies, is also associated with prominent springs. Two of the Hilgen Spring mounds were excavated in 1968 by the Public Museum of the City of Milwaukee just before the construction of a subdivision on the site.[12] The larger of these mounds was forty feet in diameter and six feet high. Construction destroyed the third mound. The two excavated mounds were similar in construction and have much in common with other Early Woodland mounds in eastern North America. Both were built over large grave pits, one containing the remnants of an extended, presumably "in the flesh" burial, and the other, three reburials in the form of bone bundles. Over the pits, a layer of black organic soil was mounded up; on top of the black soil were the burial mounds, consisting of soil and sand from the surrounding area. The black soil was apparently taken from a nearby camp, since it included such debris as chips from stone-tool making, food remains, broken artifacts, and charcoal. In one of the two mounds, an infant burial was put in the mound fill, and sometime later, a bone bundle was placed in a pit dug into the mound surface.

No grave goods were found, but there were other features in the pits that were the remnants of burial rituals and probably symbolized the concept of the renewal of the earth. Pieces of limestone and brightly colored fieldstone were concentrated alongside the burial pit in one mound, and around it, at roughly the cardinal directions, were four other such concentrations. Robert Hall has identified an identical arrangement, but made of earth, in a Woodland mound in Iowa and relates it to the widespread "Earth-Diver" origin stories and the ritual re-creation of the earth.[13] Variations of the Earth-Diver stories are found among many Native American tribes and, indeed, in some Old World cultures, suggesting that the structure of the tale is of extreme antiquity. The essence of the stories is that a water creature dives deep into a primordial ocean to retrieve some mud from which the earth is made. In a Cheyenne version, a mud hen brings up mud that is divided by the creator to form the earth. The Cheyenne have a ceremony that recapitulates this act of creation for the purpose of promoting "the fertility of all living things upon which the Cheyenne depended." Called the Sun Dance or Lodge of New Life, the rite includes the cutting of sod into five blocks, representing the creation of the earth, and then the placing of the sod pieces around a buffalo-skull altar near a central Sun Dance pole. Closer to Wisconsin, Hall has also highlighted a Ho-Chunk (Winnebago) belief that after the earth was created, it was in constant motion, so attempts were made to secure it at the four cardinal directions with four islands, water spirits, and snakes. It is also tempting to tie the four concentrations of stones surrounding the Hilgen Spring burial pit to this earth creation concept, particularly because of the association of the mound group with springs, the entrance to the underworld for water spirits.

THE MIDDLE WOODLAND STAGE:
INTERACTION WITH HOPEWELL

The construction of mound groups increased during the following Middle Woodland period, dated in Wisconsin to between about 100 B.C. and A.D. 500.[14] Several dozen locations, largely in the southern part of the state, have now been identified, almost all on terraces or bluff tops overlooking major bodies of water. Middle Woodland mounds sometimes occur singly, but most frequently are found in small groups. At many locations, later mound builders added their own mounds to the groups, so it is difficult to determine just how many were constructed during the Middle Woodland period. Like earlier mounds, Middle Woodland mounds are conical (figure 4.4). Some are very large according to Wisconsin standards. The Nicholls Mound, near Trempealeau, measured about ninety feet in diameter and was twelve feet high, making it among the largest burial mounds ever built in Wisconsin.

The ceremonies, rituals, and artifacts associated with this major wave of mound building show influences from Hopewell centers in Illinois and Ohio, particularly at those Wisconsin mound centers along the major mid-continental transportation route, the Mississippi River. Along the Mississippi, many Middle Woodland mound centers were built on river terraces between the mouth of the Wisconsin River near Prairie du Chien, to the south, and the mouth of the Trempealeau River, to the north. In the lower Illinois River valley, Hopewell mound centers are spaced about twelve miles apart, and this distance may represent the length of territories along the river that the centers served.[15] Present information suggests similar spacing and territorial distances for Hopewell-related centers in Wisconsin. Mound groups are found at virtually every major drainage valley, called hollows or coulees in southwestern Wisconsin. The mound centers typically consist of clusters of mound groups or several mound groups within a short distance of one another. This pattern suggests that several social groups, such as families or clans, were involved in the construction of the centers and/or that the focus of mortuary and other ritual activities shifted location over time.

Most of what is known about the mound groups along the Mississippi River derives from the excavations conducted in the nineteenth century by the Smithsonian Institution and, especially, from the work undertaken in the 1930s by the Public Museum.[16] Excavations of selected mounds revealed that, like Hopewell mounds to the south, mounds in the upper Mississippi River valley covered rectangular burial pits or subterranean crypts that were used continually for many years before a mound was erected over them. Some burials were placed in stone crypts or encircled by rocks, later

Figure 4.4. This mound, sixty feet in diameter and seven feet high, at the Outlet site in Monona is typical of the conical mounds built during the Early and Middle Woodland stages in Wisconsin. (Photograph by Robert Birmingham)

to be covered by earth. The dead were laid in the crypts in extended positions not long after they had died or as bundles of cleaned bones. As with mounds in the Ohio and Illinois River valleys, there is evidence that bones, decayed of flesh, were set aside as new corpses were placed in the crypts. Beneath a mound at the Schwert Mound Group, near Trempealeau, a shallow twelve- by eight-foot pit contained the remains of seven extended "in the flesh" burials and many more bone bundles. On an earthen shelf framing the pit was a continuous line of bundled bones. In all, the remains of at least forty-six people lay buried in the pit beneath the mound. In the Nicholls Mound, a thick layer of bark covered the area of the tomb, suggesting that before its construction, the chamber was sheltered by a house or roof of some kind (figure 4.5).

Careful excavation of some of these Mississippi River mounds by the Public Museum has added other details about burial rituals. When the Middle Woodland people dug the rectangular grave pits for several of the mounds in the Trempealeau area, they were careful to pile the dirt in four separate embankments paralleling the sides of the pit. This arrangement is reminiscent of that of the stone piles at the Hilgen Spring Mound Group, although the association with the cardinal directions is not quite exact. The Nicholls Mound has also offered a rare glimpse at the actual mound-

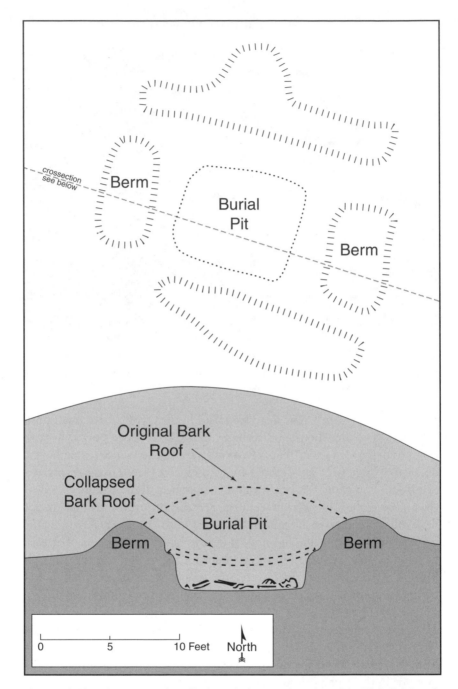

Figure 4.5. Plan view (top) and profile through the central portion of the Nicholls Mound, showing the central burial pit, embankments, and grave shelter. (Drawing by the University of Wisconsin–Madison Cartography Laboratory, after William C. McKern, "A Wisconsin Variant of the Hopewell Culture," *Bulletin of the Public Museum of the City of Milwaukee* 10, no. 2 [1931])

building methods. A cut through the mound revealed that it was built up by hundreds of small dumpings, probably basket loads, of dirt. The individual basket loads were still clearly visible in the soil profile.

Grave offerings in the mounds along the Mississippi River attest to both the status of the people buried in the mounds and their close interaction with other Hopewell centers in the Midwest. In the large Nicholls Mound, a central burial pit contained several reburials of bone bundles and the remains of seven individuals, one of whom was accompanied by silver-covered wooden beads, copper celts, a copper plate, and freshwater pearls. Another burial in the mound was accompanied by a platform pipe and chipped-stone blades made from fine cherts and obsidian from western North America and Hixton Silicified Sandstone from nearby west-central Wisconsin. Offerings and ornaments found in other mounds include ceremonial blades and other chipped-stone tools, platform pipes, pottery vessels that appear to have been traded up from Hopewell communities in Illinois, and bear canine-teeth pendants. Bear ceremonialism was an important feature in rituals throughout the Hopewell region.

Given the large number of special items from far-off places, the question arises as to what special item or items the Wisconsin people were contributing to the Hopewell trade network. The presence of ceremonial blades made of Hixton Silicified Sandstone in some of the Mississippi River mounds hints that this stone may have been one such item. The elaborate Middle Woodland mounds in the Trempealeau area are located within a few miles of the mouths of the Trempealeau River, to the north, and the Black River, to the south. The headwaters of the Trempealeau, some thirty miles to the northeast, lie in close proximity to Silver Mound, a large geologic feature that is a major source of Hixton Silicified Sandstone. Extensive Hixton deposits also can be found along a tributary of the Black River about twenty-five miles from the Trempealeau mound center. It is possible that the people interred in these mounds belonged to families or kin-groups that controlled access to and distribution of this long-prized and sacred western Wisconsin rock during the Hopewell period.

If only certain people were interred beneath mounds in these important ceremonial centers, where were other people buried? Since the Burial Sites Preservation Law went into effect in 1987, the discoveries of several suspected Middle Woodland nonmound ossuaries or mass graves have been reported along the Mississippi River, particularly in the Prairie du Chien area. These sites were brought to light by archaeological excavations of prehistoric campsites or during the course of construction activities. Although none of the sites have been completely excavated, they appear to be composed of bone bundles or, in one case, a large number of extended individuals. Since grave goods with prestige value do not appear to have been associated with these interments, it is possible that they represent less important social groups in Middle Woodland societies.

Small groups of large conical mounds were built elsewhere in southern Wisconsin along major bodies of water during the Middle Woodland period, but they show lesser degrees of Hopewell influence.[17] Middle Woodland mounds are found on the Rock River, Lake Koshkonong, Lake Mendota, Lake Monona, and the lower Fox River, among other places. Burials are usually in pits beneath the mounds, which are sometimes covered with rock or layers of burned or organic soils. Grave offerings similar to those in Hopewell mounds are occasionally found, but are not nearly as common. Among these rare offerings are freshwater pearls, shell beads, bear canines, copper artifacts, pipes, and distinctive pottery (figure 4.6).

Mound building was not a common custom in northern Wisconsin at this time. A mound center from the Middle Woodland period, however, may have been the Cyrus Thomas Mound Group, located on Rice Lake in Barron County, although some archaeologists feel that it could date much later in time. Excavations done by the Public Museum in the 1930s at the Cyrus Thomas group found burials associated with local pottery, two clay "death masks," and a bear canine-tooth pendant so typical of Hopewell ceremonialism.[18] Occasional discoveries of Hopewell trade objects at campsites from other locations in northern Wisconsin indicate that people in this region were participating in the long-distance trade networks to some extent.

The lifestyle of Middle Woodland peoples included hunting, gathering, fishing, and gardening, and there are hints that settlements were becoming more concentrated and long-lived. During the later part of the Middle Woodland, the first villages appeared on the Wisconsin landscape. Evidence for this comes from the Millville site, on the lower Wisconsin River, where excavations revealed the remains of fourteen small wigwam-like houses along with cooking fires and pits dug into the ground for the storage of food and disposal of refuse.[19] Judging from the types of animal remains found in the refuse, the village was occupied during the autumn and winter months. There probably was a complementary summer village elsewhere in the region. Evidence from rockshelters and camps indicates that small groups broke from the villages in this area for short periods to hunt deer or acquire other resources.

One Adena and Hopewell custom that was not widely practiced by Early and Middle Woodland people in Wisconsin was the construction of huge ceremonial or earthen enclosures. Several smaller rectangular, octagonal,

Figure 4.6. Middle Woodland Hopewell-inspired pot from the Mississippi River valley. (Photograph used with permission of the Milwaukee Public Museum, neg. 70292)

and circular embankments have been recorded in Wisconsin, but many of them are directly associated with effigy mound groups constructed several hundred years after the Adena and Hopewell eras. Increase A. Lapham mapped several enclosures in Milwaukee that could well have been part of the Adena–Hopewell Complex rituals, but they have been destroyed by urban expansion, so their age may never be known (figure 4.7).

Hopewell, along with the social, economic, and religious relationships it embodied, was a relatively short-lived phenomenon. After about only 300 years, the Hopewell Interaction Sphere, with its elaborate trade networks and complex cultural customs, dissipated and was gradually replaced by more regionally focused and, for a time, much simpler social arrangements.

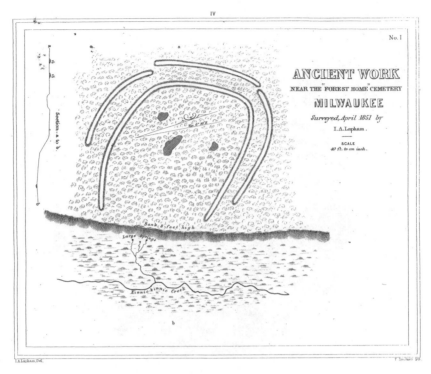

Figure 4.7. Enclosure in Milwaukee, still extant in the mid-nineteenth century but since destroyed, that may have been built by Middle Woodland people. (From Increase A. Lapham, *The Antiquities of Wisconsin, as Surveyed and Described* [Washington, D.C.: Smithsonian Institution, 1855])

The reasons for the disappearance of the Hopewell ceremonial complex are unknown. Some researchers have pointed out that around the same time, the climate in the Midwest became cooler and drier and that this change may have affected the availability of food resources.[20] Perhaps warfare erupted between rival groups, disrupting the trade routes. World history documents many such situations, although there is no evidence of large-scale warfare during the Middle Woodland period in the Midwest. Or maybe Native American societies of the time adapted to their local environments so successfully that trade with other areas simply became less important.

All that is known for sure is that the monumental mound and earthwork construction associated with this flamboyant period of North American prehistory ceased sometime between A.D. 200 and 400. This also brought to a close the first phase of mound building in Wisconsin. This phase, which began about 800 B.C., was the culmination of social, economic, and ideological trends of the Late Archaic that led to the custom of prominently marking social territories with the tombs of a social elite. Mound groups served as important ceremonial centers and played a significant role in the continuation of long-distance trade networks. On a more spiritual level, the rituals that attended the construction of mounds joined the concepts of birth, death, and the symbolic renewal of the world.

5

Effigy Mound Builders

The Late Woodland Stage

The far-flung Hopewell trade and ceremonial complex was gradually replaced in Wisconsin by more regionally focused social relationships. It is not possible to fully document changes in political and social organization during this transition, except to note that social status ceased to be marked by lavish grave offerings in burials, suggesting that social differentiation became less important. At the same time, the trend of expanding and intensifying the exploitation of food resources continued, as did that of a more sedentary lifestyle and larger populations. The construction of burial mounds at special locations for a variety of social, economic, and ritual purposes persisted, climaxing between A.D. 700 and 1200 in Wisconsin's most spectacular mound phenomenon—the effigy mounds.

The first evidence of village life in Wisconsin appeared at the end of the Middle Woodland stage in the verdant Wisconsin River valley of southwestern Wisconsin, where wild foods were especially abundant. The second-century Millville site, Wisconsin's oldest village recorded to date, included fourteen wigwam-like houses and numerous pits for food storage. Woodland people lived there during the autumn and winter and supported themselves chiefly by hunting deer and elk.[1] At about the same time, Woodland people elsewhere in Wisconsin were expanding their food alternatives by planting squash in their small gardens and perhaps gathering wild rice, which grew in shallow lakes and rivers.[2]

After about A.D. 500, the tempo of change quickened as new technologies and other food resources were introduced from elsewhere and were rapidly integrated into the existing Woodland culture. The bow and arrow replaced the spear as both a hunting and a fighting weapon. Better pottery vessels, often decorated with symbols of elaborate and ancient belief systems, were made. Most important, two Mexican domesticated plants, corn and, much later, beans, joined squash in the diet and in the economic strategies of people in the Midwest. The spread of corn northward into Wisconsin may have been facilitated by a climatic fluctuation beginning about A.D. 700, called the Neo-Atlantic, that led to weather that was warmer and wetter in some places than that of today, conditions ideal for plant growth.[3] Diffusion of corn also may have been promoted by the northward movement of horticultural tribes into Wisconsin.

With the incorporation of corn into the economy, Native Americans began a shift to village-based farming as a way of life. After A.D. 1000, virtually all people living in areas of the Midwest where agriculture could be successful were cultivating crops, especially corn, to one extent or another. Some groups eventually established large permanent agricultural towns. This shift from an economy based on hunting and gathering to one centered on growing corn brought about enormous cultural change that affected not only economic and settlement patterns, but social relations and ideology as well. It is perhaps one of the most revolutionary developments to have occurred in the 12,000-year cultural history of North America.

In the wake of these changes, the midwestern United States witnessed the flowering of three remarkable and different lifeways or traditions: Late Woodland (A.D. 500–1200), Mississippian (in Wisconsin, A.D. 1000–1200), and Oneota (A.D. 1000–European contact). The peoples of all three of these traditions built earthen mounds of various types, although Oneota tribes commonly did so only very early in their history. The relationship among Late Woodland, Mississippian, and Oneota cultures is currently a matter of intense debate in the archaeological world.

THE LATE WOODLAND STAGE: THE EFFIGY MOUNDS

The earliest of these three cultures to make its appearance in the archaeological record was composed of a number of bands and tribes that, throughout the northeastern part of the United States, are commonly referred to as Late Woodland. As the term implies, the Late Woodland cultures are regarded as direct descendants of the Middle Woodland cultures, and the Late Woodland is viewed as simply a later stage within the Woodland tradition.[4] It was the Late Woodland people who constructed the ubiquitous effigy mound ceremonial centers in southern Wisconsin. Until recently, in fact, it was common to use the labels "Late Woodland" and "effigy mound culture in Wisconsin" interchangeably. However, archaeologists now believe that effigy mounds were not built throughout the Late Woodland stage and, according to some, perhaps not by all Late Woodland people living at the same time in Wisconsin.

Agriculture and Settlement

The Late Woodland appears in the archaeological record about A.D. 500 and disappears around A.D. 1200, when it is replaced over much of Wisconsin by an entirely new lifeway known as Oneota. As did peoples of earlier cultures, Late Woodland people for a long time moved with the rhythm of the seasons within defined territories, relying heavily on hunting and gathering wild food resources. Small seasonal villages and seasonal camps were established in different parts of the territories to take advantage of food at its optimum availability.

No doubt, the people of the Late Woodland supplemented their diet with produce from gardens of such indigenous plants as chenopodium, sunflower, and sumpweed, which had been domesticated in former times, as well as squash, a cultigen that was introduced into Wisconsin from the south about 2,000 years ago.[5] From Late Woodland habitation and burial mound sites in Wisconsin, archaeologists have collected evidence that the cultivation of corn became increasingly important in the diet of Late Woodland people after A.D. 900. This evidence comes in the form of the actual remains of the tiny corn kernels and cobs as well as the examination of human remains for clues to dietary propensity. For example, the chemical analysis of human skeletons from Poor Man's Farrah, a mound group near the Mississippi River in Grant County dated to between A.D. 900 and 1000, suggested that some of the people were eating corn.[6] Likewise, an examination of the teeth of a large number of people interred in a mound at Raisbeck, an effigy mound group also in Grant County, found evidence of cavities, an expected consequence of a diet rich in carbohydrates, such as corn.[7]

The adoption of corn horticulture by Late Woodland people seems to have been gradual and have occurred at different rates in different areas. This may have to do with variations in the intensity of social contact between the various Wisconsin bands or tribes and people living to the south who had made the transition to farming a bit earlier.

Archaeologists have recorded a dramatic growth of population in the Midwest throughout the Late Woodland, as reflected in the large number of Late Woodland habitation and mound sites as compared with earlier times.

People pushed out of the main river valleys and lake regions, settling in remoter upland regions that had not been particularly attractive to earlier Woodland people.[8] As with the diffusion of southern crops, the settlement of marginal areas during this time also may have been stimulated by the wetter climate, which made headwater areas better watered and lush. Because of general population growth in the Midwest, whole bands and tribes appear to have been expanding into areas already occupied by other Late Woodland peoples, causing friction and warfare. A growth of population may have created other problems as well. At Poor Man's Farrah, specialists have found lesions on the bones of those buried in the mounds, suggestive of tuberculosis, a disease most commonly found where human populations are concentrated.[9]

Late Woodland habitation sites include small villages and special hunting, fishing, and gathering camps of various types. As in earlier times, there was a great deal of variation in lifestyles from region to region, reflecting adjustments to local environmental conditions and food resources. As already mentioned, people were congregating in small seasonal villages like Millville as early as the second century, but current evidence suggests that village life did not become widespread until after Late Woodland people had made the shift to small-scale corn agriculture in the tenth century. From a few known Late Woodland villages, archaeologists surmise that they were small, with populations of fewer than 100 people, and may have been moved several times a year. In rugged southwestern Wisconsin, small groups of hunters and their families broke off from the villages to hunt deer in the sheltered valleys, temporarily occupying caves and rock overhangs, or to fish and harvest clams along rivers and lakes.

The houses in Late Woodland villages were small, each accommodating perhaps only a single family. A house type that evidently was common throughout much of the northeastern United States during the Late Woodland was the pithouse, partially dug into the earth and covered with bark attached to wooden poles. The living space was circular or rectangular, and there often was a long narrow entranceway, giving the pithouse a keyhole-shaped appearance. Examples of Late Woodland keyhole houses have been found in several places in southern Wisconsin. One, the Statz site, is located in the headwaters of the Yahara River near Waunakee and dates to between about A.D. 700 and 1100. The community apparently was an autumn camp or a winter village consisting of three pairs of small keyhole houses. Each pair of houses may have been occupied by a single extended family.[10]

Pottery

Like earlier Woodland people, people of the Late Woodland crafted pottery by tempering the clay with crushed rock and decorating the surface with cord impressions. Compared with earlier types, however, Late Woodland pottery is thinner walled and more elaborately embellished. The vessels are also more globular in form than Middle Woodland pottery types. Intricate decorations were made by impressing woven fabrics or single cords into the moist clay surface of the pot. A variety of styles known collectively to archaeologists as Madison Ware, which appeared early in the Late Woodland stage, are among the most exquisitely decorated pottery ever made in the midwestern United States (figure 5.1*a*).

After about A.D. 900, and coinciding with the appearance of corn horticulture, another Late Woodland pottery form, bearing a distinctive collar around the rim, became increasingly common (figure 5.1*b*). Before the disappearance of the Late Woodland from the archaeological record around A.D. 1200, this collared ware, with its simplified cord-impressed decorations, is the predominant form of pottery found at Late Woodland sites in southern Wisconsin. Some archaeologists have speculated that the appearance of collared, cord-impressed pottery signals an invasion of new groups into Wisconsin: Late Woodland farming tribes from Illinois and other places to the south and east that began expanding or migrating into southern Wisconsin in the ninth century, at first living side by side with the local effigy-mound-building hunter-gatherers, and then replacing or absorbing them completely.[11] Others suggest that the collared pottery simply represents a style that became more popular over time among many Late Woodland peoples in the Midwest as they became increasingly horticultural.[12] Both Madison Ware and collared styles, dated to between A.D. 700 and 1100, were found mixed together at the Late Woodland Statz site, but the collared styles increase in frequency later in the site's history. This supports the interpretation that the makers of collared ceramics in Wisconsin were not necessarily different Late Woodland people, but simply the descendants of earlier local people. Perhaps both hypotheses are true. Unfortunately, the picture is quite hazy, since only a few Late Woodland villages have been examined and most of them, only quite recently. It is expected that the internal relationships and organization of Late Woodland societies will become clearer as more sites are discovered.

As do those on earlier pottery, the designs on Late Woodland pottery offer insights into the structuring of the belief systems of the makers. David Benn and Kelvin Sampson, both of whom have examined decorations on Late Woodland pottery of the Midwest, observed that upperworld and low-

Figure 5.1. Late Woodland pottery: (*a*) Madison Ware pot; (*b*) collared Late Woodland pot from Aztalan. ([*a*] Photograph by Robert Granflaten; used with permission of the State Historical Society of Wisconsin; [*b*] photograph used with permission of the Milwaukee Public Museum, neg. 70606)

Figure 5.2. Upperworld and lowerworld symbolism on Late Woodland pottery from Illinois: a bird-dancer and a long-tailed water spirit. (Drawing by Richard Dolan, after Kelvin W. Sampson, "Conventionalized Figures on Woodland Ceramics," *The Wisconsin Archeologist* 69, no. 3 [1988]; used with permission of the Wisconsin Archeological Society)

erworld imagery appears on pots, as it did on Early Woodland pottery, but in the form of cord-impressed figures (figure 5.2).[13] The figures include birds and, in some examples, human beings dressed as birds. Such bird impersonators are interpreted as shamans, calling on upperworld forces during rituals and dances. Benn has noted that bird and upperworld images, particularly of raptors, generally became more common on Late Woodland pottery over time. He suggested that this reflected the increasing frequency of warfare and therefore an increasingly aggressive, and perhaps even a more male-oriented, society. His observation is supported by dramatic evidence of increasing hostilities. After A.D. 1000, for example, some Late Woodland villages were fortified by wooden walls or stockades.[14] Other signs of warfare come from several Late Woodland mound burials in Wisconsin, where human skulls bear cut marks closely resembling those made by scalping.[15] Evidence of violent death, including arrowheads embedded in bone, has also been found at a number of Late Woodland sites in Illinois, Iowa, and other places in the Midwest.[16]

The lowerworld on the Illinois pottery that Sampson examined is represented by images of long-tailed "water spirits," who, in Native American belief systems, are often conceived of as inhabiting a watery world under the earth. Throughout North America, such spirit beings are variously thought of as taking the form of horned serpents, underwater panthers, rattlesnakes, and composite animals that include the features of cats, snakes, fish, birds, other animals, and humans.[17] Horned monsters and an underwater feline or panther with a long tail are believed to be denizens of the lowerworld by modern Great Lakes tribes. The powerful and somewhat malevolent beings whom the Ho-Chunk (Winnebago) call water spirits and the Menominee and others call Underground Water Panthers are viewed as being complementary to or in dynamic opposition to the equally powerful and hugely benevolent thunderbird of the upperworld. In recent times, Great Lakes tribes decorated twined bags with images of the thunderbird on one side and water spirits or panthers on the other side.[18]

This dualistic cosmological theme is also found represented on pottery and other objects in Wisconsin from Late Woodland times, indicating that it was the underlying structure of Native American belief systems. Sometimes the symbolism is clear, but usually it occurs in more abstract form. On Late Woodland pottery, as on earlier ware, chevrons may symbolize the upperworld, and parallel lines, the lowerworld: earth and water.[19] Depictions of menacing water spirits from the lowerworld that appear on several Late Woodland clay pipes found in Wisconsin offer a rare view of how Late Woodland people actually perceived these powerful spirits—as horned lizard-like creatures with long tails and clawed or taloned feet (figure 5.3).

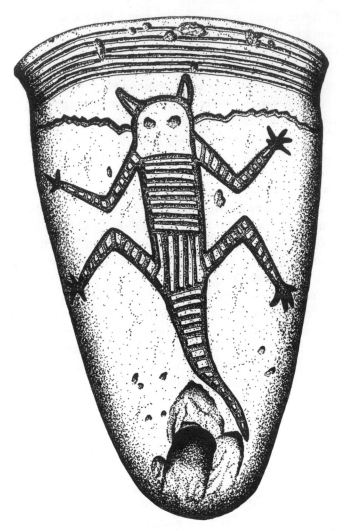

Figure 5.3. Depiction of a horned water spirit on a Late Woodland pipe found near Mauston, Wisconsin, and documented by the Mississippi Valley Archaeology Research Center. (Drawing by Richard Dolan; used with permission of the State Historical Society of Wisconsin)

Images of water spirits that may or may not date from the Late Woodland are also carved into and/or painted on the walls of caves and rockshelters. One such creature, at the Lemonweir Rock Art Site, overlooking a roiling stretch of the Wisconsin River, has a carved human head with horns or a headdress and a painted serpentine body. Other rock-art sites, those usually associated with bluffs or heights, bear clear images of thunderbirds. Upper-world imagery—especially hawks, falcons, and bird-men—eventually became important in the Middle Mississippian and Oneota cultures, appearing on a variety of art forms.

THE EFFIGY MOUNDS

The Early and Middle Woodland custom of building earthen mounds in which to bury the dead, with which to mark social territories, and around which to ceremonially renew the world was continued by Late Woodland people, but with some stunning differences. Sometime after A.D. 700, the construction of mounds greatly accelerated, and Late Woodland people throughout southern Wisconsin and parts of adjoining states began a spectacular custom that involved sculpting hilltops and other prominent locations into sometimes huge ceremonial complexes that consisted of effigy mounds—those in the shapes of birds, other animals, and even human beings—as well as innumerable low conical (round and oval) mounds and long, low embankments known as linear mounds. At some complexes, round or rectangular, ridged earthen enclosures accompanied the mound groups, defining spaces for perhaps dances and ceremonies.

Effigy mound groups were frequently built around the large conical Middle Woodland mounds, indicating shared cultural understanding of the sacred places involved, if not outright cultural links between the people of the different mound-building traditions. The effigy mounds, however, represented a new ceremonial, one that was more narrowly regional in scope than Hopewell and that seems to have helped bring together Late Woodland local groups in the upper Mississippi River valley to form a large new social confederation.

Before the custom ended around A.D. 1200 or shortly before, more than 900 effigy mound centers had been created in Wisconsin, perhaps comprising over 15,000 individual mounds. Of these, between 2,000 and 3,000 were actual effigies, while the remainder were low conical, oval, and linear mounds, all of which may have been effigies in the minds of the builders. These ceremonial centers are astounding not only because of the monumental effigy mounds they contain, but also because of the sheer number of groups and mounds that were built within a comparatively short period of time. Long a mysterious part of the Wisconsin landscape, the effigy mounds are now regarded by some as monumental representations of the same underlying belief systems encoded on Woodland pottery and other artwork and, as long suspected, reflect the kinship-based social divisions that existed among Late Woodland people who lived in the effigy mound region. In the words of R. Clark Mallam, effigy mound ceremonialism represents ancient "ideology from the earth."[20]

Wisconsin is the heartland of the so-called effigy mound culture, although the effigy mound region also includes parts of Illinois, Iowa, and Minnesota. The effigy mound region was first formally defined by Cyrus Thomas in his monumental study of the mounds.[21] To the south, it extends from Lake Michigan near the Wisconsin–Illinois border westward to the Rock River valley in Illinois and then northwestward for a short distance into Iowa. To the west, the area runs along a north–south line that takes in corners of Iowa and Minnesota. Turning eastward just north of La Crosse, the boundary extends generally east to Green Bay. There are some outliers, but these boundaries encompass the major concentrations of effigy mound groups (figure 5.4).

In his environmental study of the distribution of effigy mounds in Iowa, Mallam pointed out that this region generally corresponds to a distinct environmental area characterized by mixed southern hardwood forests, oak savannas, and some prairie. In addition to the abundant aquatic resources found in its many lakes, rivers, and wetlands, the region offered a great diversity of wild plant- and animal-food resources important to Native Americans.[22] Among the most important of them would have been deer, whose population density is greatest in this large region. Immediately to the north lie the coniferous–hardwood forests, and to the west and south, broadly speaking, is prairie—environments with a much narrower, albeit still abundant, selection of food resources. Deer are not as plentiful in these areas.

Within this extremely food-rich region, Late Woodland people built mound groups that ranged in size from just a few to many hundreds of mounds. A typical group contains between twenty and thirty mounds. Single effigy mounds occur, but rarely. One of the largest mound groups in Wisconsin is the Cranberry Creek Mound Group, near Necedah on the Yellow River, which consists of several hundred low conical mounds, typical of Late Woodland construction, and two effigies: a bird and a bear. The group appears to have been built around a small Middle Woodland center consisting of several large conical mounds. The largest effigy mound group ever recorded is on the Mississippi River in northeastern Iowa. The Harper's Ferry Great Mound Group once contained 895 mounds![23]

Individual effigy mounds are generally low, only a few feet in height, but sometimes gigantic in scale. The largest existing effigy mound in the Midwest is located on the state-owned grounds of Mendota State Hospital, on Lake Mendota near Madison. The wingspan of one huge bird is 624 feet (Figure 5.5). An even larger bird may have existed as part of the remarkable Eagle Township effigy mounds in Richland County, where it appears now as only a soil shadow in a plowed agricultural field. Preserved in Man Mound

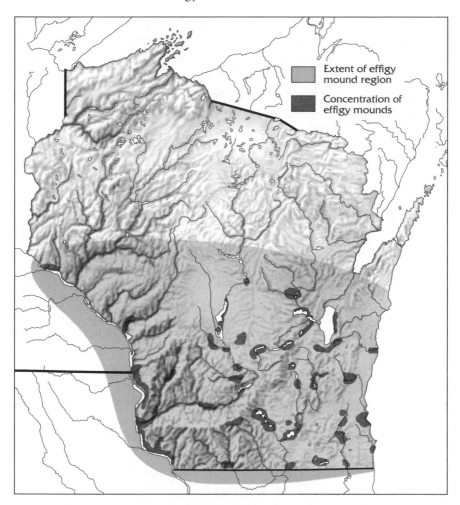

Figure 5.4. The extent of the effigy mound region (*shaded area*), with the distribution of major clusters of Late Woodland effigy mound groups in Wisconsin. (Map by Amelia Janes, Midwest Educational Graphics)

County Park, near Baraboo, is an effigy in the shape of a human being with horns or a horn headdress that was originally 218 feet long. Some linear mounds associated with effigy mounds near Lake Monona in the Madison area reached lengths of 700 feet and more. Most effigy mounds are less than 100 feet long.

Effigy mound groups are not evenly distributed throughout the effigy mound region. The groups occur in discrete clusters and, with some notable exceptions, tend to be located on high ground, bluffs, or terraces overlooking major rivers, streams, lakes, and large wetlands. One large concentration

Figure 5.5. Aerial photograph of bird effigies on the grounds of Mendota State Hospital. (Photograph by James B. Stoltman, Department of Anthropology, University of Wisconsin–Madison; used with permission)

of groups containing effigies is in south-central Wisconsin along lakes associated with the Rock River drainage system. The lake region around Madison once had more than 100 effigy mound groups with over 1,000 mounds, while 13 mound centers with nearly 500 mounds could be found on nearby Lake Koshkonong. Other areas with remarkable densities of effigy mound groups are along the lower Wisconsin River, near the confluence of the Mississippi and Wisconsin Rivers, and along the Fox River.

Examining the location of effigy mound groups in Iowa, Mallam found that they tend to be associated with the richest areas of seasonally recurring food resources.[24] Similarly, Lynne Goldstein, who has studied the distribution of effigy mounds in southeastern Wisconsin, discovered that mound groups tend to be located near large areas of wetlands, which are extremely rich in seasonally available food: waterfowl, small mammals, turtles, fish, and a variety of such edible plants as wild rice.[25] She suggested that effigy mound groups may be resource maps. Mound groups were constructed in areas whose resources could support the gathering of a large number of people on a seasonal basis. But the locations of effigy mound groups may not have been based solely on topographic and economic considerations. Like earlier mounds, many effigy mound groups were built near springs and other natural features that have spiritual connotations for Native Americans.

The Meaning of the Mound Forms

Effigy mounds were built in a variety of forms, most of which are easily recognizable as birds, animals, and even human beings. Some mound shapes, however, elude easy identification, such as the ubiquitous linear mounds and a number of other puzzling shapes.

In his classic study of effigy mounds, Chandler Rowe counted thirteen different forms, including bear, beaver, bird, buffalo, canine, deer, panther, turtle, and "problematical," or unknown.[26] He also included in his classification biconical, conical, linear, and oval mounds, all of which the builders may or may not have considered to be effigies. To these can be added the spectacular "chain" or compound mounds of southwestern Wisconsin—long strings of conical mounds connected by linear embankments. In the past, mound researchers also labeled some mounds as lizard, mink, raccoon, squirrel, and the like, but these identifications seem to have been wild guesses or based on erroneous reports and depictions.

The meaning of the various effigy mound forms has been the source of speculation ever since the mounds came to public attention in the early nineteenth century. Much of the conjecture was done in the context of a Euro-American worldview and without reference to Native American belief systems, past or present. As is that of the earlier burial mounds, the key to the meaning of the effigy mounds can be found in Native American belief systems and cosmology.

In 1980 R. Clark Mallam provided the insight that most effigy mounds fall into three classes corresponding to the three natural realms—air, earth, and water—that provide the resources on which humans depend (figure 5.6). Because of this, he theorized that mounds had been built to symbolize and ritually maintain balance and harmony with the natural world. Relating effigy mounds to the concept of periodic rituals to renew the world, he argued that the construction of effigy mounds is similar to the Navajo practice of "thinking and singing the world into existence." The effigy mounds, "in this interpretation, can be considered as 'areas of social reproduction'; places to which people returned again and again for the purpose of life-way reinforcement and renewal. It is more than just a coincidence that these places were also areas which contained, nearby, large quantities of high-yielding and annually renewable natural resources."[27] Robert Hall took this theory a step further, providing the long-awaited and needed breakthrough for interpreting the meaning of the effigy mounds. He noted a close parallel between the major forms of effigies and the depictions of powerful spirits who inhabit the upperworld and lowerworld in the cosmology of many Native American tribes of the Midwest and argued that the primary organizing

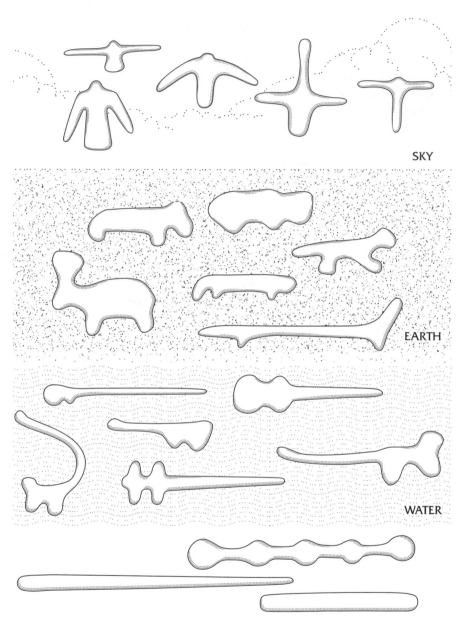

SKY

EARTH

WATER

Figure 5.6. Common effigy mound forms, showing the natural realms that they symbolize. (Drawing by Amelia Janes, Midwest Educational Graphics)

Table 5.1. Effigy mound forms in selected counties

Milwaukee (east)		Dane (central)		Grant (west)	
Water spirit or panther	34	Bird	119	Bird	56
Bird	6	Water spirit or panther	67	Bear	22
Unknown	2	Other animals	43	Unknown	22
Other animals	—	Bear/bear-like	33	Other animals	17
Bear/bear-like	—	Unknown	32	Water spirit	5
TOTAL	42		294		122

Source: George Christiansen III, "Burial Mound and Earthwork Research Project," 1998, Office of the State Archaeologist, State Historical Society of Wisconsin, Madison.

principle for mound groups is into these two major divisions.[28] Thunderbird and other bird effigies symbolize the air or upperworld. The lowerworld is subdivided into earth and water and is represented by bears and water spirits, respectively. Hall made the convincing case that the long-tailed forms, variously known as panthers, lizards, and turtles, can be viewed as variable depictions of the water spirits that are so important in midwestern Native American belief systems and that were part of Late Woodland ideology and artistic symbolism. Using this Native American worldview, Hall regards effigy mound groups as "monumental constructions of the cosmology of their builders and represented the division of the world into earth/water and sky divisions."[29]

A recent study of the shapes and distribution of effigy mounds supports Hall's thesis.[30] Reexamining data from Wisconsin with Hall's ideas in mind, the Office of the State Archaeologist of the State Historical Society of Wisconsin found that of the 1,863 identifiable zoomorphic mounds, the most common classes of effigy forms are birds (34 percent), bear and bear-like forms (15 percent), and the long-tailed forms variously referred to as panthers, lizards, and turtles, but can be considered water spirits (37 percent). The remainder are various kinds of other animals. These data generally correspond to the results of an analysis of effigy mound forms in Iowa done by Mallam.[31] The study also determined that while each of these categories can be found throughout the effigy mound region, there are significant differences in distribution: birds predominate in mound groups located among the rugged hills and bluffs of western Wisconsin; bears (and other earth animals) are concentrated in central and western Wisconsin; and water spirits are most commonly found in mound groups in watery eastern Wisconsin (table 5.1). Moreover, whatever the predominant form, or "world," in a particular mound group, the complementary or opposing world is almost always represented. This fact supports Mallam's contention that the effigy mound groups reflect concerns about maintaining balance and harmony in the world. In mound groups dominated by water spirits (lowerworld) in eastern Wisconsin, there is almost always at least one bird present, representing the upperworld. In mound groups dominated by birds (upperworld) in western Wisconsin, representatives of the lowerworld are the earth-related bears. In between these extremes in the south-central part of Wisconsin, around the Four Lakes area of Dane County, mound groups containing all three forms—birds, bears, and water spirits—are very common (figure 5.7).

If many effigy mounds represent spirit beings of the upperworld and lowerworld, do they also symbolize the clan or totems of the people who built or are buried in them? This is a very old idea and one that many modern Ho-Chunk (Winnebago) endorse.[32] The question was awkwardly examined and ultimately dismissed by Rowe in an attempt to find a connection between effigy mounds and historically known tribes.[33] He could not find a close match between his categories of mound forms and the historically reported clans of tribes that are indigenous to Wisconsin, such as the Santee Sioux, or Dakota, Ho-Chunk, and Menominee, or of several tribes that had immigrated to the state in the early historic period. So he rejected the idea that the mounds are clan symbols.

Rowe, however, did not delve into Native American ideological and social systems, a reflection of archaeological research of the time. In his reanalysis, Hall has pointed out that Rowe ignored some vital pieces of information presented by the mound researchers Arlow B. Stout, Charles E. Brown, and Paul Radin almost a half century earlier.[34] Notably, one of the most common effigy mound forms, the long-tailed panther, is equivalent to the depiction of water spirits found not only in the belief systems but also in the clans of the Ho-Chunk and other people. Furthermore, he pointed out Rowe had failed to see the association between the Thunder clans found among many tribes and the spirit beings called thunderbirds, and can be recognized among common effigy mound forms. Hall concluded that had Rowe taken this information into account, he may have seen a very close match between the effigy mound forms and the clan structure of modern Native American tribes, particularly the Ho-Chunk, who occupied parts of the effigy mound region in the historic period.

According to Radin, the Ho-Chunk are socially divided into two groups: "those who are above" (*wangeregi herera*) and "those who are on earth" (*manegi herera*).[35] These divisions or moieties, as anthropologists call them, are exogamous; that is, people are prohibited from marrying into their own division. Each moiety is subdivided into a number of clans, each with its own origin story. The largest and most important clan in the upper

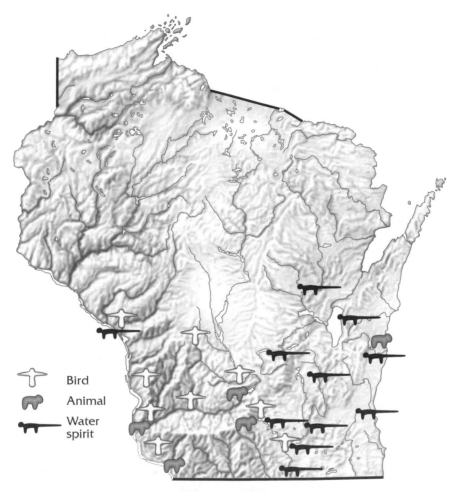

Figure 5.7. The distribution of effigy mound forms shows general patterns. Birds, which represent the air, and land animals (especially bears), which represent the earth, predominate in mound groups in western Wisconsin, while water spirits cluster in the eastern part of the state. In south-central Wisconsin, effigies symbolizing air, earth, and water are commonly found in the same mound group. (Map by Amelia Janes, Midwest Educational Graphics)

division is Thunderbird. Thunderbirds are powerful spirits who are approachable by humans as guardians and helpmates. Lightning flashes from their eyes, and thunder is caused by the flapping of their wings. Other members of the upper division include the Warrior or War-People, Eagle, Hawk, and Pigeon. Ho-Chunk people told Radin that the Warrior clan is paired with the Hawk clan, but could be symbolized by the depiction of a human being. The lower division is represented by clans of the earth and water: Bear, Buffalo, Deer, Elk, Fish, Snake, Water Spirit, and Wolf. Of these, the

Bear and Water Spirit clans are the most important, with some Ho-Chunk maintaining that the Water Spirit clan ruled over the lower division in former times. Some water spirits are usually thought of as water monsters and are supposed to be in eternal opposition to the thunderbirds. While capable of malevolence, they are also "capable of bestowing great blessings on man."[36] Regarding the water spirit, Ho-Chunk people told Brown that "it is sometimes regarded as a 'bad spirit,' destroying men by overturning their canoes and in other ways. Its good must be gained by offerings."[37] Radin wrote that a constant theme in Ho-Chunk society was the renewal of order in a chaotic world, which was accomplished by the performance of certain rituals, and the maintenance of the balance of social power between the upperworld and the lowerworld, as represented by the Thunderbird and Bear clans.[38]

The moiety system of the Ho-Chunk closely resembles the symbolism of the effigy mounds, but it is important to point out that other midwestern tribes were organized by similar concepts. For example, the Algonquian-speaking Menominee also have a dualistic belief system, with a multitiered universe organized into halves: an upper and a lower. As are those of other tribes, the denizens of the upperworld are the thunderbird and other avians. In the lowerworld is the Great White Bear, from whom all Menominee are descended, and the Underground Water Panther, White Deer, and a great serpent that inhabits lakes and rivers. Clans were grouped into two divisions: the Thunderers and the Bears. The Menominee were neighbors of the Ho-Chunk in northeastern Wisconsin during the historic period, although Ronald Mason has recently called into question whether this was always the case.[39]

An interesting alternative to the two-division model was given to Radin by some Ho-Chunk: the clans are divided into three groups headed by the thunderbird, bear, and water spirit. What is significant about this arrangement is that it not only more finely defines the realms of the natural world (sky, earth, and water), but also represents three common types of effigy mounds.

Upperworld

In the class of mounds associated with the sky or upperworld are found a number of bird forms. This is one of the commonest classes of effigies, excluding conical and linear mounds. The bird category includes straight-winged eagle-like figures that closely resemble modern Native American depictions of the thunderbird. Bird-shaped mounds are among the largest effigies ever constructed. As noted earlier, one bird on the grounds of Mendota State Hospital on Lake Mendota has a wingspan of 624 feet. Aerial photography documented the soil shadow of a straight-winged bird near the Wisconsin River in Richland County that had a wingspan of a quarter mile. While it is tempting to associate these giant mounds solely with the thunderbird theme, Robert Salzer and Robert Hall have identified a depiction of a falcon that is almost certainly also meant to be a thunderbird in the famous 1,000-year-old Red Horn paintings in the Gottschall Rockshelter in Iowa County.[40] As we shall see, peregrine falcons emerged as powerful symbols in the later Mississippian and Oneota cultures. Other bird effigy forms include such falcon- or hawk-like figures and occasional waterfowl, such as geese, which, not surprisingly, are almost exclusively associated with large wetlands.

Some mounds in this upperworld class have the characteristics of both birds and human beings. These effigies are typically anthropomorphic in form, with long wing-like arms and either human or bird-like heads. In the past, many of them were dismissed simply as birds with long bifurcated tails that only look like human legs. Even just a glance at figure 5.8, however, makes it clear that some of these effigies are "bird-men." Bird-men effigies were constructed primarily in southwestern Wisconsin along the Wisconsin River, although few exist today. Significantly, depictions of dancers dressed as birds (probably hawks or falcons) appear on Late Woodland pots in Illinois, but are more common in later Middle Mississippian and Oneota iconography. As with that of some other imagery, the presence of bird-man mounds in Wisconsin suggests that aspects of effigy mound ideology were shared with Middle Mississippian and Oneota cultures.

Upperworld or sky mounds, particularly in the shape of birds, occur throughout the effigy mound region, but are most common in western Wisconsin, especially in the hill country of the southwestern area and along the bluffs and terraces of the Wisconsin and Mississippi River valleys. The natural association of birds with high places such as cliffs, bluffs, and ridges is obvious, and this portion of the state is also part of the Mississippi flyway—the migration route of millions of waterfowl and other birds. Bird imagery, specifically that of the hawk and falcon, remained an important element in Native American iconography in western Wisconsin right up to European contact.

Sharing a close geographic association with southwestern Wisconsin are the most awe-inspiring effigy mounds ever constructed—those built in the form of colossal human beings. Some Ho-Chunk elders told Paul Radin that such human representations were associated with the Warrior and Hawk clans.[41] The War-People or Warrior clan was an upper-division clan and was closely linked with hawks and the Hawk clan. Radin himself was of the opinion that hawk-like effigy mounds had been built by the Ho-Chunk War-People or Warrior clan. Because of these historic links, it seems appropriate to include this mound form in a consideration of sky or upperworld mounds.

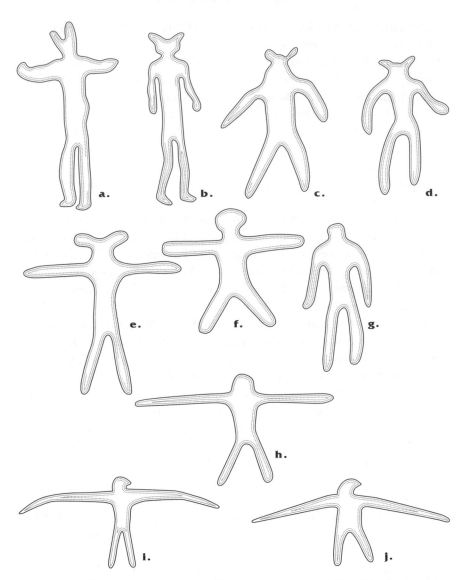

Figure 5.8. Effigy mounds in the shape of humans and bird-men: (*a*) La Valle Man Mound, Sauk County; (*b*) Man Mound County Park, Sauk County; (*c–e, g, h, j*) Eagle Township, Richland County; (*f*) near Mount Horeb, Dane County; (*i*) Devil's Lake State Park, Sauk County. (Drawing by Amelia Janes, Midwest Educational Graphics)

At least nine human or man mounds were constructed in Wisconsin, all but one in the lower Wisconsin River drainage system. A unique concentration of four mounds in the shape of human beings once existed in Eagle Township in Richland County among a spectacular array of upperworld-oriented mound groups that included birds of various sorts and bird-men. The mound groups were mapped by Theodore H. Lewis in the late nineteenth century, and these maps were recently brought to public attention by mound researcher James Scherz.[42] Most of the many mound groups in Eagle Township have been destroyed by farming. Only one man mound remains fairly intact, preserved in Man Mound County Park near Baraboo. Remnants of a second are located within the city limits of Black Earth. Both of these mounds were immense, 218 feet and 700 feet long, respectively.[43] Unlike other effigy mounds, both appear to have been built as solitary monuments on the floors of valleys well away from major streams and rivers, suggesting that they served a ceremonial purpose different from that of other effigy mound groups.

Most of the human effigies depict humans with horns. The horns may represent buffalo-horn headdresses, which are commonly associated with shamans in more modern times. David Benn suggested that man mounds are representations of Red Horn, a warrior hero who is the focus of a cycle of stories told by the related Ho-Chunk and Ioway.[44] Among these stories are accounts of epic battles with giants as well as the death and rebirth of Red Horn himself. In the Gottschall Rockshelter, a cave in a remote upland valley in Iowa County, a story of Red Horn is told in painted figures on the cave wall. Archaeologist Robert Salzer believes that the site was used in ancestor-worship ceremonies 1,000 years ago.[45] The paintings are dated to around A.D. 900 to 1000.

The Gottschall paintings were executed in a style identical to that associated with the Middle Mississippian culture, which was emerging at the time in southern Illinois. These Mississippian-style paintings, however, are archaeologically associated with an occupation level in the cave that has yielded pottery of the Late Woodland effigy mound culture. Even more intriguing is the fact that following the creek that runs in front of the cave to its confluence with the Wisconsin River, eight miles away, one comes to the Eagle Township effigy mound groups and their unique cluster of human, bird-man, and bird mounds, including quite possibly the largest bird effigy ever recorded in the state. The physical link between these two spectacular ceremonial places can hardly be coincidental. It may represent initial ceremonial contact between the effigy mound people of Wisconsin and the emerging Mississippian culture from the south that eventually led to a dramatic transformation of the Late Woodland effigy mound culture.

Lowerworld: Water

Water, one part of the lowerworld, is represented principally by long-tailed forms that historically have been referred to as panthers, turtles, or lizards and that together compose the second largest class of effigy mounds. As Robert Hall pointed out, the so-called turtle mounds do not even look like turtles: they and the so-called lizard mounds appear to be panther or water spirit mounds as viewed from above. The real difference among these mound types may be only in the perspective that the builders wanted to provide. The association between the long-tailed effigy mounds and water spirits was made quite some time ago and has long been a part of Wisconsin archaeological literature. In 1910, Arlow B. Stout of the Wisconsin Archeological Society asked Fred Dick, a Ho-Chunk man camping with his family near the Wisconsin Dells, about the long-tailed "panther mounds." After consulting with elders, Dick reported that the effigy represented a spirit animal that lived in water.[46] The following year, several well-informed Ho-Chunk men from Nebraska provided Charles E. Brown of the State Historical Society with the same information: that long-tailed panther mounds were representations of water spirits.[47]

Long-tailed water spirit mounds are found throughout the effigy mound region, but are concentrated in the low-lying eastern part of Wisconsin, where large lakes, swamps, and marshes abound. The association of the water spirits with water is quite obvious from this distribution. Moreover, water spirit mounds tend to be near springs, which bubble up from beneath the earth and have been held in sacred reverence by ancient people around the world. They are the source of life-giving water, symbolic of rebirth and renewal. Fine sands, like those in springs, are occasionally found in mounds of all periods, perhaps as a metaphor for this concept. For Native Americans, springs are also entrances to the watery underworld for the powerful water spirits. Brown was told in 1926 by Oliver La Mere, a Ho-Chunk from Nebraska with ties to Wisconsin, that springs and other waters were under the care of the Water Spirit clan.[48] In Madison, an unusually dense cluster of effigy mound groups that include water spirit forms found on the shore of Lake Wingra, a tiny body of water off the main water transportation route, may be explained by the fact that the lake is fed by a number of large, prominent (and still visible) springs. Some of these springs were still considered sacred by the Ho-Chunk residents of the Madison area in the early twentieth century.[49]

The presence of sacred springs may alone account for the location of the spectacular and enigmatic Lizard Mounds Group near West Bend (figure 5.9). The group once consisted of more than fifty mounds, two birds and a

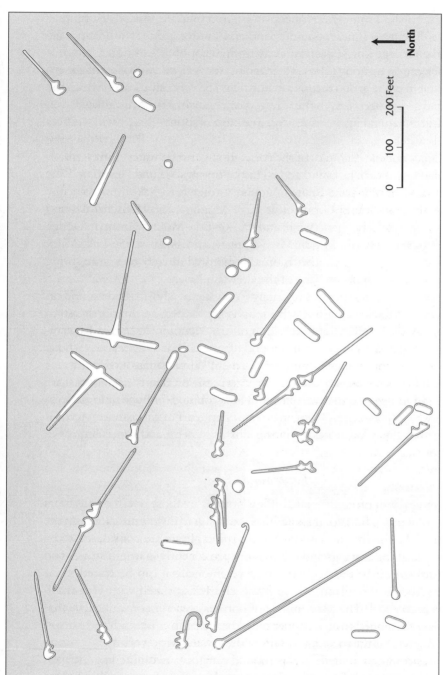

Figure 5.9. Like many mound groups in eastern Wisconsin, the Lizard Mounds Group in Washington County is heavily dominated by water spirit symbolism, although several birds are present in the center of the group. Many of the mounds at the western end of the group (*far left*) were destroyed by farming. (Drawing by Amelia Janes, Midwest Educational Graphics, based on a drawing by Kermit Freckman in "The Hagner Indian Mounds," *The Wisconsin Archeologist* 23, no. 1 [1942])

large number of mounds erroneously referred to in the nineteenth century as lizards, but are almost certainly panthers or water spirits. The group is situated on a large low plateau far away from major bodies of water. This unusual location has long puzzled archaeologists. A close inspection of the environment of the group reveals a major clue. The very elevation on which the mound group sits forms the headwaters of a branch of the Milwaukee River. Virtually surrounding the plateau are a number of springs that provide sources of this water.

Other notable examples of the correlation between water spirit symbolism and springs can be found at the Harbor Springs Mound Group on Lake Mendota, the Pheasant Branch Mound Group near Lake Mendota, the Nine Springs Mound Group near Lake Monona, the Henschel Mound Group on the Sheboygan Marsh, and the Nitschke Mound Group in Dodge County. At the famous Middle Mississippian site of Aztalan near Lake Mills, a large water spirit or panther mound is oriented directly to a large spring complex on the opposite bank of the Crawfish River.

Perhaps another form representative of water is a short-tailed mound often referred to as a catfish. Such mounds are located on the northeastern periphery of the effigy mound region on the Menominee Indian Reservation. Elongated versions of this mound type occasionally appear elsewhere. The distribution of such mounds in northern Wisconsin is outside the area where effigies are usually found. The interpretation that these mounds are fish is, of course, speculative, but could be accounted for by their location in areas where fish were and remain an important part of subsistence. Accordingly, they figure prominently in the kinship systems and supernatural beliefs of Native Americans.

Lowerworld: Earth

The most common earth-related effigy mounds are those referred to as bears and, sometimes, buffalo. It sometimes is difficult to distinguish between the forms. Like the thunderbird and water spirits, bears are considered to be very special spirit beings and often figure prominently in origin stories and clan structures. In the Midwest, bear ceremonialism can be traced as far as the Middle Woodland, where it was clearly associated with Hopewell-influenced ritual. The Menominee of northeastern Wisconsin believe that they are descended from a copper-tailed bear that lives beneath the earth.[50] The Bear clan is the most important of the lower-division clans.

Less common animals in this mound category are canine-like, perhaps representing wolf or fox, and antlered animals, such as deer and elk. All these forms are subjective categories, being the best guess about the animal form that is being represented. What they really are was, unfortunately, known to only the original builders. Animal effigies of this class, especially bear-like mounds, are found mainly in the western and central parts of Wisconsin, but occasionally in other places.

Linear and Conical Forms

Robert Hall has argued that even the ubiquitous linear and conical mounds fit the cosmological classification that divides mounds by their associations with the upperworld and lowerworld. The linear mounds, he has suggested, are representations of the long tails of the water spirits and, hence, are symbols of water spirits (and the lowerworld) themselves.[51] Some support for this interpretation comes from the fact that some linear mounds are curved or hooked, much like the tails of some panther or water spirit mounds. David Lee Smith, historian of the Ho-Chunk of Nebraska, has related a Ho-Chunk perspective on linear mounds: they represent snakes.[52] In one Ho-Chunk version of the story of the creation of the world, snakes anchored the earth. Snakes are also viewed as guardians of the underworld, and the Snake clan is one of the lower-division clans. Considering that linear mounds are often spatially associated with water spirit mounds, this is a perspective worth keeping in mind in future analyses of the arrangement of mound groups. Many linear mounds, though, are interspersed among upperworld and lowerworld mounds, suggesting that their symbolism or function may be more complex. Round and oval mounds, Hall believes, represent the bodies of the upperworld birds, but, again, the symbolism is far from clear.

Construction of the Mounds

The aboveground part of effigy mounds seems to have been constructed in a single (but perhaps lengthy) building episode. The mounds are rarely layered or stratified. In many cases, there does not appear to have been any special preparation of the ground surface before the mounds were built. Occasionally, however, an intaglio, or "reverse cameo," in the form of the effigy to be constructed was first dug several feet into the ground. The archaeological evidence indicates that the intaglio component of a mound was left open for a long time, suggesting that ceremonial preparation for effigy mound building could be a lengthy process. This sacred area was eventually filled in, sometimes with offerings of specially colored soils, ash, and charcoal. The mound was then built up in an effigy shape out of dirt from the surrounding area.

Sometimes either this process was interrupted or the intaglios were intentionally left open. Early mound researchers noted the presence of at least eleven open intaglios associated with mound groups near Baraboo, Fort Atkinson, and Milwaukee (Figure 5.10).[53] Significantly, all were lower-

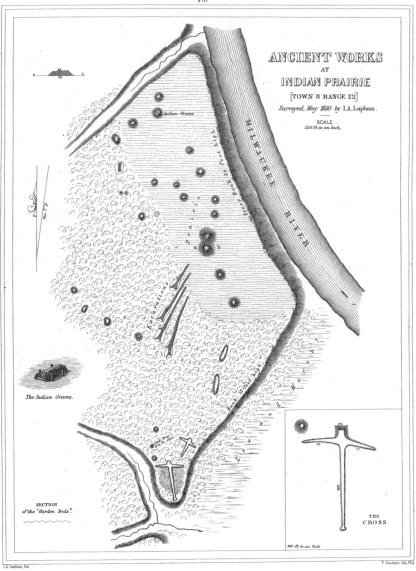

Figure 5.10. The mound group in present-day Glendale, just north of Milwaukee, as mapped in 1850, included four water spirit intaglios, labeled as excavations. Separate bird effigies appear at the bottom of the site, and grave houses, probably Potawatomi, are shown on a mound at the upper portion of the map. (From Increase A. Lapham, *The Antiquities of Wisconsin, as Surveyed and Described* [Washington, D.C.: Smithsonian Institution, 1855])

world forms: nine long-tailed water spirits and two bears. This may indicate that the intaglios, *dug into the earth or lowerworld,* were deliberately left open as part of the same ceremonial that accounts for the construction of effigy mounds on the earth. Only one, a water spirit or panther on the Rock River in Fort Atkinson, has survived land development.

Purpose of the Mounds

Burial Sites

In most of the mounds, Late Woodland people placed their dead. Burials in effigy mounds can be in pits below the mound, on the former surface of the ground, or in the mound itself. Burials and other features were characteristically placed in the head and/or heart region of the effigy, indicating an intimate relationship between the deceased and the particular effigy form.

In addition to human burials, effigy mounds often contain concentrations and arrangements of rocks and stones that traditionally are referred to as altars because of their obvious ritual functions. Indeed, many are associated with evidence of fire and burning. Small clay and rock receptacles called cists, whose purpose is unknown, are also commonly found. Like burials, these rock concentrations and cists are usually located in the head and heart regions of the effigy. Sometimes, only these features, instead of burials, are present. In some rare instances, neither burials nor features occur in the effigy mounds. As in earlier mounds, other symbolic offerings—including colored soils, mucks, charcoal, and ash—were occasionally made that speak of the continuing practice of earth renewal ceremonialism.

Effigy mound burials differ in many respects from earlier Middle Woodland burials and reflect significant social differences. First, burial pits or chambers do not appear to have functioned as long-term family crypts, used continually for interments for a long time before mounds were built over them. Unlike Middle Woodland crypt-mound burials, primary extended burials (that is, laid out in a prone position before the body decays) are rare in Late Woodland effigy mounds. Effigy mound burials often occur as cleaned bundles of bones, but flexed "in the flesh" interments are also fairly common. Most of the latter are so tightly flexed that the bodies must have been tightly bound and brought from another place long after decomposition had started. Cremations occur, but they are rare.

The pattern of effigy mound burials supports the theory that burials usually were not made immediately after death, a practice that would have produced extended burials. Rather, burials were performed at only certain appointed times when appropriate ceremonials were conducted. Corpses would be brought from temporary resting places, perhaps scaffolds, for final burial in a mound. Both the number of Late Woodland mounds and the presence of so many partly decomposed flexed burials indicate that mound ceremonials occurred at fairly frequent intervals, perhaps annually. These ceremonials probably coincided with important calendar and symbolic occasions, such as the summer or winter solstice and the spring or fall equinox.

Second, effigy mounds characteristically do not contain a large number of burials. A minority include no burials at all. Many contain a single burial. Others have a small number—all made at the same time. Mass burials do occur, but they are rare and seem to be restricted to conical mounds. For example, one conical mound at the Raisbeck Mound Group yielded the disarticulated remains of sixty five people.

Finally, in contrast to many Middle Woodland mound burials, there is no evidence that mound burial during the Late Woodland was restricted to important or "chiefly" families. Few objects were placed with the deceased in effigy mounds. Grave offerings that are present are simple in nature: pottery containers, smoking pipes, a stone knife, miscellaneous bone or copper tools—objects that could conceivably assist the spirit in the next world, but do not mark elite status. That the grave goods do not have prestige value has been used to argue that the society or societies that built the effigy mounds were not marked by the types of social differences found earlier or at least that social status did not determine access to mound burial. An argument could be reasonably made, however, that the grave structure itself, the effigy mound, is an elaborate marker of status.

Because so few villages from the effigy mound era have been investigated, it is not yet possible to estimate the human population of the effigy mound region. Given the sheer number of conical, linear, and effigy mounds built during this time (possibly over 15,000), however, the fact that most contain burials and these burials include men, women, and children of all ages, and the absence of other types of Late Woodland cemeteries, it is likely that many of the Late Woodland effigy mound people were accorded burial in a mound of one type or another. The distinct possibility that people buried in different types of mounds belonged to different kinship groups, such as clans or moieties, or even other social groups, such as warrior societies or shamanistic associations, is an interesting idea, but one that unfortunately cannot be addressed with current information.

Maps of Belief Systems or Astronomical Observatories?

One aspect of effigy mound ceremonialism that both puzzled and fascinated early researchers is that the mounds had been built in curiously nonrandom patterns. Among several novel and rather Eurocentric explanations that recently have received a great deal of public interest is that mounds are so arranged that their alignments can be used to predict or observe the movements of the sun, moon, and stars and that encoded in the angles and alignments of the mounds are "ancient geometries" shared by the mound builders with other peoples on earth.[54] However, armed as archaeologists now are with the insight that effigy mound groups are monumental expressions of Native American ideology and social structure, the organizing principles of effigy mound groups are becoming quite clear.

The underlying structure of effigy mound ceremonialism is the division of the universe into the upperworld and lowerworld and the subdivision of the lowerworld into the realms of earth and water. The spatial relationship of effigy mound forms mimics or models this ideological structure. In short, effigy mound groups are maps of ancient belief systems. They recapitulate the structure of the universe and model the relationship of the social divisions and clans of the effigy mound builders. Upperworld mounds, mostly in the shape of birds, often occupy the highest elevation on the landscape. If both animal and water spirit mounds are present in a mound group, the animals, usually bears, are intermediate between the birds and the water spirits, since they represent the lowerworld realm of earth. Water spirit mounds are typically found lowest on the terrain, close to bodies of and sources of water, to or from which they seem to be crawling (figure 5.11).

Within this broad organizing scheme, other factors account for the specifics of the arrangement of a particular mound group. One recurring explanation, consistent with Native American concerns for harmony and balance, is that many mounds appear to have been built to conform to the landscape. As was frequently observed in the past, and is very clear to all who have visited mound groups, the orientation and arrangement of mounds often follow the contours of the landform on which they were built, apparently artistically inspired by the topography (figure 5.12). Birds fly gracefully across ridge tops. Animals parade across ridge tops and slopes, changing direction, sometimes subtly, with the orientation of the terrain. Water spirits move up and down elevations, crawling to and from water sources. So closely do mounds relate to the landscape that it sometimes is difficult to see where the mounds end and the rest of the terrain begins. The concept of harmony is also illustrated by the absence of holes or borrow pits in the landscape, despite the mounds' having been built of dirt from the surrounding area. The only depressions are the rare intaglios, which obviously were of ceremonial importance. In all these regards, we are reminded of R. Clark Mallam's interpretation that effigy mounds were built to symbolize and ritually maintain balance and harmony with the natural world within the context of ceremonialism to renew the world.

Are astronomical orientations also present in the arrangement of effigy

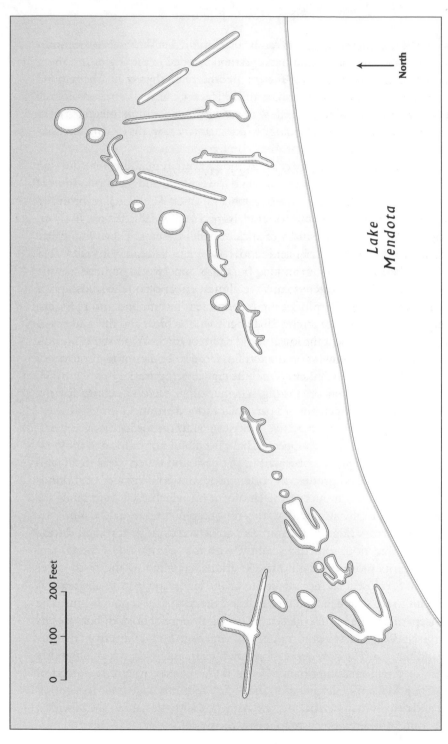

Figure 5.11. The Woodward Shores Mound Group, on the northern shore of Lake Mendota, is typical of effigy mound groups in the Four Lakes region of Dane County. Groups containing effigies that symbolize air, earth, and water are common and often are neatly divided into zones of bird, animal, and water spirit mounds. (Drawing by Amelia Janes, Midwest Educational Graphics, based on survey maps by Theodore H. Lewis, map compilations by James P. Scherz, and field data of the State Historical Society of Wisconsin.)

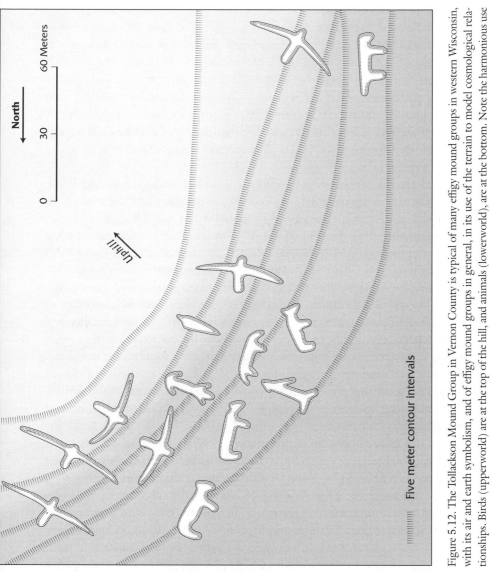

Figure 5.12. The Tollackson Mound Group in Vernon County is typical of many effigy mound groups in western Wisconsin, with its air and earth symbolism, and of effigy mound groups in general, in its use of the terrain to model cosmological relationships. Birds (upperworld) are at the top of the hill, and animals (lowerworld), are at the bottom. Note the harmonious use of the landscape: both forms primarily follow the contours of the hill or are oriented up- or downslope. (Drawing by Amelia Janes, Midwest Educational Graphics, based on survey map by the State Historical Society of Wisconsin)

mounds? Ancient people the world over were attuned to the heavens and extremely knowledgeable about the movements of various celestial bodies. Furthermore, they attributed supernatural qualities to the sun, moon, stars, and planets, which often were perceived and personified as deities and spirit beings who played major roles in creation stories and cultural epics of mythic heroes. The Ho-Chunk of Wisconsin, for example, include Sun, Moon, and Morning Star in a pantheon of deities. The use of astronomical references, particularly tracking the movements of the sun, moon, and major stars and planets, has been well documented for the ceremonial life of Native Americans and other ancient peoples throughout the world.[55] The pyramids of Egypt and Mexico as well as the stone monuments and barrows of northwestern Europe, such as Stonehenge in England and Newgrange in Ireland, all incorporated celestial observations, to one extent or another, in their design and use.

Perhaps the earliest North American example of solar tracking is the monumental earthwork at Poverty Point in Louisiana, where there may have been observation of the vernal and autumnal equinoxes.[56] Somewhat closer to Wisconsin and to the time of the effigy mounds are the remains of huge circles of posts at the Mississippian site of Cahokia in southern Illinois, built around A.D. 1100.[57] Dubbed "woodhenges," the structures were almost certainly used to observe the solstices and equinoxes, positions of the sun that mark the change of seasons. Such observations are especially important to agricultural peoples, who used such astronomical markers for fertility and crop-related ceremonies and celebrations. Since the construction of mounds seems to have been about the death and rebirth of the soul and the world and the effigy mound people were making the first steps to the cornfields, it would be surprising if they did not consider the observation of the solstice and equinox to be very important. Furthermore, because of the death and rebirth symbolism involved, the mound groups, like the great Neolithic tombs of Europe, would be appropriate places for such ritual activity.

Unfortunately, the search for astronomical alignments among the effigy mounds in Wisconsin has had equivocal results. If alignments do exist, they involve a relatively few mounds and do not appear to account for the complex mound arrangements. One researcher of this matter in Wisconsin is James Scherz, who has studied alignments at Lizard Mounds County Park, among other places.[58] While he suggests a variety of solar, lunar, and planetary alignments, others, including E. C. Krupp, director of the Griffith Observatory in Los Angeles, are somewhat skeptical about their existence. Krupp, an expert on ancient astronomy, points out that proving astronomical alignments in ancient monuments is a tricky business and is most often based on circumstantial evidence. In reviewing the Lizard Mounds data,

Krupp found that there was not sufficient evidence that the arrangement of the mound group in general was astronomically inspired. While he believes that it is plausible that a few linear mounds in the group were used to observe solar events, such as the solstices, he regards most other conjectural alignments as arbitrary or, at best, not clear. At the Lizard Mounds site, he concludes, "intentional astronomical alignment remains unresolved."[59]

The eleven mounds of the Maples Mills Mound Group in Whitewater Indian Mound Park have also been closely examined for astronomical alignments. The group was surveyed by Scherz, Frank Stekel, a physics professor, and mound researcher Larry A. Johns, who concluded that a few mounds appear to have special orientations, such as to the cardinal directions and possible solstice points.[60]

A third study of mound alignments was completed by Gary Henschel, owner of the Henschel Mound Group overlooking the Sheboygan Marsh in Sheboygan County.[61] Henschel hypothesized that a number of panther (or water spirit) effigy mounds and earlier large conical mounds were employed to observe the solstices and equinoxes as well as lunar movements. While this is possible, an alternative ideological explanation (and one that is not mutually exclusive) for the alignment of most of the panthers is that they were oriented in order to be viewed as coming from or going to the entrance to the underworld—a major spring that is now used as the source for several trout ponds on the property.

Although unproved, it is possible that at least some mounds in effigy groups have astronomical alignments, and the search for such patterning should continue, especially among the mysterious linear mounds that do not seem to conform to the division into upperworld and lowerworld. Given the complex, multilevel symbolism, metaphors, and allegories embedded in mound building by Native Americans, it is quite likely that mound arrangements owe their complexity to a variety of factors, including the relationship of effigies to actual and supernatural habitats, harmony with the landscape, the relationship of the effigies to one another, and even solar events, such as the winter and summer solstices, that observe the birth and death of the seasons and hence the ritual renewal of the earth.

Ceremonial Centers

In Early and Middle Woodland times, mound ceremonialism functioned on several levels. Mounds were burial places that marked territories and were the focus of ceremonials that integrated groups through the practice of rituals related to the renewal of the world and its resources. The effigy mound people brought forward and elaborated these concepts, building ceremonial centers that went beyond mortuary concerns. That some effigy mounds do not contain burials indicates that unlike Early and Middle Woodland mounds, Late Woodland mounds did not depend for their construction on the inclusion of human burials. During the 1970s and 1980s, archaeologists began to hypothesize instead that effigy mound groups had been built to represent ceremonial activities that were directed primarily at socially integrating segments of Late Woodland society. In this view, effigy mound groups marked the places at which highly mobile hunting and gathering families periodically rendezvoused with one another during the year to undertake a number of social, economic, and ceremonial activities that linked the families together in a band (figure 5.13). The Middle Woodland burial mounds and, indeed, cemeteries in general functioned to integrate social groups, but directly through rituals that focused on the burial of the dead. During the era of the effigy mounds, burial of the dead and accompanying mortuary rituals may have been only one part of a complex and continual ceremonial.

While the interpretation that effigy mound groups represent ceremonial centers has not changed, the view that the effigy mound people were hunters and gatherers who spent much of the year living in small family groups away from other members of the band is being challenged. Although this lifeway may have characterized groups very early in Late Woodland times, the recent discovery of Late Woodland villages, such as the Statz site, indicate that at least some families were living in villages during major portions of the year and, after A.D. 900, had turned increasingly to corn agriculture. Rather than linking families into bands, effigy mound ceremonialism and ceremonial centers may have integrated bigger groupings, such villages, bands, or lineages, into a much larger social identity extending throughout the entire effigy mound area.

The similarity of mound forms, mound arrangements, and other customs attending mound construction found throughout the large effigy mound area argues for a shared sacred knowledge that may have been controlled by a society (perhaps secret) of religious specialists, such as shamans, who directed the mound-building ceremonials. Such societies are common in historic and modern Native American cultures and cross-cut social and village organizations. For example, members of the Grand Medicine Society, which is found among both Siouan- and Algonquian-speaking tribes in the Midwest, are the keepers of origin stories and other sacred knowledge, especially that concerning medicine and healing rituals that frequently involve the restoration of balance and harmony in the world.

Unfortunately, the relationship between the effigy mound ceremonial centers and the villages and populations they served is unclear because there have been few investigations around effigy mound groups, and until recently, few Late Woodland major camps and villages had been identified.

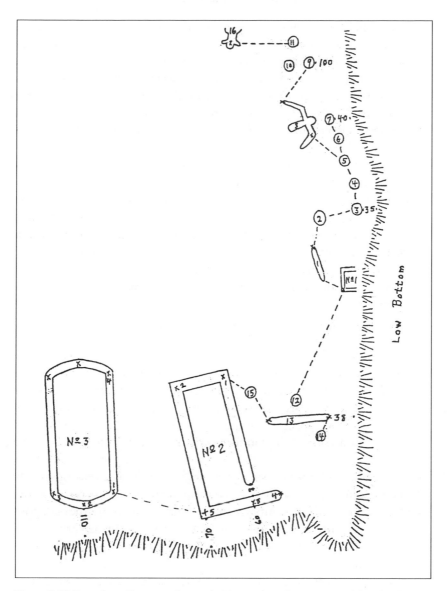

Figure 5.13. Part of an effigy mound group in Trempealeau County mapped by Theodore H. Lewis in 1888, showing enclosures probably used for ceremonies. (From Theodore H. Lewis, field notebook 23, Northwestern Archaeological Survey, Notebooks and Related Documents, Minnesota Historical Society, St. Paul; used with permission of the Minnesota Historical Society)

What evidence there is, however, suggests that the distance between effigy mound groups and associated habitations may have been determined by local geography. In many areas, like the Four Lakes region around Madison, mound groups tend to have been built on high elevations, while villages or camps were located on the shores of the lakes, which were more suitable for living. Mound groups constructed along rivers might have habitation areas immediately adjacent. In the 1960s, William Hurley found evidence of a village or major seasonal camp at the Sanders site, on the Wisconsin River.[62] Farther down the river, archaeologists from the State Historical Society working with staff from a Native American preservation office located a major Late Woodland settlement that had been neatly enclosed by a spectacular effigy mound group first surveyed by Theodore H. Lewis in the 1890s. In areas of great mound density, it is not clear whether each mound center served a separate group of people or whether a single band or village of people was responsible for building a number of mound groups—shifting the location of mound construction from time to time as desired space (hilltops, for example) became filled.

MOUNDS IN NORTHERN WISCONSIN

The region of the effigy mounds in Wisconsin corresponds to the highly productive deciduous forests and parklands to the south of and including the tension zone in Wisconsin. This zone, which consists of a mixture of southern and northern plants and animals, runs westward across central Wisconsin and arcs northward in the northwestern part of the state. Above the tension zone lies the coniferous forest that we associate with northern Wisconsin. Except for fish and wild rice, northern Wisconsin was not nearly as productive in wild food resources in the past as southern Wisconsin. Before the logging period of the nineteenth century, for example, the deer population was extremely low. In addition, because of the short growing season, horticulture never became an important part of the Native American economy, with a few notable exceptions.

This region of the state supported a comparatively small, dispersed population of fairly mobile hunters, gatherers, and fishers who shifted locations to take advantage of food resources when and where they became available. The construction of burial mounds began in northern Wisconsin on a very small scale in the Middle Woodland period and, as in southern Wisconsin, accelerated during the Late Woodland, when most mounds were built. Mounds and mound groups were erected at strategic locations along rivers and lakes, where they appear to have functioned as central gathering places for an otherwise dispersed population. Reflecting a small population and lifestyles and

Figure 5.14. Large conical mound on Clam Lake in northern Wisconsin, before its excavation in the 1930s, that was built in stages over a long period of time. (From William C. McKern, *The Clam River Focus* [Milwaukee: Milwaukee Public Museum, 1963]; used with permission of the Milwaukee Public Museum, neg. 414536)

belief systems different from those of the people of southern Wisconsin, burial mounds are not as numerous as one moves north. Of the tens of thousands of mounds constructed in Wisconsin, only about 1,500 were built above the tension zone, and most of them near where the tension zone and its abundant resources and milder climate loops up into northwestern Wisconsin. In the "snowbelt"—the northernmost tier of counties adjacent to Lake Superior and the Upper Peninsula of Michigan (Douglas, Bayfield, Ashland, and Iron)—fewer than three dozen mounds have been recorded.

Burial mounds in northern Wisconsin are of several types, probably reflecting different traditions or tribal groups. Most are conical, but oval and linear mounds occasionally can be found. Effigy mounds are rare, but the "catfish" mounds in Menominee County and some other areas may embody similar concepts. Most mounds in northern Wisconsin are part of small groups, but a considerable number of mound locations (about 30 percent) consist of a single conical mound of considerable size, often reaching heights of more than twelve feet. Early archaeological excavations at a few of these sites revealed that they had been built in stages over a long time, perhaps several generations, reflecting periodic "feast of the dead" burial ceremonies. At the Clam Lake Mound, William McKern of the Public Museum of the City of Milwaukee documented a sequence of periodic ceremonial activities that eventually had created a mound fourteen feet high and ninety feet in diameter (figure 5.14).[63] The initial mound had been only four feet high and thirty-four feet in diameter. No burials had been made, but the mound was covered with red ocher, a symbol of death and burial ceremonialism for Native Americans since ancient times. After a time, beach sand and six bundles of cleaned human bones, wrapped in birch bark, had been added. McKern and many others believed that such bone bundles represented a periodic "feast of the dead" ceremonial that involved the burial of the remains of people brought down from mortuary scaffolds much like those that the Dakota and other tribes maintained in this region. This level was capped by dirt, and eventually two other stages were built on top, each one with many bone bundles (figure 5.15). McKern felt that this mound had indeed been built by the Dakota who lived in this area during the historic period, but radiocarbon dates obtained later from the nearby Spencer Lake Mound as well as the type of pottery found in the Clam Lake Mound indicate that the mound had been constructed hundreds of years earlier (figure 5.16). It is possible, of course, that the mound builders were the ancestors of the historic Dakota.

THE RISE AND DEMISE OF THE EFFIGY MOUND CULTURE

The dates of effigy mound construction have been a source of controversy. This is because of the many thousands recorded—and several hundred excavated—only a handful of effigy mounds (excluding conical and linear mounds) have been radiocarbon dated, and these from only six mound groups: Sanders in Waupaca County; Bigelow in Portage County; Utley, Kolterman, and Nitschke in Dodge County; and Effigy Mounds National Monument in Iowa.[64] To complicate matters, some of these dates were taken when the technique was not as accurate as it is now, resulting in possible errors of several hundred years. In his study of the effigy mound culture, William Hurley used these radiocarbon dates, along with much indirect and circumstantial evidence, to argue that in Wisconsin the culture lasted from about A.D. 400 right up to the appearance of the Europeans.[65] But recent and critical examinations of radiocarbon dates, along with data from habitation sites, suggest that effigy mounds were built during a comparatively brief period in the Late Woodland, beginning around A.D. 700 and ending, for the most part, by about A.D. 1100.[66] At the very least, there is general agreement among archaeologists that effigy mound construction ended by A.D. 1200.

At this point, two fundamental questions still have to be answered: What stimulated Late Woodland people to coalescence in the first place, displaying their ideology on the landscape in such an extraordinarily visible fashion? And what caused them to stop?

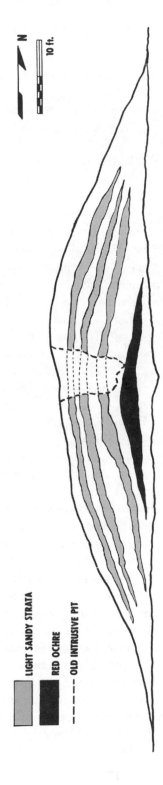

Figure 5.15. Profile of the Clam Lake Mound. (From William C. McKern, *The Clam River Focus* [Milwaukee: Milwaukee Public Museum, 1963]; used with permission of the Milwaukee Public Museum, neg. 414537)

Figure 5.16. Pottery found in the Clam Lake Mound. (From William C. McKern, *The Clam River Focus* [Milwaukee: Milwaukee Public Museum, 1963]; used with permission of the Milwaukee Public Museum, neg. 71951)

The origins of effigy mound ceremonialism are unclear, but may be related to both the events taking place elsewhere in the Midwest at the time and the role that mound building generally played in rituals of world renewal. The Late Woodland was an unstable period of rapid technological, economic, and social change; population growth; warfare; and physical movements of tribes and bands. Much of this change was emanating from regions to the south of Wisconsin. Perhaps the Late Woodland people of the effigy mound region were unsettled by change, even as they accepted new ideas. Perhaps they began to perceive ideological and even physical threats that undermined their sense of cultural well-being. When faced with similar challenges brought about by continuing contact with Euro-Americans, Native Americans in the nineteenth century responded by developing new religious movements that cross-cut social boundaries, such as the Ghost Dance and Dream Dance, and that sought to define who they were and restore their way of life: bringing the world back into balance and harmony. The effigy mounds are monumental representations of the cosmology of their builders. Perhaps effigy ceremonialism also began as an attempt by a people to define themselves in relation to intruders and competing ideologies. Perhaps, through the physical modeling of an orderly universe, the effigy mound people sought to call on the power of their spirit beings to restore harmony to a quickly changing world.

If the origins of effigy mound construction are still a mystery, the demise of the culture is less so. We believe that the effigy mound ceremonial helped bind people together in Wisconsin and adjacent areas, forming a new horticulturally based social confederation with distinct clan structures organized into upper and lower divisions. This new social entity that emerges in the archaeological record in Wisconsin sometime after A.D. 1000 is what archaeologists refer to as Oneota. The comparatively rapid transition to this new way of life was to a large part stimulated by direct and indirect interaction with a new and powerful cultural presence on the Wisconsin landscape between A.D. 1000 and 1200: the Middle Mississippian. By the time the transition was complete, the Oneota had developed social mechanisms (such as permanent villages and well-organized social structure) and ceremonials adapted to a new horticultural lifestyle that eventually replaced the various social and spiritual functions of mound building. Robert Hall believes that the end of the period of burial mound construction (which was supplanted in Oneota culture by large belowground cemeteries with individual graves) occurred as ceremonialism shifted emphasis from world renewal in general, symbolized in various ways by the periodic construction of mounds, to new agriculturally based concerns for the fertility of the earth, which became a matter separated from the death ritual.[67] In short, culture had dramatically changed, and the building of earthen mound ceremonial centers was a custom that was no longer needed.

But the culture of the Woodland mound builders did not completely disappear after A.D. 1200 in Wisconsin. The probable descendants of the Oneota—the Ho-Chunk (among others, perhaps even the Menominee)—retained major aspects of an ancient belief system and social structure that can be traced back to the mound builders. In addition, some people maintaining a Late Woodland lifestyle may have continued to build conical burial mounds in areas of northern Wisconsin into the period of European contact.

6

Temple Mound Builders

The Mississippian Tradition

The fate of the Late Woodland mound builders and the emergence of the Oneota culture in Wisconsin were inextricably tied to the evolution of a new civilization that was springing from the vast fertile Mississippi River floodplains of southern Illinois. Around A.D. 800, local Late Woodland people in this "American Bottom" made the shift to corn horticulture and within a few hundred years had organized one of the most complex societies in prehistoric North America. This new culture has been referred to as the Middle Mississippian because it developed in the central part of the Mississippi River valley. Because of its spectacular nature, the Middle Mississippian culture or tradition is exceptionally well studied. In addition, this remarkable society was documented in the writings of early explorers. The last vestige of Middle Mississippian culture was still thriving in parts of the present-day southeastern United States when Spanish and French explorers arrived.[1] Among the first was Hernando de Soto. His famous and ill-fated *entrada* brutally rampaged through the region in the sixteenth century. Tribal names associated with the Mississippian civilization in the historic period include the Natchez, Creek, and Chickasaw.

CAHOKIA

At the heart of prehistoric Mississippian culture is the largest Native American settlement ever to have been constructed in North America, a place that is now called Cahokia. Many archaeologists would trade their careers to learn by what name it was known to most of the people of eastern North America around A.D. 1150—for there resided North America's first great lords.

Cahokia is situated on the Mississippi River floodplain in Illinois, across the river from St. Louis, Missouri. The site draws its name from an Indian tribe that lived in the area in the eighteenth century, although the tribe had little to do with the site itself. Archaeologists have traced Cahokia's development from a concentration of villages and mound ceremonial centers to a veritable city. At its greatest power about 900 years ago, this city covered more than five square miles and accommodated a population estimated at 10,000 or more (figure 6.1).[2]

Cahokia was a fabulously vital and complex community. A huge wooden wall, complete with watchtowers, enclosed the central 200 acres of the city. Within this central precinct, the seat of Cahokia civic and religious power, lay a public plaza and a number of very large earthen mounds and flat-topped pyramids, on top of which apparently stood ceremonial structures and the houses of the ruling families. At one end loomed Monk's Mound, a flat-topped or platform pyramid that was 100 feet high and covered 14 acres at its base. It is the largest prehistoric earthen structure ever constructed in the world. Here lived the paramount chief, the lord of Mississippian society. Such figures were referred to by the Spanish as *caciques* (or *cacicas,* if women), a word borrowed from Caribbean natives describing a ruler or chief. According to European observers, these rulers among the Natchez and other Mississippian tribes of the historic period belonged to the Sun clan and were believed to have descended from the sun, one of the principal deities of the Mississippians.

Members of Cahokia's ruling family or lineage were buried in nearby mounds covered by a larger ridged-topped mound, called mound 72, which was excavated in the 1960s. The offerings that accompanied them to the spirit world, which included fabulous grave goods and many human sacrifices, tell a great deal about the power of both the rulers and Cahokia from the tenth through the thirteenth century. One such individual, almost certainly a *cacique,* lay in death on a bed of 20,000 shell beads arranged in the form of a large hawk or falcon, an ancient upperworld icon that had clearly become the fierce symbol of Cahokia aggressiveness. He was surrounded by the corpses of human sacrifices. Near the grave were pits containing clusters of arrows, each cluster tipped with a stone distinctive of a midwestern region, offerings from the hinterlands that had come under Mississippian influence or control. Among them was a bundle of arrows whose heads were made from Hixton Silicified Sandstone from the Silver Mound area of western Wisconsin.

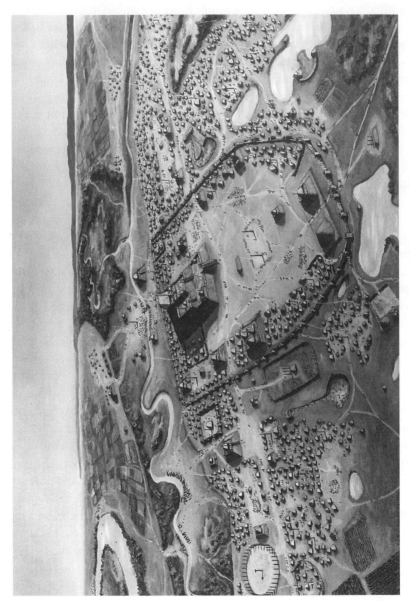

Figure 6.1. Cahokia, around A.D. 1150. (Painting by William R. Iseminger; courtesy of the Cahokia Mounds Historic Site)

Other human offerings in mound 72 included four men whose heads and hands had been chopped off. They could well have been leaders of enemy chiefdoms and their presence meant to symbolize power and military prowess. Later Mississippian iconography on shell and other media often depicts war themes, such as elaborately ornamented people dressed as hawks or falcons holding decapitated human heads. An even more dramatic and grim representation of the power of these lords of Cahokia was a central mass grave in mound 72 containing the remains of more than fifty young women who apparently had been sacrificed after the death of a *cacique* so they could accompany their ruler into the afterlife.

Outside the central precinct of Cahokia were more large mounds, residential districts consisting of houses made of poles and thatch, and circles of large poles that archaeologists have dubbed "woodhenges" because of their probable function as calendrical or astronomical observatories. Radiating from Cahokia itself were smaller subordinate towns and ceremonial centers as well as dozens of hamlets and farmsteads. Surrounding all these places were thousands of acres of cornfields that produced much of the Mississippian food.

Cahokia and Mississippian society was so vast and complex at about A.D. 1100 that some archaeologists in the past believed that it formed the first state or nation in North America: a Native American empire. In this scheme, the ruling family could be compared to those of early Old World city-states. Most now agree that at the very least, Mississippian society consisted of chiefdoms, although much more elaborate than those of earlier times (figure 6.2). One scholar likened Cahokia and other Mississippian towns to medieval Italian principalities.[3]

As is characteristic in chiefdoms, food and other resources were not distributed by markets but through ceremonial redistribution during the course of important seasonal ceremonies and feasts controlled by the chief. Such festivals reflected well on the chief, increasing his or her prestige and influence. One important ceremony found among the Mississippians of the southeastern United States in the historic period was the Green Corn Ceremony or Busk, an annual fertility or "first fruits" ceremony.[4]

It is easy to imagine the impact that the rise of Cahokia and Mississippian society had on adjoining regions. Feeding and clothing tens of thousands of people must have quickly strained the local resource base. The Mississippians turned thousands of acres of fertile bottomland into farmland, but there must have been a continuing need for other staples — such as meat, hide for clothing, stone for tools, and wood for construction — as well as goods that were symbols of prestige for the ruling families. Trade as well as other social and political processes expanded Cahokia influence out into

Figure 6.2. Artist's conception of the Mississippian elite. (Illustrations by Lloyd Kenneth Townsend; courtesy of Cahokia Mounds Historic Site)

much of eastern North America. Given Cahokia's massive fortifications, militaristic imaginary in some art, notably men dressed as hawks, and evidence of human sacrifice, this probably was not always a cooperative venture. Furthermore, Cahokia itself may have been competing for land and other resources with other powerful Mississippian chiefdoms that began developing throughout the Mississippi River valley. Some have even suggested that Mississippian intrusions in the north were by political refugees.

THE MISSISSIPPIAN TRADITION: THE TEMPLE MOUNDS

Mississippian trade interest in the northern frontier of Wisconsin may have focused on such resources as lead (for white paint), found in the southwestern part of the state; stone (Hixton Silicified Sandstone is found at Cahokia in small quantities); meat and hides from the vast and productive southern deer country; and other food. Trade for copper from northern Michigan almost certainly involved Wisconsin people as well. Several archaeological sites in Wisconsin have unmistakable evidence of interaction with Cahokia or at least the Middle Mississippian sphere of influence, and new sites are being discovered all the time (figure 6.3).[5]

It is possible that the expansion of Mississippian trade and influence into Wisconsin followed a pattern similar to that of the French fur trade many centuries later, by which trade between the French and the western Great Lakes tribes was initially conducted indirectly through a series of Native American intermediaries. In this way, European goods and ideas (as well as infectious diseases) traveled in advance of the Europeans themselves. Armed with goods that conferred great prestige, the middlemen became powerful and vied with one another for valued trade routes and prominent roles in the trade network. Sometimes they expanded into the territories of others involved in the trade, stimulating intertribal warfare. Alliances between tribes frequently shifted. This unstable and frequently violent situation was exacerbated by the immigration of eastern tribes into Wisconsin as the European colonial presence grew in the East, displacing local tribes westward through a vast "domino effect." After a short time, fur-trading posts, often garrisoned with European soldiers, were established throughout the region to secure the trade by mediation or force. During one period in the era of French trade, a virtual war of extermination was waged by the French and their Native American allies on the Fox, originally from Michigan, who had attempted to monopolize the fur trade in Wisconsin. Accompanying European fur traders were missionaries intent on converting the Indians to Christianity. Missions were established at important fur-trading centers; the European

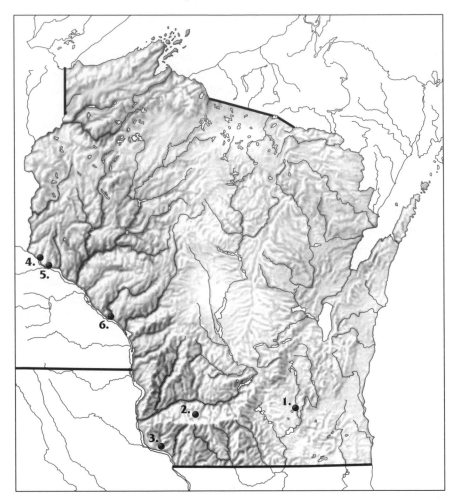

Figure 6.3. The distribution of Mississippian-related sites in Wisconsin: (*1*) Aztalan; (*2*) Gottschall Rockshelter; (*3*) Fred Edwards site; (*4*) Diamond Bluff site; (*5*) Adams site; (*6*) Trempealeau mounds. (Map by Amelia Janes, Midwest Educational Graphics)

nations well understood that the best trading partners are those that share an ideology.

Although the Middle Mississippians never sought to colonize or even directly control all of the hinterlands, Middle Mississippian trade in Wisconsin appears to have been conducted first through intermediaries, some of whom migrated into the region, undoubtedly competing with and otherwise unsettling the indigenous population. At strategic points, the Mississippians themselves built ceremonial centers that apparently served as trading stations. At one of them, Aztalan on the Crawfish River in Jefferson

County, they built and occupied a fortress to secure their interests in that district.

Gottschall Rockshelter

Although Cahokia did not reach its zenith until after A.D. 1100, there is increasing evidence that trade and ceremonial relationships had been established between the emerging Mississippian culture in Illinois and the Late Woodland people in Wisconsin a century earlier. One of the Mississippians' first long-distance trading partners in Wisconsin may even have been the effigy mound people. Such a link is suggested by the findings at the Gottschall Rockshelter.[6] Mississippian paintings, dated to between A.D. 900 and 1000, are associated with effigy mound–era pottery in the cave floor, and the site is geographically linked to a spectacular effigy mound ceremonial complex a relatively short distance away. No Middle Mississippian artifacts have been found at Gottschall, but the paintings are rendered in an undeniable Mississippian art style that is completely foreign to Wisconsin (figure 6.4). Depicting a story about the mythic Siouan culture hero Red Horn, the paintings feature human beings adorned as Mississippian warriors, one with "forked-eye" face paint in imitation of the markings of the peregrine falcon. The falcon was revered by the Mississippians because of its hunting technique: the bird swoops down at high speeds and immobilizes

Figure 6.4. Researchers believe that the paintings in the Gottschall Rockshelter tell a story associated with the mythic hero Red Horn and are rendered in a Mississippian artistic style. Red Horn and the opposing warriors are dressed and decorated as Mississippian warriors. (Drawing by Mary Steinhauer; used with permission of Robert Salzer, Beloit College)

its prey with a blow much like that dealt with a war club. The Gottschall Rockshelter may represent the initial expansion of Mississippian influence into the northern frontier in an attempt to secure trade relationships for the emerging Mississippian entity in the American Bottom.

Fred Edwards Site

More direct evidence of Mississippian trade and influence in Wisconsin dates to a bit later—between A.D. 1050 and 1150—when the effigy mound ceremonialism appears to have been in decline. Located in southwestern Wisconsin along the Grant River, the Fred Edwards site was a large village enclosed by a defensive log wall and occupied by a people who had migrated to the area from Iowa or northern Illinois.[7] Among the broken ceramic pots they left behind were Late Woodland styles that are foreign to Wisconsin and Mississippian styles that link the Fred Edwards people to Cahokia. The purpose of their comparatively short sojourn in Wisconsin can also be deduced from village debris. Lead, deer bones, and stone hide scrapers were found in comparatively large quantities, leading the investigators to conclude that the visitors had been extracting or trading for lead and deer hides. Lead was used by both Native Americans and later white settlers as a base for white paint. Native American use probably focused on body decoration, which, judging from the Mississippians' artistic renditions of themselves, was considerable and elaborate. The southwestern part of Wisconsin contains extensive lead deposits and drew thousands of Euro-American miners in the early nineteenth century. This area, along with southern Wisconsin in general, also supported a large deer population.

Trempealeau Mounds

The archaeological evidence at the Fred Edwards site suggests that intermediary traders with Cahokia connections were moving northward into Wisconsin by the eleventh century. The migration into Wisconsin of small groups of Mississippians themselves also may be traced to about the same time. In what is now the tiny town of Trempealeau on the Mississippi River north of La Crosse, Mississippians sculpted the summit of a high bluff into three low platform mounds generally reminiscent of the monumental platform mounds at Cahokia (figure 6.5).[8] Archaeologists have not yet found a habitation area associated with this ceremonial center, but pottery sherds from vessels identical to forms manufactured in Cahokia early in its evolution have been found below the bluff. Much of the mound complex was disturbed by the construction of a water tower that serves the town of Trem-

Figure 6.5. Platform mounds on a high hill overlooking the town of Trempealeau as they appeared in the early twentieth century. (State Historical Society of Wisconsin, neg. no. WHi [X3] 51038)

pealeau, but fortunately the site had been well documented by pioneering mound researcher Theodore H. Lewis in the late nineteenth century and later by amateur archaeologist George H. Squier.[9]

A clue to the function of this Mississippian ceremonial center can be gleaned from its location. As are Middle Woodland burial mound centers in the same area, the platform mound site at Trempealeau is within twenty-five to thirty miles of outcroppings of Hixton Silicified Sandstone, including the famous Silver Mound. This colorful, workable, and apparently sacred rock was used for 10,000 years by Native Americans to fashion spear points, arrowheads, knives, and other tools. It is possible that the Mississippian ceremonial complex at Trempealeau operated as a trading center symbolized by Hixton Silicified Sandstone. Trade apparently would have been with the local Late Woodland people, who probably mined the rock and provided it to the Mississippians, along with such other goods as food and hides, in the context of ceremonials conducted at the platform mounds. Significantly, one of the arrow bundles found with the burial of the *cacique* in mound 72 at Cahokia included exquisitely crafted arrowheads made from Hixton. This may represent an offering from the dead leader's trading partners in the upper Mississippi River valley.

Red Wing Locality

Farther north, another center of intense Mississippian-influenced activity appeared after A.D. 1000, along the banks of the Mississippi River in what is now Goodhue County, Minnesota, and Pierce County, Wisconsin. At what has been called the Red Wing Locality, there developed a series of large fortified villages surrounded by dense Late Woodland–like burial mound complexes. In the two-county area, more than 2,000 mounds were built over several hundred years. Two small Mississippian-style platform mounds at sites in Minnesota suggest Mississippian presence. In Wisconsin, the village and mound complexes include the Diamond Bluff site, where Late Woodland, Mississippian-like, and Oneota pottery have been found (figure 6.6).[10] Some researchers have suggested that Diamond Bluff and the other Red Wing Locality sites are places to which Late Woodland people from throughout the region were drawn by Mississippian trade, giving birth in that area to the Oneota lifeway or culture. James B. Stoltman and George Christiansen have argued that effigy mound people vacated the whole of southwestern Wisconsin and migrated to such places as the Red Wing Locality. Their theory is that the rapid cultural transformation of the Late Woodland effigy mound builders into Oneota was accomplished through their intense interaction with the Middle Mississippians.[11] Aside from their pottery, Late Woodland presence is indicated by the fact that effigy mounds are among the thousands of small conical burial mounds constructed around these villages. The Diamond Bluff site contains mounds in the shapes of a bird, an animal, and a panther or water spirit. The water spirit mound was excavated in the 1940s, providing provocative evidence of interrelationships among Late Woodland, Mississippian, and Oneota peoples: several pottery vessels and sherds found with burials in the mound include Middle Mississippian and Oneota styles.[12]

Aztalan: A Mississippian Outpost

The largest and most famous Mississippian site in Wisconsin is Aztalan, located on the Crawfish River near the town of Lake Mills. The name Aztalan comes from a greatly mistaken idea prevalent in the early nineteenth century that the site had been the place of origin of the Aztecs of Mexico. Because of its uniqueness in Wisconsin, the site has been the focus of intensive archaeological investigations beginning in the nineteenth century. Increase

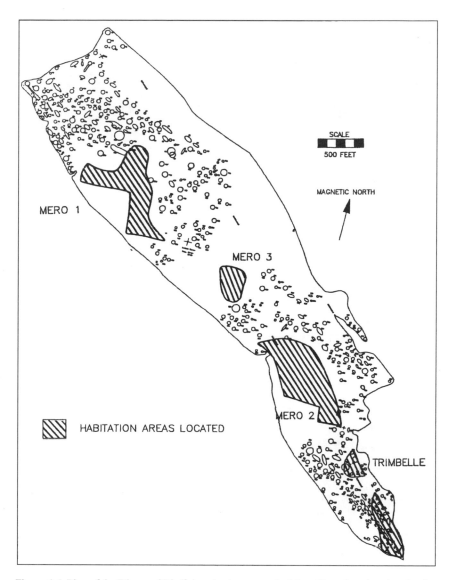

Figure 6.6. Plan of the Diamond Bluff site, also known as the Mero Complex, showing the distribution of mounds and habitation areas. (Map by Clark Dobbs, based on modern surveys and Theodore H. Lewis, field notes, Northwestern Archaeological Survey, Notebooks and Related Documents, Minnesota Historical Society, St. Paul; used with permission of the Institute for Minnesota Archaeology)

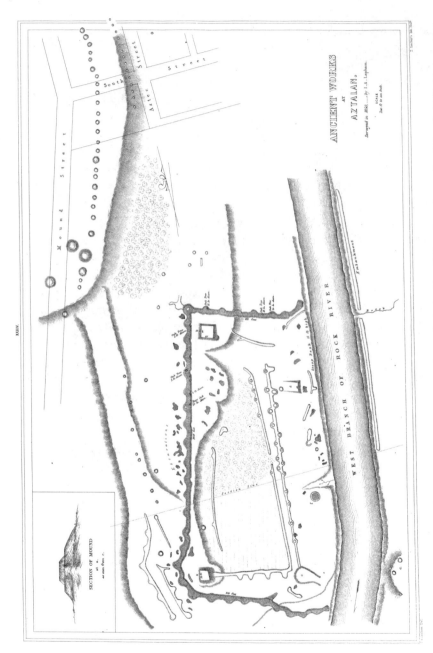

Figure 6.7. Aztalan, as mapped in 1850. (From Increase A. Lapham, *The Antiquities of Wisconsin, as Surveyed and Described* [Washington, D.C.: Smithsonian Institution, 1855])

A. Lapham examined some mounds before 1855 (figure 6.7). Large sections were excavated by Samuel Barrett of the Public Museum of the City of Milwaukee in the 1920s and by investigators from the University of Wisconsin and the Wisconsin Archaeological Survey in the 1940s and 1950s. The later work resulted in the reconstruction of two platform mounds and of a segment of a defensive wall. Researchers from the University of Wisconsin–Milwaukee recently conducted more limited and focused investigations at the site.[13]

At its heyday around A.D. 1150, Aztalan covered fifteen acres and was enclosed by a formidable wall made of huge posts interwoven with willow branches and thickly plastered with clay and mixed grass, a type of construction known as wattle and daub. Large buttresses located at intervals along the wall not only helped support the massive structure, but also probably served as watchtowers and defensive positions for warriors. Two sets of progressively smaller enclosures subdivided the town. They may have separated it into different social spaces and/or reflect expansion (or retraction) of Aztalan over time (figure 6.8).

At roughly the four corners of the town were earthen platform mounds, smaller versions of those at Cahokia. The southeastern mound is actually a natural knoll incorporated into the town design, and not much is known about it. The other three platform mounds were civic and religious structures, and each appears to have played a distinct role in Aztalan life. The southwestern mound—the largest at the site—was two-tiered and built in three stages over time. The top surface was covered with a clay facing, enhancing the dramatic appearance of the mound. Steps led to the top of the mound, where there was a large structure or house, measuring forty-two feet on a side, built of upright posts (figure 6.9). Inside the structure were storage pits containing remains of corn. This may have been the house of the *cacique* of Aztalan, the place where the ruling Mississippian family lived.

The northwestern mound functioned as a platform for a mausoleum, most likely for the resident Mississippian elite. It also was built in three stages. On top of the second stage, archaeologists found the remains of a burned mausoleum, also called a charnel house, containing the charred bones of ten people who had been placed side by side in the five- by twelve-foot structure. The bones of an eleventh individual were bundled together by a cord. Charnel houses were common repositories for the remains of important Mississippian families. After learning of this custom, Hernando de Soto and his conquistadors raided mound-top charnel houses in the southeastern United States in search of valuables, no doubt enraging the local inhabitants. As were those of Hopewell times, the Mississippian mortuary structures were periodically burned, which stimulated a phase of new

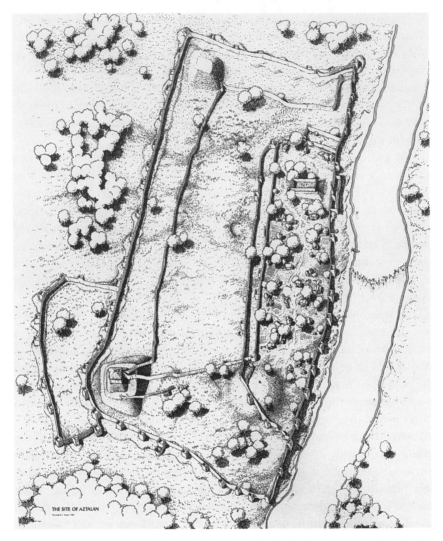

Figure 6.8. Artist's conception of Aztalan, based on archaeological investigations. (Drawing by Eric Paulson; used with permission of the Department of Anthropology, University of Wisconsin–Milwaukee)

mound construction. The remnants of a second charnel house may have existed on a top stage of the northwestern mound or elsewhere on the site. According to a report written in 1838, mound diggers excavated the top of a large unidentified mound within the enclosure at Aztalan and recovered the charred remains of more than fifty bundles of human bones still tied by cords.[14]

The northeastern platform mound at Aztalan was excavated in the

Figure 6.9. The reconstructed southwestern platform mound at Aztalan. (Photograph by Robert Birmingham)

1950s, but, unlike the southwestern and northwestern mounds, was never reconstructed. It functioned as a platform for a temple or religious structure. The mound was built in one stage, but it was raised over the remains of large building, measuring forty-five by ninety feet, that had been constructed on the ground surface. Another building, identical in size to the first, was built on top of the mound. It was open-walled and constructed of upright posts. Inside the structure, the Aztalan people maintained sacred fires in large pits. Periodically, the fires were extinguished and the pits were cleansed or re-consecrated by lining them with pure white sand. Eyewitness accounts by Europeans tell that sacred fires were carefully maintained in temples by Mississippian peoples in the Southeast, where they were perceived as the personification of the sun deity. The ritual fires were extinguished and re-kindled during the annual Green Corn Ceremony.[15]

Aztalan's residential district accommodated about 350 people and occupied the eastern side of the village. It appears to have been set off from several of the platform mounds by another wall. In this precinct, archaeologists discovered the remains of small but substantial single-family pithouses built of wattle and daub. Some were circular and others rectangular with pronounced entranceways, much like the keyhole houses of the Late Woodland. In the 1990s, investigators from the University of Wisconsin–Milwaukee discovered a specialized precinct at the northern end of the town. It con-

Figure 6.10. The conical mounds built in a line overlooking Aztalan were not for burials, but marked the location of large ceremonial posts. (Photograph by Robert Birmingham)

sisted of a large number of huge clay-lined pits in which food was stored. The existence of a centralized food depot suggests that food distribution was controlled by town leaders, a practice that was common in Mississippian communities.

A map of the ruins of Aztalan made in about 1837 shows that remnants of agricultural fields, to the north of the town proper, were still visible in the nineteenth century.[16] Immediately to the west and overlooking this area originally stood a line of at least twenty-nine large conical mounds that followed a high ridge that trended north–south (figure 6.10). A line of ten smaller conical mounds was situated just below this. Farther to the west was a third group of about a dozen conical mounds that has been called the Greenwood Mound Group. By the twentieth century, many of the Greenwood mounds had been obliterated by farming, but Barrett examined some of those that remained. They contained large central pits with cremated human remains and bundle burials, but no grave goods. It is probable that this mound group was constructed by Woodland people before the establishment of Aztalan.

Barrett also explored the large conical mounds in the long central line on the ridge top. His findings resulted in two surprises. The first was that many of the mounds were not burial mounds at all, but covered deep pits in which large, and presumably very high, wooden posts once stood. The diameter of the posts was approximately fifteen inches. In one mound, the basal remnants of a large oak post were still in place. The function of these posts is not obvious, nor is the reason that their locations were covered by high prominent mounds. Barrett suggested that the seasonal Green Corn Ceremony, as widely practiced by southeastern Mississippian peoples in the historic period, was a possible reason for the erection of large poles. European observers described dances associated with the ceremony as taking place around a special pole erected for the purpose.[17] Perhaps each of the mounds, which overlook Aztalan's cornfields, commemorates an annual observance of the Green Corn Ceremony. Alternatively, the posts could have played a role in year-round calendrical observations, as did the woodhenges at Cahokia.

The second surprise came toward the northern end of this unusual line of mounds. Lying in a grave pit beneath a low conical mound nearly fifty feet in diameter, Barrett discovered one of the most lavish Native American burials ever found in Wisconsin: the famous "princess" burial. This was the burial of a woman in her early twenties who had had a spinal deformity and whose corpse had been wrapped in three belts of several thousand beads made from local river clams and Gulf coast marine shell. The presence of so many shell beads is reminiscent of that of the bead bed found in the burial of a chief in mound 72 at Cahokia. It could be that this woman was from the elite Mississippian family that ruled Aztalan. Perhaps she was a chief, or *cacica,* herself. In historic times, the Mississippians of the southeastern United States traced family descent through the female line, and women appear to have had much social power. Occasionally, women directly ruled. In his search for plunder, Hernando de Soto in 1540 sought out a storied Mississippian empire called Cotifachequi in what is now South Carolina that was headed by young "queen" who recently had inherited her status. In an attempt to secure the cooperation of the natives, de Soto kidnapped the ruler, but she escaped. Whatever her status, the important young Aztalan woman was buried in a peculiar place—at the end of a line of mounds that marked the locations of ritual posts to the northwest of the town. Why she was interred in this place is a mystery.

History of Aztalan

The history of the town of Aztalan is becoming clearer as a result of work undertaken by archaeologists from the University of Wisconsin–Milwaukee.[18] Excavating layered middens, or garbage deposits, along the bank of the Crawfish River, they were able to piece together a chronology of events that spanned the life of the town. Aztalan started as a Late Woodland farming village between A.D. 800 and 900. The inhabitants were not the local effigy mound builders, but a group of farmers who had migrated from the south, perhaps from north-central Illinois, as part of an initial expansion of Late Woodland people following their adoption of corn agriculture.

This early village was situated at a place that had been used by previous Woodland people for quite some time as an important ceremonial center. Middle Woodland artifacts are commonly found at the site, and the Greenwood Mound Group, to the northwest, may have been built by earlier Woodland peoples. Effigy mound people also used the locale for ceremonial purposes at some point: directly across the river from Aztalan is a large water spirit or panther effigy mound and two small earthen enclosures, one of which contained other mounds.

The particular Late Woodland group that settled at Aztalan had connections to the emerging Mississippian society in southern Illinois, perhaps serving as intermediaries in the trade network. Just before A.D. 1000, pottery sherds similar to early Mississippian styles appear in the archaeological deposits. The pottery, however, seems to be locally made copies of Mississippian pottery rather than trade vessels. After A.D. 1000, there is unmistakable evidence, in the form of Mississippian pottery and extensive modifications to the site, that the Mississippians were present themselves, perhaps to take direct control of trade that had been conducted through their Late Woodland middlemen from Illinois or for other reasons that are unclear. At this time, Aztalan was expanded and built along the lines of Cahokia and other Mississippian communities, including platform mounds and a formidable wall. Mississippian ceremonies, perhaps including the Green Corn Ceremony, probably accompanied the Mississippians and would have been introduced to the indigenous Late Woodland people. Evidence from the earlier excavations of the platform mounds indicates that Aztalan underwent a total of three major waves of expansion under the Mississippians. These episodes probably corresponded to major earth renewal ceremonies.

Archaeological work done at Aztalan indicates that throughout the history of the town, many of its residents were drawn from Late Woodland populations. Most of the ceramics found at the site, even those dated to after the arrival of the Mississippians, are Late Woodland collared types, and even pottery of the effigy mound people is present. Again, using a historic period fur-trade analogy, the social composition of Aztalan brings to mind the social organization at many a fur-trading post, where the European traders lived surrounded by communities of Native Americans who were drawn to the post by the trade. But if Aztalan was a trading outpost, what were the Mississippians and their close allies trading for? Archaeologists Lynne Goldstein and John Richards have pointed out that Aztalan is located immediately adjacent to large wetland areas that could have produced any number of food resources.[19] Furthermore, Aztalan lies in an area character-ized by mixed forest and prairie. The immediate environment would have supported (and still does) a large deer population. Perhaps, as at the Fred Edwards site, the acquisition of deer meat and hides was a major focus of Mississippian trading activity.

Aztalan and Its Neighbors

The presence of several types of Late Woodland pottery, including that of the effigy mound people, would lead one to believe that the Mississippians at Aztalan enjoyed peaceful relationships with at least some of the local Late Woodland people. This notion is reinforced by the recent discovery of con-temporaneous and unfortified Late Woodland sites within a short distance of the town. Small amounts of Mississippian pottery have been recovered from these sites, indicating interaction between the Late Woodland and the Mississippian people. But Aztalan itself has provided undeniable evidence of a town at war, if not under siege. It is massively fortified. Throughout the town proper, early archaeologists exhumed many discarded, burned, and butchered human body parts, some of which show unmistakable signs of cannibalism—a grisly by-product of intense warfare. Human sacrifice and ritual cannibalism were common during periods of warfare in many parts of the New World. Historical accounts, for example, detail the practice among such tribes as the Huron, Creek, and Tunica, who tortured, burned, cut into pieces, and sometimes ate their prisoners in order to gain their power and courage.[20]

The Mississippians and their allies at Aztalan clearly had enemies. Among them could have been other Late Woodland people who were not allied with the Mississippians. Conflict among many bands and tribes may have arisen as competition for trade routes and even prime agricultural land, creating an unstable situation in which alliances frequently shifted. How-ever, most probably one enemy of Aztalan was a large group of *former* Late Woodland effigy mound people: the Oneota. It could be that the Oneota in Wisconsin were the descendants of the indigenous Late Woodland trading partners of the Mississippians who evolved a dramatically new lifestyle and material culture though their adoption of agriculture and their intense cul-tural contact with the Mississippians. Near Aztalan, one group of Oneota lived in large villages on the shores of Lake Koshkonong, which until about A.D. 1000 had been a major center for the effigy mound people. Some ar-chaeologists have long recognized that Lake Koshkonong was also a point for subsequent Mississippian cultural contact, as indicated by characteristic Mississippian decorations on the earliest Oneota pottery in the area, as well as other Mississippian characteristics. Some believe that the Oneota became the enemy of the Mississippians at Aztalan and use radiocarbon evidence from sites on Lake Koshkonong to argue that the Oneota may have been temporarily driven from the shores of the lake as a result of conflict.[21] Fierce warfare eventually may have erupted between the Oneota and the Mississippians as the former became more settled and proprietary over their lands and resources, and the latter, more expansionist and aggressive.

THE DEMISE OF THE TEMPLE MOUND CULTURE

Between A.D. 1200 and 1300, Cahokia and its remarkable society evaporated. The city itself was abandoned, as was its daughter community of Aztalan in Wisconsin. After having dominated events for several hundred years, the Mississippians vanished from the landscape of the Midwest. The reasons for their disappearance are not yet known. Some have cited such factors as the overexploitation of local resources, the loss of political and ideological power, and the onset after A.D. 1200 of a lengthy period with a cool climate that may have affected crops and other food resources. Mississippian culture continued to flourish in the Southeast until the appearance of the Europeans, but it no longer exerted influence in the upper Midwest. And North America never again saw the likes of Cahokia, the ancient Mississippian capital.

7

Mound Construction and Use
in Later Times

Oneota, Northern Wisconsin,
and the Historic Period

Nonindigenous travelers in southern Wisconsin between about A.D. 1300 and 1650 would have found an eerie place. Moving westward across what is now Milwaukee and Waukesha Counties, they would have stumbled across several hundred large ceremonial centers consisting of clusters of curious earthen mounds built in the shape of birds and animals, now abandoned and grown over. In what is now Jefferson County, they would have come upon the burned and ruined walls of Aztalan, still plainly visible. Our mythical travelers, like nineteenth-century Euro-American settlers at the same spot, might even have wondered about the great war that had brought down this large fortress. In the Four Lakes region of Dane County and westward through the Wisconsin River valley and the hilly southwestern area of the state, they would have encountered more groups of effigy mounds, even larger and more numerous than the others and sometimes containing mounds in the shape of human beings, further testaments to furious human activity in some distant past. But where, the travelers would have asked, are the people now? Where have all the mound builders gone?

THE ONEOTA

After the collapse of the Mississippian civilization in the Midwest, and the apparent disappearance of the ubiquitous Late Woodland people, including the effigy mound builders, what is now central and southern Wisconsin appears to have been populated by culturally similar groups of people: the Oneota.[1] The Oneota are distinguished in the archaeological record from other people by a characteristic form of pottery, large villages occupied during much of the year, and a subsistence pattern based on corn horticulture. Unlike the Mississippians, the Oneota did not build temple mounds, and unlike the Late Woodland people, they did not build burial mounds, except perhaps very early in their history. Also unlike Late Woodland people, who had widely dispersed camps and villages, the Oneota were concentrated into widely separated village clusters in various parts of Wisconsin. Similar Oneota population centers emerged elsewhere in the Midwest in what is now Michigan, Illinois, Iowa, Minnesota, South Dakota, Nebraska, and Missouri.

Who Were the Oneota?

The origin of the Oneota in Wisconsin is another archaeological issue that has been hotly debated.[2] Noting a similarity between some Oneota and Mississippian customs, one early but now discarded theory suggested that the Oneota had been simply the descendants of Mississippian migrants to Wisconsin. Another theory proposes that the Oneota developed independently of the Late Woodland and Middle Mississippian cultures from a common Woodland base as part of the same broad trajectory toward increasing agricultural life. According to one version of this theory, the Oneota then migrated northward into Wisconsin, eventually eliminating or displacing the indigenous Late Woodland people. Some Oneota, particularly in the western part of the state, became briefly allied with the contemporaneous Middle Mississippians, while others, especially in the eastern region, were not as much affected.

The most likely situation is that the Oneota in Wisconsin were the descendants of the Late Woodland effigy mound builders whose lifestyle had been transformed by both the adoption of corn agriculture and contact with the Mississippians. It is likely that the nature and intensity of cultural contacts between the Late Woodland and the Mississippian peoples varied from region to region, ranging from indirect trading to cohabitation, such as at Aztalan.[3] This accounts for the different rates at which the transition was made and the reason that some Late Woodland populations persisted in certain areas of Wisconsin, particularly the east, for at least two centuries after the appearance of Oneota culture in other areas. Among the competing theories about the origin of the Oneota, this best explains the fate of the effigy mound builders and the very close ideological links between the effigy mound people and the modern descendants of the Oneota. It is also supported by other lines of evidence, such as linguistics and geographic continuity of the various cultural entities.

The name Oneota is drawn from the Oneota River valley in Iowa, where this cultural tradition was first identified. It has also been known in archaeological literature as the Upper Mississippian tradition, as opposed to the Middle Mississippian. As with all these matters, archaeologists do not know for sure the name or names by which the people referred to themselves, although most scholars are quite certain of the many tribal names by which their midwestern descendants have been known by the Euro-Americans in historic times: the Siouan-speaking Ho-Chunk (Winnebago), Ioway, Kansa, Missouria, Omaha, Osage, and Otoe. Recent archaeological work in northeastern Wisconsin even hints that the Algonquian-speaking Menominee also may have shared in this tradition, but the prehistory of these peoples has not been archaeologically documented.[4]

At the time of contact with Europeans in the seventeenth century, the Ho-Chunk lived in east-central Wisconsin. The Ioway lived in eastern Iowa, but apparently had migrated from west-central Wisconsin a century or so earlier. Both Ho-Chunk and Ioway traditions relate that they were once part of one tribe, separating in some distant past. Indeed, the languages of the two tribes are very similar, as are aspects of their social structures, belief systems, and other cultural traditions. It is possible that the single tribal entity remembered in oral history and reflected in similarity of language and culture is the Late Woodland effigy mound people. This view is supported by some linguistic data. Employing glottochronology, a technique that dates the divergence of languages by using known rates of changes in words, James Springer and Stanley Witkowski estimated that the language group that includes Ho-Chunk, Ioway, Missouria, and Otoe differentiated from other Central Siouan language groups sometime between A.D. 700 and 1000.[5] Significantly, these dates coincide with the coalescence of the effigy mound culture and immediately predate the appearance in the archaeological record of the Oneota in Wisconsin. The subsequent separation of at least Ho-Chunk and Ioway within this common language group may be traced in the archaeological record of the Wisconsin Oneota to between A.D. 1300 and 1500.

Settlement and Nucleation

The first communities that archaeologists call Oneota appeared sometime around or just after A.D. 1000 in certain areas, some of which had been centers of intense Middle Mississippian trade and activity. Within these areas, Oneota farming villages were established on river terraces and lakes on or near easily tillable light sandy soils. Like that of the Middle Mississippians, the economy of the Oneota was based on farming. Corn, beans, squash, and other crops were cultivated around large villages that were occupied mainly during the warmer months (figure 7.1). The Oneota also relied heavily on river and lake resources, such as fish, clams, and wild rice. They hunted deer, elk, and bison as well as a variety of small animals for meat, hides, and bone that could be fabricated into tools. In the winter, the Oneota traveled to hunting grounds to take deer, and perhaps buffalo.

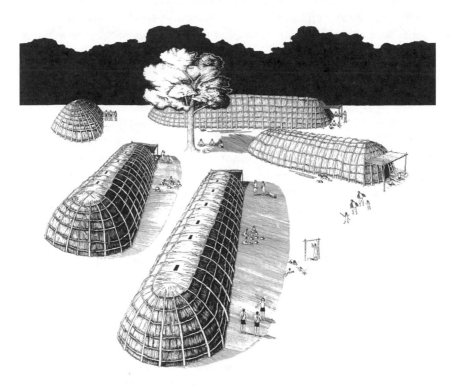

Figure 7.1. Oneota village scene in Wisconsin, around A.D. 1450. (Drawing by Nancy Hoffman, Museum Archaeology Program; used with permission of the State Historical Society of Wisconsin)

The Oneota never developed huge towns, temple mound ceremonial centers, or complex chiefdoms. Instead, the evolution of Oneota society over its 600-year history is reflected in changing household patterns. The first identifiable Oneota communities consisted of small, single-family pole-and bark-covered pithouses. Just before the time of European contact, many of the Oneota appear to have been living in longhouses, sometimes 150 feet in length, that would have accommodated many families of a single lineage or clan.[6]

After 1300, the Oneota in Wisconsin seem to have consolidated into two principal densely populated centers: a western concentration on the sandy Mississippi River terraces around present-day La Crosse, and an eastern concentration along the Middle Fox River, including Lake Winnebago. There are sites as well at nearby Green Bay and on the Door Peninsula (figure 7.2). There is radiocarbon evidence to suggest that some Oneota may have returned to the shores of Lake Koshkonong at this time after having been driven off by the Mississippians, but little is known about these people.[7]

The consolidation of the Oneota in Wisconsin into essentially two large groups may reflect the separation, recounted in oral history, into the Ioway (western Oneota) and Ho-Chunk (eastern Oneota) people. Outside Wisconsin, widely dispersed Oneota population centers similarly have been linked to the homelands of modern tribes that lived in these areas.[8] Throughout the late prehistoric period, the areas between the Oneota enclaves in Wisconsin and among the Oneota settlements elsewhere in the Midwest seem to have been thinly populated, suggesting the maintenance of vast buffer zones. That warfare continued through this period is evident by the presence of some fortified villages.

Sometime before the arrival of European explorers, fur traders, and missionaries, many Oneota villages in Wisconsin were decimated or wholly abandoned. The western Oneota at La Crosse seem to have migrated into Iowa, where combined archaeological and historical evidence brings them into history as the Ioway. Archaeological evidence indicates that the eastern Oneota were reduced to a few villages in the sixteenth century: most of the large sites seem to have been abandoned at that time. Both warfare and the spread of infectious diseases carried by the Europeans may have been responsible for this decimation.[9] Almost certainly, the ancestors of the Ho-Chunk are among the eastern Oneota. Although there is no unequivocal archaeological evidence making this link, there is much circumstantial documentary evidence and oral history. Accounts written by the Europeans place the Ho-Chunk in the same area as the late prehistoric eastern Oneota, and oral traditions of the Ho-Chunk state that this area was always a part of their homeland. Furthermore, Ho-Chunk oral traditions as well as early his-

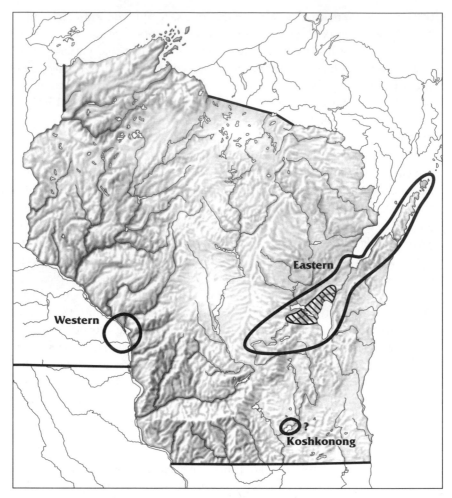

Figure 7.2. The distribution of late prehistoric Oneota population centers in Wisconsin. Hatched area shows dense settlement around A.D. 1350 to A.D. 1500. (Map by Amelia Janes, Midwest Educational Graphics)

torical documents support archaeological evidence of a population calamity in eastern Wisconsin.[10] The Ho-Chunk told Paul Radin that they had been a populous tribe, but had been almost exterminated by disease and wars with the Illinois.

Pottery

As are other ancient pottery-making societies, the Oneota are distinguished from other cultures in the archaeological record by the appearance of a distinctive style of pottery. The Oneota made thin-walled globular pottery vessels that, like many of the Middle Mississippian pottery forms, were tempered with crushed shell. Oneota pottery, which began appearing around A.D. 1000, is often decorated with designs made by trailing a blunt tool along the wet clay or punching a blunt tool into it. With some notable exceptions, the Woodland practice of impressing cords into the clay was not employed. The earliest Oneota decorations were also clearly inspired by beautiful Mississippian motifs, which include interlocking scrolls, curved lines, chevrons, and other geometric patterns on a smooth surface. These Mississippian designs appear to be elaborations on the upperworld and lowerworld themes and so would have been easily understood and absorbed by Late Woodland people who shared a generally similar worldview.[11]

After the disappearance of the Mississippians and their influence, Oneota decorations took on a more distinctive flavor, but continued to deal with ancient midwestern upperworld and lowerworld themes that, like the earlier effigy mounds, seem to have geographic associations (figure 7.3). Probably as a legacy of both the Mississippian ideology and continuing warfare, a prominent upperworld image is a stylized peregrine falcon or hawk. As are the ancestral effigy mounds in the form of birds, Oneota upperworld symbolism seems to be strongly, although not exclusively, associated with western Wisconsin. Hawk or falcon symbolism on pottery and other art extended to the south and west of Wisconsin and is found associated with Oneota population concentrations in Illinois, Iowa, Minnesota, and Missouri.[12]

Lowerworld symbolism seems to predominate on Oneota pottery from eastern Wisconsin, as it does in the lizard- or water spirit–shaped mounds of this region. Curvilinear designs, probably water motifs, are common on pottery made in the thirteenth and early fourteenth centuries, and they give way, after A.D. 1350, to rectilinear patterns of vertical and, especially, horizontal lines that may be general representations of the earth, as they appear to be on Woodland pottery. Significantly, the Ho-Chunk (Winnebago), believed to be descended from the eastern Oneota, were associated by other tribes with water. Winnebago is an Algonquian name for the tribe that probably refers to dirty or muddy water, and the Ho-Chunk were known to the French as "people of the sea."[13]

Although lowerworld symbolism appears to predominate in eastern Wisconsin, pottery with upperworld hawk or falcon imagery, almost identical to western Oneota pottery, has been found at some eastern Oneota sites on Green Bay and the Door Peninsula and in small quantities at other sites in the region.[14] It is referred to as Allamakee Trailed and Perrot Punctate.

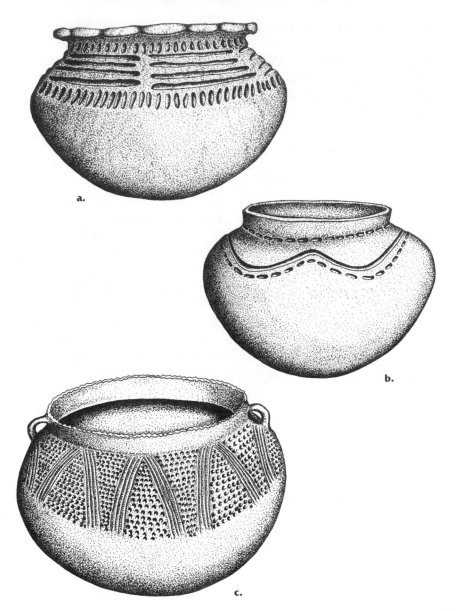

Figure 7.3. Oneota pottery: (*a*) the trailed designs on this pot, characteristic of some parts of eastern Wisconsin around A.D. 1350 to 1500, may be lowerworld (earth) symbolism; (*b*) this earlier pot, also from eastern Wisconsin and dated to around A.D. 1150 to 1350, features a curvilinear design, symbolic of water, and may reflect Mississippian contact or influence; (*c*) this pot, with its upperworld (bird) symbolism, is characteristic of western Wisconsin (La Crosse area) around A.D. 1400 to 1650. (Drawings by Richard Dolan; used with permission of the State Historical Society of Wisconsin)

That both upperworld and lowerworld iconographies are present may reflect the existence among the Oneota of moieties or dual social divisions, which exist in many modern tribes, such as the Ho-Chunk and Menominee. That is, people who belonged to upperworld clans were making pottery with upperworld symbolism, and members of lowerworld clans were making pottery with lowerworld symbolism.

Mounds

Like their Woodland ancestors, some Oneota (or emerging Oneota) continued to build small conical burial mounds around their villages, sometimes in great numbers. This appears to have been a transitional phase: by A.D. 1200, this custom diminishes, along with the demise of the great mound-building era. Among these transitional sites are the Diamond Bluff and Adams sites on the Mississippi River, which probably are places where the Oneota culture appeared, and the later Armstrong site, farther downstream in Trempealeau County. Elsewhere in Wisconsin, mounds do not appear to have been common, even at early Oneota sites. Some Oneota—for example, those at the Grand Village site in Green Lake County—enhanced natural knolls by adding dirt to accommodate ongoing burials.[15] These hills took on the appearance of large low burial mounds. After about A.D. 1200, all Oneota typically interred people just after death in individual graves in flat underground cemeteries at their villages. In addition, people often were buried beneath the floors of their houses, a practice that, in the case of young children, was already present with the appearance of the first Oneota communities just after A.D. 1000.[16]

The change from burial in mounds to burial in cemeteries seems to have been related to a general shift from the mobile hunting and gathering lifestyle to the more sedentary farming lifestyle. Ceremonies of world renewal, which had been part of burial mound ritual, became associated with crop fertility rites rather than mortuary rites, and new ceremonies and institutions evolved to socially integrate segments of tribal society.

Among the new ceremonials was one that appeared later in the evolution of the Oneota and was specifically directed at social integration: the Calumet Ceremony. Through the Calumet Ceremony, as widely practiced by North American tribes in the historic period, outsiders are symbolically adopted into the tribe, taking the name of a deceased member. The ceremony involves dancing and smoking a calumet pipe, consisting of a special, elaborately carved wooden stem and a bowl of red pipestone. Robert Hall has drawn a parallel between the Calumet Ceremony and earlier mound ceremonialism, pointing out that during the Calumet Ceremony, the dead are symbolically reborn.[17] Red pipestone "disk" pipe bowls believed to be from calumets and dated to after A.D. 1350 are commonly found at Oneota sites.

MOUNDS IN NORTHERN WISCONSIN

Although the custom of building burial and other types of earthen mounds had ended in most of Wisconsin by A.D. 1200, there is intriguing evidence that mound ceremonialism may have persisted among some less agricultural people in the northern part of the state who continued to follow a Woodland lifestyle until the time of contact with Europeans. As William McKern predicted many years ago, the people appear to have been the Dakota, who occupied northwestern Wisconsin until the Chippewa drove them out in the early eighteenth century.[18]

In the 1950s, Leland Cooper excavated a large conical mound in the Rice Lake Mound Group and found some European trade items that may have accompanied burials. The mound was one of fifty-one original mounds, making the group one of the largest in northern Wisconsin. Earlier excavations had been done at the group under the direction of Cyrus Thomas of the Smithsonian Institution in the late nineteenth century during his quest for the "mound builders." The mound that Cooper dug had been badly disturbed by looters.[19]

As were the famous Clam Lake and Spencer Lake Mounds in Burnett County, the mound at Rice Lake appears to have been accretionary, or built in stages over time. Cooper suggested that the remains of people buried in the mound, like those buried in the Clam Lake and Spencer Lake Mounds, had been brought down from nearby scaffolds, where they had awaited periodic mass burials in a mound. Few datable grave goods accompanied the burials, but among them were a steel spring and a lead button. The spring may have been a component of a "hair puller," a device for removing facial hair that was a popular European trade item during the fur-trading period in northern Wisconsin. Since such objects were not available until after European contact, the burials and the mound itself, Cooper believed, must necessarily date to after that time. As did McKern in reference to the Clam Lake and Spencer Lake Mounds, Cooper identified the inhabitants of northwestern Wisconsin during the early historic period, the Dakota, as the likely people who had built at least some of the mounds at Rice Lake.

Cooper did not believe that the historic items in the Rice Lake Mound were intrusive—introduced into an ancient mound after the mound had been completed—but the fact that the mound had been heavily disturbed before being excavated by Cooper has led archaeologists to be cautious about accepting it as historic rather than prehistoric and ascribing a specific tribal affiliation to its builders. Minnesota provides better evidence that burial mounds were occasionally built in the historic period and specifically by the Dakota, who also occupied parts of Minnesota until being displaced in the eighteenth century by the Chippewa. The Cooper Mound site, located in Mille Lacs, consists of a series of conical mounds. One was excavated in 1967 by Minnesota archaeologists who found that it covered a grave pit that contained a vessel of Ogechie Ware, a style that archaeologists feel certain was made by a branch of the Dakota known as the Mdewakanton in the early historic period. Other offerings in the grave pit were trade goods acquired from French fur traders between 1670 and 1740, consisting of glass beads, copper cone-shaped "tinkling" ornaments, and a copper ring.[20]

REUSE OF PREHISTORIC MOUNDS IN THE HISTORIC PERIOD

Of any time in the eventful and dramatic history of Native Americans, contact with Europeans was the most catastrophic. Within a comparatively brief period, as much as 80 percent of the indigenous population of North America died from infectious diseases. Whole tribes probably disappeared, and entirely new tribes were created by the survivors. In Wisconsin, Native Americans engaged in economic enterprises with Europeans, such as the fur trade, that changed their material cultures and eventually led to a dependence on European goods and the market system. Ceramic pots, with their ancient and deep symbolism, were supplanted by generic brass and copper containers. Iron implements and weapons replaced stone tools. By the mid-eighteenth century, the material cultures of the different tribes that occupied the western Great Lakes region were indistinguishable from one another. On the Great Plains, the introduction of the horse created a buffalo-oriented culture that drew tribes to the plains in great numbers. Competition and the westward migration of Euro-Americans led to great tribal movements, exacerbating intertribal warfare that further changed traditional societies and reduced populations. So much cultural disruption occurred during the early part of the historic period that it is frequently difficult to connect known tribes to their prehistoric ancestors. Archaeologist Carol Mason characterized this break in the record as an "archaeological Grand Canyon, more easily looked across than spanned or jumped."[21]

According to early historical documents and tribal oral traditions, the tribes living in what is now Wisconsin when the Europeans arrived were the

Ho-Chunk (Winnebago), Menominee, and Dakota.[22] Close relatives of the Ho-Chunk, the Ioway, apparently also had resided in western Wisconsin until soon before European contact, but had migrated westward. Other tribes may have lived in Wisconsin, but had been pushed out, drawn to the Great Plains to hunt buffalo on horseback, or completely wiped out by disease and warfare before their existence in the state could be documented.

When the Europeans first encountered the Ho-Chunk, they lived in villages apparently restricted to the upper Fox River region in east-central Wisconsin.[23] Recovering from a drastic loss in population, they eventually expanded into (or reoccupied) parts of southern Wisconsin. The Algonquian-speaking Menominee lived along Lake Michigan just north of the Ho-Chunk, but they also expanded over large parts of Wisconsin. The Dakota originally occupied northwestern Wisconsin. By the late seventeenth century, waves of new Algonquian people were moving westward into Wisconsin. In the north, bands of Chippewa or Ojibwe migrated westward from the eastern end of Lake Superior, leading to an extended period of warfare with the Dakota and resulting in displacement of Dakota westward. The more southerly areas of Wisconsin were briefly occupied by tribes that had migrated to or had been pushed into Wisconsin during the early part of the historic period. Among them were the Sauk, Fox, Kickapoo, and Miami. In eastern Wisconsin, the Potawatomi, immigrants from Michigan related to the Ottawa and Chippewa, settled vast tracts of land along with scattered mixed settlements of other tribes that had originated elsewhere in Wisconsin and the Midwest, such as the Sauk, Chippewa, and Menominee.

Of all these, the Dakota may have been the only (and last) tribe to build burial mounds in Wisconsin in the historic period. As the first European explorers and settlers swept into the state, they made note of the ubiquitous mounds on the Wisconsin landscape, but repeatedly stated that they never saw local Native American people build mounds, although cultural customs, including burials, were often noted. In addition, later anthropological studies, based on historical accounts and oral histories, described in detail the mortuary practices of the tribes in the historic period. All these studies document in-ground flat cemeteries or, as with the Potawatomi, Chippewa, and some other groups, occasional aerial burials on scaffolds or in trees. When asked about mounds in more recent times, Wisconsin Native Americans themselves generally ascribed them to customs that had been practiced in some distant past.

One curious exception to tribal oral history is found in an article written by John Blackhawk, a Ho-Chunk from Black River Falls. Blackhawk had been asked by Charles E. Brown, of the State Historical Society of Wisconsin, to give an account of Ho-Chunk beliefs concerning mound building. In the article, Blackhawk repeated information published by Paul Radin earlier in the century, but added: "My grandfather related once of an instance where he saw a bird mound being built in front of a chieftain's lodge. This was perhaps the last of the custom. He noted that it was placed to the east of the lodge or lodges."[24] Taken at face value, this uncorroborated report would indicate that effigy mounds were also occasionally built, in imitation of existing mounds and unnoticed by neighboring white settlers, well into the nineteenth century. But there are other more likely explanations. One is that the oral information had been garbled, and what was meant to be transmitted was that the village was simply located near an ancient bird effigy mound. Throughout the chaotic historic period, bands of Native Americans settled or resettled on the very same sites that had been used by the mound builders for the same reasons that the ancients had established them—access to critical food resources or to transportation and trade routes. The reoccupation of desirable locations is a pattern that was repeated over several thousand years, often leading to stratified archaeological sites that have provided a record of human occupation in Wisconsin. Early maps of mound groups by Increase A. Lapham and others depict corn cultivated by Indians in the historic period running up and over low effigy mounds.[25] Even the ancient site of Aztalan was occupied briefly in the nineteenth century by a Ho-Chunk band.

An even more likely explanation is that in his story, Blackhawk recorded not the construction but the use of an existing mound for a burial, a common practice in many parts of southern Wisconsin during the nineteenth century that is well documented in both the historical and archaeological records. Nineteenth-century observers made frequent mention of the custom as practiced by various tribes, especially those living in central and southern Wisconsin, such as the Ho-Chunk, Menominee, and Potawatomi.[26] According to Richard C. Taylor, for example,

Successive tribes have occupied, by turns, the region of the country where these apparent animal and human effigies abound. The Winnebago ... have held possession of that part of the Wisconsin Territory that lies immediately south of the Wisconsin River, and east of the Mississippi, only from sixty to eighty years. Previous to this time the district was in the hands of the Sauk and Fox Indians ... who dug and smelted the lead ore, but were driven out by the Winnebagos. Neither of these tribes now erect monuments of this character, to the memory of their dead. *We have seen them, it is true, in numerous places, excavate graves, and deposit the remains of the deceased on the summits of the ancient circular tumuli, which they appear to conceive were constructed for such purposes.*[27]

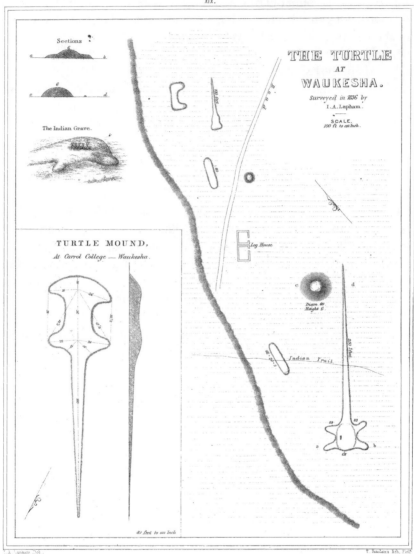

Figure 7.4. "Turtle" effigy mound, mapped in 1836, in present-day Waukesha, with a recently made grave and grave house, probably Potawatomi. A detailed rendering of the grave structure is at the upper left. (From Increase A. Lapham, *The Antiquities of Wisconsin, as Surveyed and Described* [Washington, D.C.: Smithsonian Institution, 1855])

The reuse of these mounds for graves often involved the erection of small wooden structures such as log grave houses, as was customary of the Potawatomi, in which were left offerings of food and tobacco (figure 7.4). Archaeological reports, some dating back to the nineteenth-century mound-digging era, contain many references to the diggers encountering "intrusive burials"—graves dug into the mounds—accompanied by European or American trade goods, such as silver ornaments, glass beads, iron axes, and metal kettles.[28] Before the time of detailed soil observation, this misled some to conclude that the mounds themselves were of recent origin.

The reuse of mounds for burials seems to have been primarily a nineteenth-century phenomenon, but the custom apparently continued into the twentieth century in some areas. The practice appears to have been related to the removals suffered by Native Americans through treaties and Euro-American settlement (Figure 7.5). The earliest treaties, such as that at Prairie du Chien, were directed at establishing the land claims of the various tribes. After the 1830s, treaties divested Native Americans of their land for white settlement, restricting some tribes, like the Menominee and Chippewa, to small reservations in northern Wisconsin and forcibly removing others, notably the Potawatomi and Ho-Chunk, ultimately to western "Indian lands" in Nebraska and Kansas. Many Ho-Chunk and Potawatomi simply refused to move and continued to live where they could as fugitives and refugees until white settlement drove them to remoter areas, where they were joined by relatives who defiantly returned from the western reservations (Figure 7.6). These "stray bands" and "lost tribes," as they were referred to, fiercely resisted repeated attempts at removal and finally were provided some small lands by the federal government.[29]

With the sudden loss of family or tribal burial grounds brought about by the treaties and white settlement, these people may have perceived the ancient mounds, especially the effigy mounds with their spirit being and clan symbolism, as eternally sacred and sanctified places where their relatives could be most appropriately and safely interred. Lapham reported many new Native American graves on mounds in Milwaukee, Waukesha, and Dodge Counties during his survey of mounds in southern Wisconsin in the late 1830s and the 1840s—after all the tribes in this area were supposed to have been relocated.[30] Despite white settlement of the region, Lapham observed that Native American families, probably Potawatomi, continued to visit these mound-top graves in Milwaukee on an annual basis. At Theresa in Dodge County, Lapham noted a mound entirely covered by graves, apparently from a small nearby Ho-Chunk and Menominee community. As a sad footnote, most of the ancient mounds used by nineteenth-century Native Amer-

177

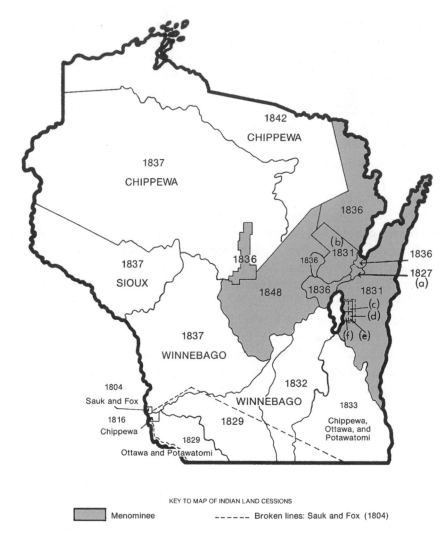

KEY TO MAP OF INDIAN LAND CESSIONS

▨ Menominee   –––––– Broken lines: Sauk and Fox (1804)

Figure 7.5. Land ceded by Native Americans to the United States in the nineteenth century. Only Chippewa bands and the Menominee retained reservations, located in northern Wisconsin. The Ho-Chunk and Potawatomi who refused to be removed obtained small parcels of land from the federal government in the late nineteenth and twentieth centuries in western Wisconsin (Ho-Chunk) and northern Wisconsin (Potawatomi). The letters *a–f* on the map refer to land ceded by some Wisconsin tribes for use by eastern U.S. tribes. (Map by Judy Patenaude, from Nancy Lurie, *Wisconsin Indians* [Madison: State Historical Society of Wisconsin, 1987]; used by permission of the State Historical Society of Wisconsin)

Figure 7.6. Ho-Chunk, who had refused to resettle in Nebraska, in the Wisconsin Dells in the late nineteenth century. Seated at the right is the war chief Wa-con-jaz-gah (Yellow Thunder). (Photograph by H. H. Bennett; State Historical Society of Wisconsin, neg. no. WHi [X3] 14208)

icans as burial places have been obliterated by urban and residential development, road building, and modern farming.

It would not be until the late twentieth century that federal and state laws would be enacted to protect Native American mounds and other burial places.

8

Indian Mounds in the Modern World

The great era of Indian mounds, which began in Wisconsin around 800 B.C., lasted for about 2,000 years. The earliest mounds, large and round or conical, were built as crypts in which to inter community leaders and their families and as landmarks to visually anchor mobile bands and tribes in the natural and supernatural worlds. Rituals that attended periodic mound building sought to renew the world and the resources on which Native Americans depended, eventually linking people over wide areas by means of common ceremonials. During the spectacular effigy mound period, between roughly A.D. 700 and 1200, people in Wisconsin and adjacent states constructed giant cosmological maps that modeled the underlying structure of their belief systems and social structure. These earthen effigies of powerful spirits also frequently served as tombs. What stimulated this monumental construction at that particular time remains a mystery. After A.D. 1000, the Mississippians briefly appeared on the stage, building on the Wisconsin landscape great temple mounds: high platforms for a variety of civic, religious, and funerary activities. And then quite suddenly, comparatively speaking, the era of mound building came to an end, except perhaps in northern Wisconsin. By A.D. 1200, economic and social change attending corn cultivation swept through the Midwest, leading to a new agricultural way of life. New customs relating to death and burial evolved that replaced the practices that had required the construction of imposing earthen tombs and ceremonial centers.

The custom of building burial mounds and other earthworks was shared by many Native American peoples throughout eastern North America. In Wisconsin, mounds were found everywhere. Accordingly, it is possible that

180

most Native American groups with ancient roots in the state are descendants of mound builders. The Dakota or Santee Sioux may have built mounds into the historic period.

As for the effigy mounds built over 800 years ago mainly in the southern half of the state, we view these as constructed by Woodland people who coalesced into what archaeologists called Oneota. It is widely held that Oneota in Wisconsin are ancestral to the Ho-Chunk, Ioway, and related groups. Indeed, there are similarities between mound symbolism and Ho-Chunk beliefs and kinship systems. It is likely that these people have the effigy mound ceremonial in their distant ancestry, but this is far from proven. Further effigy mound ceremonialism could have crossed social boundaries. The ancient neighbors of the Ho-Chunk, the Menominee, have similar beliefs and social structure and there is provocative evidence, still unfolding, that they shared in the Oneota tradition. There are some effigy mounds, primarily the "catfish" mounds, in places that strong oral tradition says are ancestral areas. Further research will clarify matters.

LEGISLATION TO PRESERVE MOUNDS

Archaeological and historic sites have gained a measure of protection under state and federal laws, beginning in the 1960s, but this legislation usually applies only to public lands or to cultural resources that would be destroyed as a result of projects undertaken by the federal or state governments. In 1985, however, Wisconsin joined thirty-one other states with the passage of a law designed specifically to protect marked and unmarked burial places, including those used by ancient Native Americans. Most of the nationwide legislation was enacted in the 1970s and 1980s, when sensibilities were heightened about the treatment of Native American grave sites and remains recovered from them, including gratuitous displays in museums. Events leading to the passage of the Burial Sites Preservation Law in Wisconsin can only be described as lengthy and complicated. The legislation was stimulated by the realization of Native Americans, archaeologists, and other interested people that they were jointly unable to protect a large eighteenth-century Chippewa cemetery in northern Wisconsin from condominium development.[1] Input from the Native American, academic, and legislative communities was incorporated into 1985 Wisconsin Act 316, which later became Wisconsin Statute 157.70: the Burial Sites Preservation Law. Under Administrative Rules written for the law, Indian mounds are defined as "grave markers" and, as such, are entitled to protection from disturbance. The first time the law was invoked was to protect a long-tailed water spirit or panther mound on the shore of Lake Monona in the community of Monona.

Figure 8.1. Since the passage of the Burial Sites Preservation Law, Wisconsin now protects all human burial sites, whatever their age and cultural association. A panther or water spirit mound is preserved in Forest Hill Cemetery in Madison. (Photograph by Robert Birmingham)

The Burial Sites Preservation Law protects all burial sites on public and private land from disturbance, regardless of age and cultural, ethnic, or religious affiliation (figure 8.1). Burial sites are defined simply as any places where human remains are buried and include marked and unmarked recent cemeteries, ancient Native American graves, farm family plots, and Indian mounds. These burial places receive their greatest protection after they are "cataloged"—when professionally surveyed boundaries of the cemetery, grave site, or mound are recorded on the deed for the property at the county Register of Deeds.

By law, Indian mounds and other defined grave sites are surrounded by a five-foot buffer zone within which disturbance cannot take place. Dane County, which has taken a leadership role among Wisconsin counties in the protection of Indian mounds, has enlarged that zone to twenty-five feet in unincorporated areas, but only with the permission of the landowners. Once cataloged, these burial locations "run with the land" and are identified in every title search of the property. In addition, landowners who catalog burial sites through the State Historical Society of Wisconsin are entitled to a reduction in property taxes that is calculated by the local assessor's office on the basis of site size. Cataloged sites can enhance property values and ensure the preservation of Wisconsin's rich cultural and archaeological heritage. Today, most landowners are thrilled and fascinated to have an Indian mound or mound group on their property and consider themselves to be stewards of a special part of Wisconsin history. They take mound preservation very seriously. Even though sites may be officially cataloged by the state of Wisconsin, privately owned mounds are still private property and visitors still have to obtain the landowners' permission to see the sites.

A provision of the Burial Sites Preservation Law permits the disturbance of a burial site with the prior approval of the director of the State Historical Society, which today causes many Native Americans great concern. Disturbances are unavoidable—for example, when there are no other routes for a new highway—and the respectful and tightly controlled removal of burials is the only prudent and reasonable alternative. When Native American graves are concerned, such decisions are made by the State Historical Society in consultation with interested tribes. Occasionally, human burials from unrecorded burial places are accidentally disturbed by earth-moving activities, ranging from small-scale gardening to excavating for new houses. Under the Burial Sites Preservation Law, work must immediately stop and the Burial Sites Preservation Office of the State Historical Society must be notified. After a careful and considered evaluation, the bones and associated grave offerings may be removed so that construction may proceed. *Preservation in place* is always the first alternative to be considered in these situations. Human remains removed from the ground probably will be reburied, ideally in a location near the original burial site.

While mounds and other burial places on public and private land in Wisconsin are protected under the Burial Sites Preservation Law, comparable sites on federal and tribal land are protected under the Native American

Graves Protection and Repatriation Act of 1990 (NAGPRA). It provides procedures to follow when the remains of Native Americans are inadvertently discovered on federal and tribal land, and addresses the issue of the possession of human remains, grave offerings, and sacred objects by museums, universities, and other federally financed institutions. Much to the great distress of Native Americans, tens of thousands of burials, many from the time of the mound-digging era of the nineteenth and early twentieth centuries, reside on shelves and in storerooms throughout the nation. A major aim of NAGPRA has been to ensure that the human remains and funerary objects, as well as sacred items used in ongoing ceremonies, are returned, or repatriated, to the appropriate tribes. For federally supported institutions, this process involves publishing inventories of relevant collections and consulting with Native American tribes about returning these collections. This procedure is not easy, but NAGPRA has provided new and exciting opportunities for dialogue and close cooperation between Native American tribes and American cultural and academic institutions. It has also led to increasing sensitivity on the part of the general public toward human remains and objects that Native Americans hold in great reverence.

NATIVE AMERICAN AND SCIENTIFIC PERSPECTIVES ON THE MOUNDS

In the past, the archaeological excavation of burial mounds and other Native American graves sharply divided the Native American and academic communities. Today, at least in Wisconsin, these communities work together on the basis of one principle that has wide agreement: these places must be saved from destruction. This collaboration has resulted in many joint projects undertaken by archaeologists and Wisconsin tribes to locate and catalog Indian mounds and other burial sites in such places as Dane County, Richland County, and northern Wisconsin.

Nevertheless, many Native Americans and members of the Euro-American–dominated scientific community still have different attitudes toward burial places, especially regarding the treatment of human remains. These perspectives reflect fundamentally different worldviews that occasionally cause misunderstanding, friction, and a certain amount of suspicion and mistrust. From the perspective of a "scientific" view, the study of human remains and burial places can provide information about social status, family relationships, diet, daily activities, place of origin, disease, life expectancy, and even the evolution of warfare. Bones and teeth can help determine the ancestry, sex, social status, and age at and cause of death of an individual who lived in the distant past. Much of the information on such matters in this book derived from the early excavations of burials and burial mounds.

New scientific advances have greatly increased the potential of the study of human remains to answer important archaeological questions: Are the Ho-Chunk (Winnebago) indeed the descendants of both the Oneota and the earlier effigy mound builders? Did some Late Woodland and Oneota populations migrate to Wisconsin from elsewhere? Did Middle Mississippians intermarry with local populations, and, if so, with whom? Who were the enemies of Aztalan who were killed and ritually eaten? Analysis of very minute quantities of the organic portions of bones and teeth can now be used to "map" the genetic building blocks known as DNA (deoxyribonucleic acid). Nuclear DNA, which comes from the nucleus of every cell, and mitochondrial DNA (mtDNA), which is derived from the cellular fluid outside the nucleus, can provide answers to questions about genetic relationships, past and present.

From the perspective of many Native Americans, the scientific rationale for the study of human remains carries little or no weight. It is not only illegal to disturb the remains of their ancestors, but immoral. Once an individual dies and is buried, many argue, this sacred site should not be touched. Some Native Americans believe that the disturbance of graves interrupts the journey of the dead to the spirit land. Many traditional people say that they know who their ancestors are and that oral traditions preserve the important and necessary elements of their history, so further analysis is unnecessary. For most, research on human remains and burials places Native Americans and their ancestors in the humiliating role of "laboratory specimens," a practice that is regarded as a holdover of racist attitudes common in the nineteenth century, when Native Americans were considered to be less than human.

It is not likely that these two different cultural views on burial places and human remains will be reconciled. From the standpoint of Native Americans, deeply held spiritual beliefs cannot be negotiated. Consequently, the philosophy adopted by most archaeologists, academics, and museum curators has been to respect the concerns of Native Americans and to make special efforts to involve tribes and members of Native American communities in archaeological studies and educational exhibits that do not involve the disruption of sacred areas, but still provide information on the ancient past. As we have seen, the incorporation of Native American viewpoints and knowledge has proved critical to the unraveling of ancient mysteries, such as those of the Indian mounds.

LEGACY OF THE MOUNDS

The construction and ceremonial use of burial mounds played an important role in integrating segments of prehistoric Native American societies into larger communities. That is why this book emphasizes their function as ceremonial centers. Archaeologists imagine that, even when burials were not being made, people gathered at these prominent places to take part in a wide variety of social celebrations, economic activities, and religious events that helped reinforce human bonds. Some Indian mounds in Wisconsin continue to play a similar role in the modern world. On October 4, 1998, the Monona Landmarks Commission hosted the dedication of a historic marker at a large 2,000-year-old conical mound preserved on a small piece of public land in a suburban neighborhood. The mound is one of the last of the Outlet Mound Group, which once covered many acres of land. Fittingly, this mound was one of those saved from destruction by residential development by Charles E. Brown and the Wisconsin Archeological Society in 1938. Through an ambitious fund-raising campaign, the mound was purchased from developers and given to the city of Monona.[2] The dedication was attended by a large crowd of neighborhood people as well as members of the local Native American community. Speeches were made, food was shared, and people talked and visited. The highlight of the event was when most of those present participated in a Native American celebration dance led by a Native American cultural teacher. For the afternoon, this ancient mound functioned much as it had two millennia ago—as the focal point of a community.

Not far away, in another residential neighborhood along the shore of Lake Monona, stands *Let the Great Spirits Soar*, a tree-stump sculpture made by Harry Whitehorse, a Ho-Chunk artist who lives in the area, as did his ancestors (figure 8.2). The sculpture includes depictions of a Native American as well as a wolf, an eagle, and bears—powerful cultural symbols for the Ho-Chunk—and it overlooks a pair of effigy mounds, also once part of a large mound group. This place, Elmside Park in Madison, has become a popular gathering spot for small groups of people who come to view the sculpture and the mounds and to learn more about the heritage of their community. Elsewhere in Wisconsin, a new appreciation of ancient earthen monuments has also resulted in the celebration of their existence as community landmarks (figure 8.3).

The legacy of the Indian mounds and the other ancient earthworks preserved on the Wisconsin landscape goes beyond the view that they are silent reminders of a long-ago people. The earthen monuments representing different mound-building periods and sometimes different Native American

Figure 8.2. A tree-stump sculpture, *Let the Great Spirits Soar,* by Harry Whitehorse commemorates the effigy mound builders and his Ho-Chunk ancestors. Located near mounds in Elmside Park in Madison, overlooking Lake Monona, it depicts a wolf, an eagle, bears, and a Native American. (Photograph by Robert Birmingham)

Figure 8.3. Depictions of effigy mounds on the northern shore of Lake Mendota are incorporated into an outdoor artwork by artist L. Brower Hatcher. Located in downtown Madison, the work includes other symbols of life in and the history of Madison. (Photograph by Robert Birmingham)

peoples are heuristic devices. Their presence teaches us that, like all peoples and societies, Native American cultures continually evolve in response to social and environmental changes and that contemporaneous Native American tribes are very different from one another, each with its unique language, customs, and beliefs. The mounds teach us that there is no one indigenous culture, frozen in time, with which later Native Americans should be compared, any more than there is one time in European or American history in which the "traditional" European or American culture can be identified. The Indian mounds of Wisconsin also remind us that, like all peoples and societies, Native Americans are a "historical" people and that their history is deep, dramatic, and complex, spanning 12,000 years or more. It is a history filled with legendary heroes, mass migrations, alliances, colorful ceremonies, religious movements, powerful families, peaceful villages, beautiful and monumental artworks, wars, the rise and fall of spectacular societies, technological innovations, and economic and social revolutions. This story is far from the simplistic and stereotypical history constructed for Native Americans in the past.

If the mounds represent change in one sense, they also represent cultural continuity in another. For Native Americans, the mounds are eternally sacred places, the graves of ancestors, that connect them to the land and the

188

supernatural. But the mounds have also become highly visible and powerful symbols of the persistence into the modern era of uniquely Native American values and beliefs. Indeed, when thunder and lightning move across the Wisconsin skies and water roils in the lakes and streams, there are still some who know that thunderbirds and water spirits are about their ancient work, which brings balance to an unsettled world.

APPENDIX
NOTES
BIBLIOGRAPHY
INDEX

Appendix

Selected Mound Sites Open to the Public

Unless otherwise noted, all sites are open year-round and there is no admission charge.

Barron County

Rice Lake Mound Group
Indian Mounds Park
Lakeshore Drive
Rice Lake, Wisconsin

Open: May 1 to October 10
Contact: (715) 234–9235

Twelve mounds of the Rice Lake Mound Group are preserved in Indian Mounds Park, a city park on the shore of Rice Lake. The group once consisted of fifty-one conical burial mounds, apparently built after about A.D. 500. The mounds were spread over a quarter mile of lakeshore. Some mounds were excavated in the nineteenth century by the Smithsonian Institution during its search for the identity of the mound builders, while others were excavated in the 1950s. Many were obliterated by city expansion.

CALUMET COUNTY

Calumet County Park

County Trunk Highway EE, off State Highway 55
Stockbridge, Wisconsin

Contact: Calumet County Park
N6150 County Trunk Highway EE
Hilbert, Wisconsin 54129
(414) 439–1008

Calumet County Park, located on the eastern shore of Lake Winnebago, is approximately two miles north of the community of Stockbridge. Six effigy mounds with lowerworld water iconography—panthers or water spirits—are situated on top of an escarpment that overlooks the lake.

High Cliff State Park

State Highway 55
Sherwood, Wisconsin

Open: 6:00 A.M. to 11:00 P.M.
Fees: State park and recreation fees
Contact: High Cliff State Park
N75475 High Cliff Road
Menasha, Wisconsin 54952
(414) 989–1106

High Cliff State Park is situated along the scenic limestone cliffs of the Niagara Escarpment, paralleling the eastern shore of Lake Winnebago, south of the community of Sherwood. An effigy mound group, which once included a bird, an animal (probably a bear), a large concentration of water spirits or panthers, and small conical mounds, is on the edge of the escarpment, overlooking the lake. The large number of water spirit mounds is characteristic of the many mound groups once found on the eastern shore of Lake Winnebago and in eastern Wisconsin in general. Six of these long-tailed effigies as well as several conical mounds are included in an interpretive trail at the park. The mounds at High Cliff were first featured in Increase A. Lapham's *Antiquities of Wisconsin.*

Appendix: Selected Mound Sites Open to the Public

COLUMBIA COUNTY

Kingsley Bend Mound Group
State Highway 16
Wisconsin Dells, Wisconsin

A portion of the Kingsley Bend Mound Group is preserved in a highway wayside approximately three miles south of the community of Wisconsin Dells. Originally there were at least twenty-two conical, linear, and effigy mounds. As is characteristic of many effigy mound groups in south-central Wisconsin, the forms are symbolic of the three natural realms of air (bird), earth (bear), and water (water spirit or panther). A highly stylized long-tailed water spirit or panther effigy as well as several linear and conical mounds are preserved in the wayside. Other mounds of the group are on private lands nearby. One of the individuals who brought the site to public attention in the late nineteenth century was the prominent photographer H. H. Bennett, of Wisconsin Dells.

DANE COUNTY

Madison, with its surrounding lakes, was the center of mound building in Wisconsin. Between 800 B.C. and A.D. 1200, Native Americans built more 1,500 mounds in the Four Lakes area. A large number of them were preserved over the years through the efforts of Charles E. Brown of the State Historical Society and other area residents.

Baum Mound Group
Goodland County Park
Goodland Park Road
Dunn, Wisconsin

The Baum Mound Group, preserved in Goodland County Park, consists of three linear mounds and one conical mound. They are located along both sides of the main park road from the park sign to Lake Waubesa.

Burrows Park
Burrows Road, off Sherman Avenue
Madison, Wisconsin

Burrows Park, a small park on the shore of Lake Mendota, contains a reconstructed bird effigy mound with a wingspan of 128 feet. A second effigy, a fox or canine-like animal, was destroyed. The bird was damaged early by looting, but was restored by workers for the Works Progress Administration under the direction of Charles E. Brown.

Edgewood Mound Group
Edgewood College
Woodrow Street, off Monroe Avenue
Madison, Wisconsin

Twelve mounds of the Edgewood Mound Group are preserved on the campus of Edgewood College. A linear mound and six conical mounds are visible along Edgewood Drive. The remains of two linear mounds are near the library, and on the other side of the library is a large bird effigy. Finally, two conical mounds can be seen near the playground.

Edna Taylor Conservancy
Femrite Drive
Madison, Wisconsin

Six linear mounds and a panther or water spirit effigy mound are located on a high glacial drumlin at the Edna Taylor Conservancy. Two very long linear mounds, one of which was more than 700 feet long, follow the crest of this hill, but were shortened by highway construction and farming. The four other linear mounds and the panther effigy are on the northwestern slope of the drumlin, part of which was sliced away by residential development.

Elmside Park
Lakeland and Hudson Avenues
Madison, Wisconsin

Hudson Park
Lakeland and Maple Avenues
Madison, Wisconsin

Elmside Park and Hudson Park were created to preserve three effigy mounds during the course of residential construction in the early twentieth century. The mounds were part of a dense cluster that extended from the Yahara River to Olbrich Park. Giant birds, one with a wingspan reported to have been 568 feet, were once found on a hill to the northeast of Elmside Park, overlooking Lake Monona. Elmside Park preserves two animal effigies: a bear and what has been referred to as a lynx. It also contains *Let the Great Spirits Soar,* a beautiful tree-stump sculpture by Harry Whitehorse, a local Ho-Chunk (Winnebago) artist. Water spirit or panther mounds were once found in a low area to the southeast, where one is preserved in Hudson Park.

Appendix: Selected Mound Sites Open to the Public

Farwell's Point Mound Group and Mendota State Hospital Mound Group

Mendota State Hospital
Troy Drive
Madison, Wisconsin

Portions of two large mound groups are preserved on the grounds of Mendota State Hospital, located on the northern shore of Lake Mendota. The Farwell's Point Mound Group includes a number of large conical mounds, part of a linear mound, and a bird effigy. These mounds evidently were built over a 1,000-year period. The large conical mounds are believed to have been built during the Middle Woodland stage, about 2,000 years ago, while the bird effigy and the linear mound date to the subsequent Late Woodland stage.

The Mendota State Hospital Mound Group, located to the east of the Farwell's Point Mound Group, contains some of the finest and largest effigy mounds preserved anywhere. Included are three large birds, two panthers (one with an unusual curved tail), two bears, a deer, several conical mounds, and one of indeterminate shape. One of the bird effigies has a wingspan of 624 feet. The deer effigy is unusual because four legs are depicted.

To see the mounds, check with the staff in the administration building, which is the first building on the right after entering the hospital grounds.

Forest Hill Cemetery

Regent Street and Speedway Drive
Madison, Wisconsin

Established in 1858, historic Forest Hill Cemetery is the final resting place of many of Wisconsin's most prominent citizens, including eight governors. Among the more modern graves is an effigy mound group that consists of most of a goose, two water spirits or panthers, and a linear mound. The head of the bird effigy, which is on a slope that leads, appropriately, to adjacent wetlands, was removed when a railroad was built through the area in the nineteenth century. Part of the tail of one panther and three additional linear mounds were destroyed during the early development of the cemetery. Efforts by Charles E. Brown of the State Historical Society saved the remaining mounds. Fittingly, Brown himself is interred at Forest Hill. His grave can be found in Lot 1 next to a large granite monolith bearing a single word: ARCHAEOLOGIST.

A brochure for a self-guided walking tour of Forest Hill Cemetery is available at the office.

Governor Nelson State Park

County Trunk Highway M
Waunakee, Wisconsin

Open: 6:00 A.M. to 11:00 P.M.
Fees: State park and recreation fees
Contact: Governor Nelson State Park
5140 County Trunk Highway M
Waunakee, Wisconsin 53597
(608) 831-3005

The 422-acre Governor Nelson State Park is located on the northern shore of Lake Mendota in Waunakee. A group of five conical mounds and a large panther or water spirit effigy mound are located in the park. The conical mounds probably were built during the Middle Woodland stage, while the effigy was added later. A stockaded Late Woodland village was located to the north of the mounds, in the vicinity of the showers and toilet near the beach. Native American cornfields were planted in this area, which also was the site of an eighteenth-century Ho-Chunk village.

Lewis Mound Group

Indian Mound Park
Burma Road
McFarland, Wisconsin

This Late Woodland mound group is located on the hill overlooking Lake Waubesa in Indian Mound Park. Called the Lewis Mound Group after Tollef Lewis, the nineteenth-century owner, it consists of a bear effigy as well as two conical, two linear, one oval, and one "hook"-shaped mounds. The unusual last mound probably was meant to represent the curved tail of a panther or water spirit, or a snake. Local volunteers have restored the mounds and rerouted trails so they no longer pass over the mounds.

Observatory Hill Mounds

Observatory
University of Wisconsin
Madison, Wisconsin

Directly to the west of the observatory on the campus of the University of Wisconsin, overlooking Lake Mendota, are the Observatory Hill Mounds: a bird effigy and an unusual two-tailed water spirit effigy. One tail is barely visible, and the other was destroyed. The mound may actually represent two water spirits placed back to back. Paired effigies are found at several other mound groups, such as that at Lizard Mounds County Park in Washington County. Two other mounds, a long-tailed panther or water spirit and a linear, were located downslope, but were destroyed by development of the campus. A plaque erected in 1914 incorrectly states that the Ho-Chunk built the mounds 500 years ago. The mounds are almost certainly at least 1,000 years old, although they indeed may have been erected by distant ancestors of the Ho-Chunk and related tribes.

Outlet Mound
Midwood and Ridgewood Avenues
Monona, Wisconsin

The large conical Outlet Mound was one of nineteen mounds overlooking the outlet of Lake Monona. Probably built 2,000 years ago during the Middle Woodland stage, it is a good example of a mound of that era. Most of the other mounds in the group, one of which was excavated and radiocarbon dated to 50 B.C., were destroyed.

The Outlet Mound was purchased with funds raised by Charles E. Brown and the Wisconsin Archeological Society to save it from residential development and then was donated to the city of Monona.

Picnic Point Mounds
Willow Drive
University of Wisconsin
Madison, Wisconsin

On the south shore of Picnic Point, halfway to the tip of the peninsula, are two linear and three conical mounds. Near the tip is a conical mound. The Picnic Point Mounds, on the campus of the University of Wisconsin, were preserved and restored in 1939 through the efforts of Charles E. Brown of the State Historical Society.

University of Wisconsin Arboretum
McCaffrey Road
Madison, Wisconsin

Two Late Woodland effigy mound groups, including a bird, a panther, and linear and conical mounds, are located on both sides of McCaffrey Road at the University of Wisconsin Arboretum. One group is situated right above several prominent springs that were considered sacred by Ho-Chunk who camped in this area into the twentieth century. Among other things, springs were considered entrances to the watery underworld realm of the water spirits. These groups were restored by Charles E. Brown of the State Historical Society.

A map is available at the McKay Center at the arboretum.

Vilas Park
Erin and Wingra Streets
Madison, Wisconsin

The Late Woodland effigy mound group in Vilas Park consists of a bird effigy, a linear mound, and six conical mounds. Two additional conical mounds and another bird effigy were destroyed. The plaque at the site is an example of the preservation efforts undertaken by Charles E. Brown and his colleagues at the Wisconsin Archeological Society.

Vilas Park Circle
Vilas Avenue, 1400 to 1500 block
Madison, Wisconsin

The small Vilas Park Circle was created to preserve a large effigy mound of a bear, which is located on the west side of the circular park. This mound was once part of a large group that included seven linear mounds and a conical mound. The group was undoubtedly constructed during the Late Woodland stage, between A.D. 700 and 1100, but the bear may have been reused for a burial in more recent times. In the early twentieth century, children digging in the mound found the remnants of an eighteenth- or nineteenth-century steel sword. Dispossessed Ho-Chunk and other tribes frequently buried their dead in ancient mounds, and this sword, obtained from Europeans or Americans, possibly accompanied such a burial.

Hornung Mound Group
County Trunk Highway Y, half mile east of U.S. Highway 12
Sauk City, Wisconsin

Located in an unusual place for an effigy mound group—away from large bodies of water—the Hornung Mound Group was not discovered until 1987. It was subsequently mapped during a project to identify mounds in Dane County, and the land was purchased by the state as part of a conservation program on the lower Wisconsin River. The site is located on Roxbury Creek, a small tributary of the Wisconsin River, one mile southeast of Sauk City. It is characteristic of mound groups in Dane County and south-central Wisconsin in that it contains bird (sky), bear (earth), and water spirit (water) forms. In this group, the three realms are neatly segregated, with the bird on the far north, the bear 300 feet to the southeast, and several long-tailed water spirits or panthers across the creek to the south. Several linear mounds and an unidentified, damaged effigy accompany the water spirit mounds.

Appendix: Selected Mound Sites Open to the Public

DUNN COUNTY

Upper Wakanda Park Mound Group

Wakanda Park
Pine Street
Menomonie, Wisconsin

The Upper Wakanda Park Mound Group consists of three large oval mounds located in Wakanda Park on a ridge overlooking Lake Menomin, a widening of the Red Cedar River. Seventeen other mounds were located below this ridge, but were flooded when the construction of a dam in the 1950s elevated the water level of the lake. Before their inundation, fourteen of the mounds were excavated. Burials and stone concentrations, or "altars," were found in them. One of the burials was of an individual who had been cremated while wearing a clay face covering or mask. The custom of placing clay coverings or masks on the faces of the dead has been documented at only two other mound sites in Wisconsin: the Cyrus Thomas Mound Group on Rice Lake and the Outlet Mound Group on Lake Monona. The lower Wakanda mounds were radiocarbon dated to sometime between A.D. 1000 and 1400. The Upper Wakanda Park Mound Group could date to that time or earlier.

GRANT COUNTY

Wyalusing State Park

County Trunk Highway C
Prairie du Chien, Wisconsin

Wyalusing State Park is located near Prairie du Chien on the high bluffs overlooking the broad floodplains at the confluence of the Mississippi and Wisconsin Rivers. High vistas offer spectacular views of the rivers and surrounding countryside. The area was very attractive to Native Americans because of its beauty, bounty, and strategic importance. Twenty-one mound sites have been recorded in the park, once totaling more than 130 mounds. In the 1880s, Cyrus Thomas of the Bureau of Ethnology at the Smithsonian Institution investigated several mounds in his search for the identity of the mound builders. In 1909, Charles E. Brown of the State Historical Society, assisted by the Reverend Drexel and Robert Glenn, mapped most of the mounds in the area. Among the groups mapped was the Signal Hill Mound Group or "Procession of the Mounds"—a single line of mounds, including conical, linear, and one effigy, that follows the crest of the bluff.

In 1911, the Wisconsin Archeological Society chose Prairie du Chien for its annual assembly, "to make known the deep interest of the Society in the proposed Mississippi–Wisconsin River state park of which it has been for several years an advocate," according to Brown. Before the park was established by the state, though, many of the mounds were destroyed by farming or stone quarrying. However, sixty-nine mounds survived and are carefully preserved, including the "Procession of the Mounds."

At least two separate periods of mound building are represented at the park. Thomas investigated several large conical mounds and found burials in stone crypts, one with shell beads, a copper celt, and a stone platform pipe. These characteristics suggest construction during the Middle Woodland stage. Most mounds, however, appear to have been built during the Late Woodland stage. They consist of small conical mounds, linear mounds, and several types of effigy mounds, including bears and other animals, several long-tailed water spirits, and compound or chain mounds, which, like the bear effigies, are common in this region of the Mississippi River valley.

Iowa County

Avoca Mound Group
Lake Side Park
East Lake Shore Drive
Avoca, Wisconsin

The Avoca Mound Group is located in Lake Side Park and campground on the shore of Avoca Lake, a backwater slough of the Wisconsin River. This mound group includes six linear and four conical mounds that may have been part of a larger group. It is undated, but probably is Late Woodland.

Jefferson County

Aztalan State Park
County Trunk Highway Q
Aztalan, Wisconsin

Open: May to October, 7:00 A.M. to 9:00 P.M.
Contact: Department of Natural Resources
1213 South Main Street
Lake Mills, Wisconsin 53551
(920) 648-8774

Located on the Crawfish River, just south of the modern village of Aztalan, Aztalan is the premier archaeological site in Wisconsin. Between A.D. 1000 and 1200, this large Native American town was home to a group of Mississippian people who had migrated from Cahokia in what is now southern Illinois. The Mississippians built earthen platform mounds and fortified the site with a huge timber and clay wall.

Beginning in the 1920s, the site was extensively excavated, and two of the four platform mounds as well as segments of the wall have been reconstructed. To the northeast of Aztalan is a line of large conical mounds that mark the locations of ceremonial posts as well as the burial of a young woman who apparently was a member of the Mississippian elite.

A brochure for a self-guided walking tour is available at the site and at the headquarters of the Department of Natural Resources.

General Atkinson Mound Group

Jefferson County Indian Mounds and Trail Park
Koshkonong Mounds Road, off State Highway 26
Fort Atkinson, Wisconsin

The southern part of the General Atkinson Mound Group is preserved in the Jefferson County Indian Mounds and Trail Park, south of the community of Fort Atkinson. These eleven mounds consist of tapering linear, conical, bird, and "turtle" mounds. The turtle mounds may actually represent panthers or water spirits as viewed from above, rather than from the side. The mounds range in length from 75 to 222 feet. The General Atkinson Mound Group originally consisted of seventy-two mounds, many of which were destroyed. The park includes an Indian trail that was documented by a land surveyor in 1835. In 1993, Hugh Highsmith of Fort Atkinson purchased the land containing the eleven mounds and, in cooperation with the Fort Atkinson Historical Society, donated the land to Jefferson County.

Panther Intaglio

State Highway 106
Fort Atkinson, Wisconsin

Just west of downtown Fort Atkinson, along the northern side of the Rock River, is the last remaining intaglio in Wisconsin. It was discovered by Increase A. Lapham in 1850 and is one of only about a dozen intaglios recorded in the state. It was once part of a large effigy mound group that was destroyed by residential development. The 125-foot intaglio is a scooped-out area in the form of a water spirit or panther about two feet deep. The excavation of this reverse image of a panther mound may be related to the fact that such water spirits were believed to originate in a watery realm below the surface of the earth. In 1919, the Fort Atkinson chapter of the Daughters of the American Revolution leased the land to preserve the intaglio.

JUNEAU COUNTY

Indian Mounds Park
Indian Mound Road
New Lisbon, Wisconsin

Open: Closed in winter

Indian Mounds Park, on the Lemonweir River on the south side of New Lisbon, preserves a mound group that consists of three conical mounds, two linear mounds, a compound or chain mound, and a water spirit or panther effigy. Originally, there were at least seven other mounds, which have been destroyed. Chain or compound mounds are rarely found outside the Mississippi River valley. Some of the mounds were reconstructed by the Lion's Club of New Lisbon.

MILWAUKEE COUNTY

Lake Park
Kenwood Boulevard and Lake Drive
Milwaukee, Wisconsin

Lake Park, on Lake Michigan, preserves one of the few remaining mounds in Milwaukee. The low conical mound is located on a high bluff overlooking the lake in the northeastern corner of the park. It is two feet high and forty feet in diameter and was one of a number of like-size mounds that were once in the park area. The mound is undated, but is believed to have been built during the Middle Woodland stage, between 300 B.C. and A.D. 400. Lake Park is significant both because of the mound and because of its more modern but unique landscape, which was designed by landscape architect Frederick Law Olmsted.

ONEIDA COUNTY

Northern Highlands/American Legion State Forest
State Highway 47
Lake Tomahawk, Wisconsin

Fees: Daily user fees

At the Indian Mounds Campground in the Northern Highlands/American Legion State Forest, about two miles north of the community of Lake Tomahawk, are four conical burial mounds. Typical of mounds built in northwestern Wisconsin during the Woodland, they can be viewed in the picnic area adjacent to Lake Tomahawk.

Appendix: Selected Mound Sites Open to the Public

SAUK COUNTY

Devil's Lake State Park

State Highway 33
Baraboo, Wisconsin

Fees: State park and recreation fees
Contact: (608) 356-8301

Devil's Lake State Park, located three miles south of Baraboo, preserves a number of effigy mounds that represent both the upperworld and the lowerworld. The Ho-Chunk name for the lake is Tamahcunchukdah, or Sacred Lake, which was mistakenly given an evil connotation and translated as Devil's Lake. According to Ho-Chunk tradition, the famous bluffs were created during a battle between the thunderbirds and the water spirits. The effigy mounds in the park reflect this tradition. A 150-foot-long "fork-tailed" bird effigy is located on the southeastern shore of the lake. It is also possible that this mound form represents a "bird-man," combining characteristics of a bird and a human being. Effigy mounds at the northern end of the lake are from the opposing lowerworld and include a bear, an unidentified animal, and a water spirit or panther.

Man Mound County Park

Man Mound Road
Baraboo, Wisconsin

Only one effigy mound in the shape of a human being has survived nearly intact. It is located near the base of a high hill in Man Mound County Park, to the northeast of Baraboo. Probably built more than 1,000 years ago, this huge mound is in the form of a walking man who has horns or is wearing a horned headdress, such as a buffalo-horn headdress, which was characteristically worn by Native American shamans in more recent times. The mound was first reported by W. H. Canfield in 1859 during a land survey. It was featured in a short article written by Increase A. Lapham in the same year. It was originally 214 feet long, but road construction in 1905 destroyed the feet and lower legs of the figure. The remainder of the mound was saved from damage by the Wisconsin Archeological Society and the Sauk County Historical Society, which purchased the mound in 1907. It is now the centerpiece of a county park and can be viewed from an elevated platform.

SHEBOYGAN COUNTY

Sheboygan Indian Mound County Park

South Ninth Street
Sheboygan, Wisconsin

Open: April 1 to November 1
Contact: (414) 459-3444
[for guide] Municipal Services Building
2026 New Jersey Avenue
Sheboygan, Wisconsin
[for guide] Department of Public Works
City Hall
Sheboygan, Wisconsin

Sheboygan Indian Mound County Park, located to the south of Sheboygan, preserves what was first known as the Kletzien Mound Group. The group originally consisted of thirty-three conical and effigy mounds, primarily deer and panthers, as well as one panther or water spirit intaglio. A number of mounds were excavated in 1926 by the Public Museum of the City of Milwaukee.

The local garden clubs saved the mound group from development in the late 1950s by raising money to purchase the site. The land was subsequently donated to the city for an archaeological park, and sixteen of the eighteen existing mounds were restored under the supervision of the Public Museum.

The Town and County Garden Club recently developed a nature trail and a guide to the trail that is available at the Municipal Services Building and the Department of Public Works.

WASHINGTON COUNTY

Lizard Mounds County Park

Half mile east of intersection of State Highway 111 and County Trunk Highway A
West Bend, Wisconsin

Open: April 1 to November 1
Contact: (414) 335-4445

One of the most unusual effigy mound groups in Wisconsin is located in Lizard Mounds County Park, northeast of West Bend. The mound group originally contained approximately sixty mounds, dominated by long-tailed effigy forms that early investigators thought were lizards. They are undoubtedly versions of water spirits or panthers. Over the years, many of the mounds were obliterated by continued cultivation, and others were reduced to a point where they are no longer visible. When archaeologist Kermit Freckman mapped the site in detail in 1941, thirty-one of the sixty mounds remained. There are now twenty-nine.

The preserved group consists of five conical mounds, one oval mound, eight linear mounds, two tapering linear mounds, two symmetrically paired "bird" effigies, and eleven panther effigies. The location of the group is unusual. It is on a low, level plateau far from any major body of water. The plateau is, however, surrounded by springs, which have many spiritual associations for Native Americans and are entrances to the underworld of the water spirits. Thus the location and underworld theme of the group may have been determined primarily by landscape features that have spiritual connotations.

In 1950, the state purchased the site for a state park and restored some mounds damaged by looting. It has since been turned over to the county. A sign-posted trail winds around the mounds.

WAUKESHA COUNTY

Cutler Park
Maple Avenue
Waukesha, Wisconsin

Three conical mounds preserved in Cutler Park are typical of those built during the Middle Woodland stage, approximately 2,000 years ago. The large central mound is nine feet high and sixty-five feet in diameter. Excavations conducted by Increase A. Lapham in the 1840s revealed that the mound had been built over a large rock-lined burial chamber dug into the ground. Lapham went on to use information from such excavations to argue that mounds had been constructed by Native Americans and not by a mysterious lost race. In 1902, the city purchased the group to preserve it.

WAUSHARA COUNTY

Whistler Mound Group and Enclosure
Whistler Mounds Park
County Trunk Highway FF
Hancock, Wisconsin

The Whistler Mound Group, located in Whistler Mounds Park on Fish Lake, just east of the village of Hancock, contains one of the few surviving enclosures in Wisconsin, as well as two straight lines of low conical mounds. The enclosure is a low double-walled oval embankment that measures 120 feet by 51 feet. Such enclosures undoubtedly defined sacred spaces where periodic ceremonies were held. The site is believed to date to the Late Woodland stage, between A.D. 500 and 1200.

CLAYTON COUNTY, IOWA

Effigy Mounds National Monument
State Highway 76
Marquette, Iowa

Open: 8:00 A.M. to 5:00 P.M. [visitor center]
Fees: Admission fee

The best interpreted mound site in the Midwest is not in Wisconsin, but in Iowa, on the western periphery of the effigy mound region. Effigy Mounds National Monument is located to the north of Marquette, Iowa, across the Mississippi River from Prairie du Chien, Wisconsin. This large, scenic park contains long lines of "marching" bear effigies, bird effigies, chain or compound mounds, linear mounds, and large conical mounds dating to earlier periods. One mound, the Great Bear, is 137 feet long. The bear effigies and compound mounds are quite typical of mounds in this part of the Mississippi River valley.

Notes

CHAPTER 1. THE MYSTERY OF THE MOUNDS

1. "Long Journal 1817—Down the Mississippi to Belle Fontaine, July 10 through August 15, 1817," in *The Northern Expeditions of Stephen H. Long: The Journals of 1817 and 1823 and Related Documents*, ed. Lucille M. Kane, June D. Holmquist, and Carolyn Gilman (St. Paul: Minnesota Historical Society, 1978), 85–86.

2. Richard C. Taylor, "Notes Respecting Certain Indian Mounds and Earthworks in the Form of Animal Effigies, Chiefly in Wisconsin Territory, U.S.," *American Journal of Science and Art* 34 (1838): 88, 90.

3. Increase A. Lapham, *Wisconsin: Its Geography, Topography, History, Minerology: Together with Brief Sketches of Its Antiquities, Natural History, Soil, Productions, Population and Government* (Milwaukee: Hopkins, 1846).

4. William M. Hurley, "The Late Woodland Stage: Effigy Mound Culture," *Wisconsin Archeologist* 67, nos. 3–4 (1986): 298 [special issue, "Introduction to Wisconsin Archeology," edited by William Green, James B. Stoltman, and Alice B. Kehoe].

5. One example is the *Ancient American*.

6. "Indian Mounds Tell History and Folklore," *McFarland Community Life,* 15 March 1995, 7.

7. Robert Hall, "Ghosts, Water Barriers, Corn, and Sacred Enclosures in the Eastern Woodlands," *American Antiquity* 41 (1976): 363.

CHAPTER 2. SPECULATION, EXCAVATION, EXPLANATION: IN SEARCH OF THE MOUND BUILDERS

1. Robert Silverberg, *The Mound Builders of Ancient America* (New York: New York Graphic Society, 1976); Gordon R. Willey and Jeremy A. Sabloff, *A History of American Archaeology* (San Francisco: Freeman, 1968).

2. Willey and Sabloff, *History of American Archaeology,* 14.

3. Willey and Sabloff, *History of American Archaeology*, 15.

4. Willey and Sabloff, *History of American Archaeology*, 28.

5. For an erudite discussion of American ideology pertaining to earthworks in the nineteenth century, see Roger G. Kennedy, *Hidden Cities: The Discovery and Loss of Ancient North American Civilization* (New York: Free Press, 1994).

6. Silverberg, *Mound Builders of Ancient America*, 159–160.

7. Silverberg, *Mound Builders of Ancient America*, 28.

8. Stephen D. Peet, "The Mound Builders," *American Antiquarian* 2, no. 3 (1880): 188.

9. Edward G. Bourne, *Narratives of the Career of Hernando de Soto*, 2 vols. (New York: Barnes, 1904).

10. Gloria Deák, *Discovering America's Southeast: A Sixteenth Century View Based on the Mannerist Engravings of Theodore de Bry* (Birmingham, Ala.: Public Library Press, 1992), 126–127.

11. Bourne, *Narratives of de Soto*.

12. Silverberg, *Mound Builders of Ancient America*, 6.

13. Caleb Atwater, *Descriptions of the Antiquities Discovered in the State of Ohio and Other Western States*, Transactions and Collections of the American Antiquarian Society, vol. 1 (Worcester, Mass.: American Antiquarian Society, 1820).

14. Ephraim G. Squier and Edgar H. Davis, *Ancient Monuments of the Mississippi Valley*, Smithsonian Contributions to Knowledge, vol. 1 (Washington, D.C.: Smithsonian Institution, 1848).

15. Willey and Sabloff, *History of American Archaeology*, 36.

16. William Green, "Examining Protohistoric Depopulation in the Upper Midwest," *Wisconsin Archeologist* 74, nos. 1–4 (1993): 290–393 [special issue: "Exploring the Oneota–Winnebago Direct Historical Connection," edited by David F. Overstreet].

17. Nancy O. Lurie, "Winnebago," in *Handbook of North American Indians*, vol. 15, *Northeast*, edited by Bruce G. Trigger (Washington, D.C.: Smithsonian Institution Press, 1978), 702–705; James A. Clifton, "Potawatomi," in *Handbook of North American Indians*, vol. 15, *Northeast*, edited by Trigger, 736–741.

18. [Increase A. Lapham,] "Antiquities of Wisconsin," *Milwaukee Advertiser*, 24 November 1836, 2.

19. Nathaniel F. Hyer, "Ruins of the Ancient City of Aztalan," *Milwaukee Advertiser*, 25 February 1837, n.p.

20. Richard C. Taylor, "Notes Respecting Certain Indian Mounds and Earthworks in the Form of Animal Effigies, Chiefly in Wisconsin Territory, U.S.," *American Journal of Science and Art* 34 (1838): 98–99.

21. Taylor, "Notes Respecting Certain Indian Mounds and Earthworks," 104.

22. Increase A. Lapham, *The Antiquities of Wisconsin, as Surveyed and Described*, Smithsonian Contributions to Knowledge, vol. 7 (Washington, D.C.: Smithsonian Institution, 1855).

23. Lapham, *Antiquities of Wisconsin*, 90.

24. Lapham, *Antiquities of Wisconsin*, 25.

25. William Pidgeon, *Traditions of De-coo-dah and Antiquarian Researches: Comprising Extensive Explorations, Surveys, and Excavations of the Wonderful and Mysterious Earthen Remains of the Mound-Builders in America; the Traditions of the Last Prophet of the Elk Nation Relative to Their Origin and Use; and the Evidences of an Ancient Population More Numerous Than the Present Aborigines* (New York: Thayer, Bridgman, and Fanning, 1853).

26. Pidgeon, *Traditions of De-coo-dah*, 44.

27. Silverberg, *Mound Builders of Ancient America*, 150.

28. Theodore H. Lewis, "The 'Monumental' Tortoise Mounds of De-coo-dah," *American Journal of Archaeology and History of the Fine Arts* 2 (1886): 69.

29. Stephen D. Peet, *Emblematic Mounds and Animal Effigies*, vol. 2 of *Prehistoric America* (Chicago: American Antiquities Office, 1898).

30. Theodore H. Lewis, *The Northwestern Archaeological Survey* (St. Paul, Minn.: Pioneer Press, 1898). The field notebooks and related documents from the survey are curated by the Minnesota Historical Society, St. Paul.

31. Charles R. Keyes, "The Hill–Lewis Survey," *Minnesota History* 9, no. 2 (1928): 96–108.

32. Quoted in Silverberg, *Mound Builders of Ancient America*, 170.

33. Bruce D. Smith, Introduction to *Report on the Mound Explorations of the Bureau of Ethnology*, by Cyrus Thomas (Washington, D.C.: Smithsonian Institution, 1985), 6.

34. Cyrus Thomas, *Report on the Mound Explorations of the Bureau of Ethnology*, Twelfth Annual Report of the Bureau of American Ethnology, 1890–1891 (Washington, D.C.: Smithsonian Institution Press, 1985).

35. Marshal McKusick, *The Davenport Conspiracy* (Iowa City: University of Iowa Press, 1970), and "A Disturbed Bear that Bears Watching and Other Remarks on an Iowa Effigy Mound Interpretive Model," *Wisconsin Archeologist* 61, no. 3 (1980): 355; Thomas, *Report on the Mound Explorations*, 91–93, 531.

36. Thomas, *Report on the Mound Explorations*, 659.

37. The mound on Lake Butte des Morts probably dates to the Middle Woodland and was destroyed in the 1850s. Late-nineteenth-century researchers assumed that there was a connection between this mound and a famous series of eighteenth-century battles between the French and the Sac and Fox, and this error was repeated by subsequent investigators.

38. R. Clark Mallam, "The Mound Builders: An American Myth," *Journal of the Iowa Archeological Society* 23 (1976): 170–171.

39. Walter Hoffman, *The Menominee Indians*, Fourteenth Annual Report of the Bureau of American Ethnology, 1892–1893 (Washington, D.C.: Smithsonian Institution, 1896), 38; S. A. Barrett and Alanson Skinner, "Certain Mounds and Village Sites of Shawano and Oconto Counties, Wisconsin," *Bulletin of the Public Museum of the City of Milwaukee* 10, no. 5 (1932): 503–504. Barrett and Skinner note that the published story is only part of a more elaborate one that accounts for the origin of the Menominee and the identity of and disappearance of the mound builders.

40. Pliny Warriner, "Legend of the Winnebagos," *Wisconsin Historical Collections* 1 (1903): 86–93.

41. George A. West, "The Indian Authorship of Wisconsin Antiquities," *Wisconsin Archeologist,* o.s., 6, no. 4 (1907): 167–256.

42. West, "Indian Authorship of Wisconsin Antiquities," 253.

43. Arlow B. Stout, "Prehistoric Earthworks in Wisconsin," *Ohio Archaeological and Historical Quarterly* 20, no. 1 (1911): 1–30.

44. Arlow B. Stout, "The Winnebago and the Mounds," *Wisconsin Archeologist,* o.s., 9, no. 4 (1910–1911): 101–103.

45. Charles E. Brown, "The Winnebago as Builders of Wisconsin Earthworks," *Wisconsin Archeologist,* o.s., 10, no. 3 (1911): 124–129.

46. Brown, "Winnebago as Builders of Wisconsin Earthworks," 129.

47. Paul Radin, "Some Aspects of Winnebago Archaeology," *American Anthropologist* 13 (1911): 517–538, and *The Winnebago Tribe,* Thirty-seventh Annual Report of the Bureau of American Ethnology, 1923 (Lincoln: University of Nebraska Press, 1990).

48. Carol I. Mason, "Archaeological Analogy and Ethnographic Example: A Case from the Winnebago," in "Indians, Colonists, and Slaves: Essays in Memory of Charles H. Fairbanks," *Florida Journal of Anthropology Special Publication,* no. 4 (1985), edited by Kenneth W. Johnson, Jonathan M. Leader, and Robert C. Wilson, 95–104.

49. W. C. McKern, "The Neale and McCaughry Mound Groups," *Bulletin of the Public Museum of the City of Milwaukee* 3, no. 3 (1928): 213–416.

50. Nancy O. Lurie, "Winnebago Protohistory," in *Culture in History: Essays in Honor of Paul Radin,* edited by Stanley Diamond (New York: Columbia University Press, 1960), 791–808.

51. Detailed information on Brown's life can be found in *Wisconsin Archeologist* 25, no. 2 (1944), and in the Charles E. Brown Papers, State Historical Society of Wisconsin, Madison.

52. Charles E. Brown, "The Preservation of the Man Mound," *Wisconsin Archeologist,* o.s., 7, no. 4 (1908): 140–154.

53. Charles E. Brown, "Archaeological Items," *Wisconsin Archeologist,* o.s., 10, no. 3 (1911): 136–137.

54. Quoted in Charles E. Brown, "The State Field Assembly at Madison," *Wisconsin Archeologist,* o.s., 9, no. 3 (1910): 68–72.

55. William Ellery Leonard, *The Locomotive God* (New York: Century, 1927).

56. Itineraries for the Lake Mendota Historical Excursions, 1936 and 1939, box 21, Brown Papers.

57. Charles E. Brown, "Lake Wingra," *Wisconsin Archeologist,* o.s., 14, no. 3 (1915): 91–92.

58. Charles E. Brown, "The Arboretum: Notes and Reminiscences by Charles E. Brown," 1935, box 9, Brown Papers.

59. S. A. Barrett and E. W. Hawkes, "The Katz Creek Mound Group," *Bulletin of the Public Museum of the City of Milwaukee* 3, no. 1 (1919): 1–138.

60. S. A. Barrett, "Ancient Aztalan," *Bulletin of the Public Museum of the City of Milwaukee* 13 (1933): 1–602.

61. Charles E. Brown, "Superstitions about Indian Mounds," 1931, box 4, Brown Papers.

62. Alice Kehoe, "The History of Wisconsin Archaeology," *Wisconsin Archeologist* 78, nos. 1–2 (1997): 13 [special issue: "Wisconsin Archaeology," edited by Robert A. Birmingham, Carol I. Mason, and James B. Stoltman].

63. W. C. McKern, "The Kletzien and Nitschke Mound Groups," *Bulletin of the Public Museum of the City of Milwaukee* 3, no. 4 (1930): 462.

64. McKern, "Kletzien and Nitschke Mound Groups," 463.

65. Robert Ritzenthaler, "The Riddle of the Spencer Lake Horse Skull," *Wisconsin Archeologist* 45, no. 2 (1964): 115–123.

66. Robert Ritzenthaler, "Radiocarbon Dates for the Clam River Focus," *Wisconsin Archeologist* 47, no. 4 (1966): 219–220.

67. "The Spencer Lake Horse Skull: Response to Mr. P.'s Letter of June 28, 1962," in Ritzenthaler, "Riddle of the Spencer Lake Horse Skull," 118–120; W. C. McKern to Holland Hague, 30 March 1977, Anthropology Section, Public Museum of the City of Milwaukee.

68. W. C. McKern, "Preliminary Report on the Upper Mississippi Phase in Wisconsin," *Bulletin of the Public Museum of the City of Milwaukee* 16, no. 3 (1945): 109–285.

69. Chandler Rowe, *The Effigy Mound Culture of Wisconsin*, Milwaukee Public Museum Publications in Anthropology, no. 3 (Milwaukee: Milwaukee Public Museum, 1956).

70. Warren L. Wittry, "The Kolterman Mound 18 Radiocarbon Date," *Wisconsin Archeologist* 37, no. 4 (1956): 133–134.

71. William M. Hurley, *An Analysis of Effigy Mound Complexes in Wisconsin,* University of Michigan, Museum of Anthropology Anthropological Papers, no. 59 (Ann Arbor: University of Michigan, Museum of Anthropology, 1975).

72. Warren L. Wittry, "Archaeological Studies of Four Wisconsin Rockshelters," *Wisconsin Archeologist* 40, no. 4 (1959): 137–267.

73. Julian H. Steward, *Theory of Cultural Change* (Urbana: University of Illinois Press, 1955).

74. Mallam, "Mound Builders."

75. Rowe, *Effigy Mound Culture of Wisconsin.*

76. Peter Mires, Jennifer L. Kolb, and Edgar S. Oerichbauer, "The Archaeological Resources of Northwestern Wisconsin: Region 1 Program, 1988–1989," 1989, Division of Historic Preservation, State Historical Society of Wisconsin; Jennifer L. Kolb, "The Archaeological Resources of Northwestern Wisconsin: Region 1 Archaeology Program, 1987–1988," 1988, Division of Historic Preservation, Burnett County Historical Society, Siren, Wisconsin.

77. Steven Hackenberger, He Ping, and Larry A. Johns, "Final Report of the Rock County Indian Mounds Project," 1993, Division of Historic Preservation, State Historical Society of Wisconsin.

78. Robert J. Salzer and Larry A. Johns, "Final Report of the Dane County Indian Mounds Identification Project," 1992, Division of Historic Preservation, State Historical Society of Wisconsin.

79. Barbara Mead, "The Rehbein I Site (47-Ri-81)," *Wisconsin Archeologist* 60, no. 2 (1979): 91–182.

80. John T. Penman, "Late Woodland Sites in Southwestern Grant County, Wisconsin," *Journal of the Iowa Archeological Society* 32 (1985): 1–36.

81. Barry Fell, *America B.C.: Ancient Settlers in the New World* (New York: Quadrangle, 1976).

82. Stephen Williams, *Fantastic Archaeology: The Wild Side of North American Prehistory* (Philadelphia: University of Pennsylvania Press, 1991).

83. Carl Sagan, *The Demon Haunted World: Science as a Candle in the Dark* (New York: Random House, 1995).

84. Brian Fagan, *Ancient North America: Archaeology of a Continent* (New York: Thames and Hudson, 1995), 16–19.

85. James P. Scherz, "Pertinent Aspects of Geometry, Astronomy, Distance, and Time," *Journal of the Ancient Earthworks Society* 3 (1991): M-51.

86. Scherz, "Pertinent Aspects," M-51.

87. T. B. Martin and Richard Flavin, "Twisting History: The Lies of the Ancient American," *News from Indian Country,* January 1995, 6–7.

88. William M. Hurley, "The Late Woodland Stage: Effigy Mound Culture," *Wisconsin Archeologist* 67, nos. 3–4 (1986): 298 [special issue, "Introduction to Wisconsin Archeology," edited by William Green, James B. Stoltman, and Alice B. Kehoe].

89. Robert Hall, "Ghosts, Water Barriers, Corn, and Sacred Enclosures in the Eastern Woodlands," *American Antiquity* 41 (1976): 363.

90. Robert Hall, *Archaeology of the Soul: North American Indian Belief and Ritual* (Urbana: University of Illinois Press, 1997).

91. Robert Hall, "Red Banks, Oneota, and the Winnebago: Views from a Distant Rock," *Wisconsin Archeologist* 74, nos. 1–4 (1993): 42 [special issue: "Exploring the Oneota–Winnebago Direct Historical Connection," edited by David F. Overstreet].

92. Robert J. Salzer, "Preliminary Report on the Gottschall Site (47Ia80)," *Wisconsin Archeologist* 68, no. 4 (1987): 419–472, and "Oral Literature and Archaeology," *Wisconsin Archeologist* 74, nos. 1–4 (1993): 80–119.

93. David W. Benn, E. Arthur Bettis III, and R. Clark Mallam, "Cultural Transformations in the Keller and Bluff Top Mounds," *Plains Anthropologist* 38, no. 145, memoir 27 (1993): 53–73.

94. Ronald J. Mason, "Oneota and Winnebago Ethnogenesis: An Overview," *Wisconsin Archeologist* 74, nos. 1–4 (1993): 418.

CHAPTER 3. WISCONSIN BEFORE THE MOUND BUILDERS: THE PALEO-INDIAN AND ARCHAIC TRADITIONS

1. T. D. Dillehay, *Monte Verde: A Late Pleistocene Settlement in Chile*, vol. 1, *Paleoenvironment and Site Context* (Washington, D.C.: Smithsonian Institution Press, 1989).

2. For a comprehensive discussion of the state of knowledge of the Paleo-Indian tradition in Wisconsin, see Ronald J. Mason, "The Paleo-Indian Tradition," *Wisconsin Archeologist* 78, nos. 1–2 (1997): 78–111 [special issue: "Wisconsin Archaeology," edited by Robert A. Birmingham, Carol I. Mason, and James B. Stoltman]. Archaeologists classify Native American cultures in Wisconsin into stages of cultural development within very broad traditions known as Paleo-Indian, Archaic, Woodland, and Mississippian. Stages and traditions are composed of cultural complexes that are generally similar to one another, reflecting very broad patterns in lifestyles. They are not necessarily the same as periods, although the terms "stage" and "period" are used interchangeably in this book for simplicity. One tradition or stage may persist in one area, although it has disappeared in another. For example, the Paleo-Indian survived for more time in northern Wisconsin than in southern Wisconsin. Finally, stages are generally subdivided into phases, or archaeological sites in a particular area that were occupied for a short time by people who shared many customs, such as those in a tribe or band.

3. David F. Overstreet, with Daniel J. Joyce, Ruth Blazina-Joyce, David Wasion, and Keith A. Sverdrup, *FY 1992 Historic Preservation Survey and Planning Grant: Early Holocene Megafaunal Exploitation, Kenosha County, Wisconsin*, Great Lakes Archeological Research Center, Reports of Investigations, no. 325 (Milwaukee: Great Lakes Archaeological Research Center, 1993); David F. Overstreet, with David Wasion, Keith A. Sverdrup, and Michael Kolb, *FY 1993 Historic Preservation Survey and Planning Grant: Ice Age Landscapes of Southeastern Wisconsin*, Great Lakes Archaeological Research Center, Reports of Investigations, no. 366 (Milwaukee: Great Lakes Archaeological Research Center, 1994).

4. David F. Barton, "Skare Site Projectile Points," *Wisconsin Archeologist* 77, nos. 1–2 (1996): 82–83.

5. Ronald J. Mason and Carol Irwin, "An Eden–Scottsbluff Burial in Northeastern Wisconsin," *American Antiquity* 26 (1960): 43–57.

6. Norman M. Meinholz and Steven Kuehn, *The Deadman Slough Site*, Museum Archaeology Program, Archaeology Research Series, no. 4 (Madison: State Historical Society of Wisconsin, 1996), 183–184.

7. For an overview of the Archaic in Wisconsin, see James B. Stoltman, "The Archaic Tradition," *Wisconsin Archeologist* 78, nos. 1–2 (1997): 112–139 [special issue, "Wisconsin Archaeology," edited by Robert A. Birmingham, Carol I. Mason, and James B. Stoltman].

8. Stoltman, "Archaic Tradition"; Robert Ritzenthaler, ed., "The Old Copper Culture in Wisconsin" [special issue], *Wisconsin Archeologist* 38, no. 4 (1957).

9. Robert Ritzenthaler, "The Osceola Site: An 'Old Copper' Site near Potosi,

Wisconsin," *Wisconsin Archeologist* 38, no. 4 (1957): 186–203 [special issue: "The Old Copper Culture in Wisconsin," edited by Robert Ritzenthaler].

10. Bruce Trigger, *The Children of Aataentsic: A History of the Huron People to 1660,* 2 vols. (Montreal and Kingston: McGill–Queen's University Press, 1976).

11. Harold Hickerson, "The Feast of the Dead among the Seventeenth Century Algonkians of the Upper Great Lakes," *American Anthropologist* 62 (1960): 81–107.

12. Robert Hruska, "The Riverside Site: A Late Archaic Manifestation in Michigan," *Wisconsin Archeologist* 48, no. 3 (1967): 145–260.

13. Katherine P. Stevenson, Robert F. Boszhardt, Charles R. Moffat, Philip H. Salkin, Thomas C. Pleger, James L. Theler, and Constance M. Arzigian, "The Woodland Tradition," *Wisconsin Archeologist* 78, nos. 1–2 (1997): 250–297 [special issue: "Wisconsin Archaeology," edited by Robert A. Birmingham, Carol I. Mason, and James B. Stoltman].

14. Brian Fagan, *Ancient North America: Archaeology of a Continent* (New York: Thames and Hudson, 1995), 371.

15. David F. Overstreet, "The Convent Knoll Site (47Wk327): A Red Ocher Cemetery in Waukesha, Wisconsin," *Wisconsin Archeologist* 61, no 1 (1980): 34–90.

CHAPTER 4. EARLY BURIAL MOUND BUILDERS:
THE EARLY AND MIDDLE WOODLAND STAGES

1. For an overview of mounds constructed during the Archaic, see *Southeastern Archaeology* 13, no. 2 (1994).

2. Jon L. Gibson, *Poverty Point: A Terminal Archaic Culture of the Lower Mississippi Valley,* Anthropological Study Series, no. 7 (Baton Rouge: Louisiana Archaeological Survey and Antiquities Commission, Department of Culture, Recreation, and Tourism, 1996).

3. Brian Fagan, *Ancient North America: Archaeology of a Continent* (New York: Thames and Hudson, 1995), 403–410.

4. Fagan, *Ancient North America,* 411–422.

5. Robert Hall, "In Search of the Ideology of the Adena–Hopewell Climax," in *Hopewell Ideology: The Chillicothe Conference,* edited by D. W. Brose and N. Greber (Kent, Ohio: Kent State University Press, 1979), 258–265, and *Archaeology of the Soul: North American Indian Belief and Ritual* (Urbana: University of Illinois Press, 1997), 18–23.

6. Constance Arzigian, "The Emergence of Horticultural Economies in Southwestern Wisconsin," in *Emergent Horticultural Economies of the Eastern Woodlands,* edited by William F. Keegan, Occasional Paper, no. 7 (Carbondale: Southern Illinois University, Center for Archaeological Investigations, 1987), 217–242; Lynn A. Rusch, "The Early and Late Woodland Occupations at the Bachman Site in East Central Wisconsin," 1988, Division of Historic Preservation, State Historical Society of Wisconsin, Madison; Philip H. Salkin, "The Lake Farms Phase: The Early Woodland Stage in South Central Wisconsin as Seen from the Lake Farms Archaeo-

logical District," in *Early Woodland Archaeology,* edited by Kenneth B. Farnsworth and Thomas E. Emerson, Kampsville Seminars in Archaeology, vol. 2 (Kampsville, Ill.: Center for American Archaeology Press, 1986), 92–120; James L. Theler, "The Early Woodland Component at the Mill Pond Site, Wisconsin," in *Early Woodland Archaeology,* edited by Farnsworth and Emerson, 137–158.

7. David W. Benn, "The Woodland People and the Roots of Oneota," in *Oneota Archaeology: Past, Present, and Future,* edited by William Green, Report no. 20 (Iowa City: University of Iowa, Office of the State Archaeologist, 1995), 103.

8. Kelvin W. Sampson, "Conventionalized Figures on Woodland Ceramics," *Wisconsin Archeologist* 69, no. 3 (1988): 163–188.

9. Alphonse Gerend, "Sheboygan County," *Wisconsin Archeologist* 19, no. 3 (1920): 121–192.

10. Cyrus Thomas, *Report on the Mound Explorations of the Bureau of Ethnology,* Twelfth Annual Report of the Bureau of American Ethnology, 1890–1891 (Washington, D.C.: Smithsonian Institution Press, 1985), 93–94.

11. David F. Overstreet, Larry Doebert, Gary W. Henschel, Phil Sander, and David Wasion, "Two Red Ocher Mortuary Contexts from Southeastern Wisconsin—the Henschel Site (47 Sb 29), Sheboygan County and the Barnes Creek Site (47 Kn 41) Kenosha County," *Wisconsin Archeologist* 77, nos. 1–2 (1996): 36–62.

12. Howard Van Langen and Thomas F. Kehoe, "Hilgen Spring Park Mound," *Wisconsin Archeologist* 52, no. 1 (1971): 1–19.

13. Hall, *Archaeology of the Soul,* 17–23.

14. Katherine P. Stevenson, Robert F. Boszhardt, Charles R. Moffat, Philip H. Salkin, Thomas C. Pleger, James L. Theler, and Constance M. Arzigian, "The Woodland Tradition," *Wisconsin Archeologist* 78, nos. 1–2 (1997): 250–297 [special issue: "Wisconsin Archaeology," edited by Robert A. Birmingham, Carol I. Mason, and James B. Stoltman].

15. Stuart Struever, "Woodland Subsistence-Settlement Systems in the Lower Illinois River Valley," in *New Perspectives in Archeology,* edited by S. R. Binford and L. Binford (Chicago: Aldine, 1968), 285–312.

16. W. C. McKern, "A Wisconsin Variant of the Hopewell Culture," *Bulletin of the Public Museum of the City of Milwaukee* 10, no. 2 (1931): 185–328.

17. Robert J. Salzer, "The Wisconsin North Lakes Project: A Preliminary Report," in *Aspects of Upper Great Lakes Anthropology,* edited by Elden Johnson, Minnesota Prehistoric Archaeology Series, no. 11 (St. Paul: Minnesota Historical Society, 1974), 40–54, and "The Woodland Tradition: An Introduction," *Wisconsin Archeologist* 67, nos. 3–4 (1986): 239–243 [special issue, "Introduction to Wisconsin Archeology," edited by William Green, James B. Stoltman, and Alice B. Kehoe]; Stevenson et al., "Woodland Tradition."

18. Leland Cooper, "The Red Cedar River Variant of the Wisconsin Hopewell Culture," *Bulletin of the Public Museum of the City of Milwaukee* 16, no. 2 (1933): 47–108. The use of puddled white clay on human remains has also been reported for Hopewell-like mounds on Lake Koshkonong and Lake Monona in southern Wisconsin and for a much later mound (ca. A.D. 1200) at Wakanda Park on the Cedar

River. This practice may be related to the earth diver myth and be symbolic of the re-creation or renewal of the world, according to Hall, *Archaeology of the Soul,* 19.

19. Joan Freeman, "The Millville Site: A Middle Woodland Village in Grant County, Wisconsin," *Wisconsin Archeologist* 50, no. 2 (1969): 37–87.

20. P. A. Delcourt and H. R. Delcourt, "Vegetation Maps for Eastern North America," *Geobotany* 11 (1981): 123–165.

CHAPTER 5. EFFIGY MOUND BUILDERS: THE LATE WOODLAND STAGE

1. Joan Freeman, "The Millville Site: A Middle Woodland Village in Grant County, Wisconsin," *Wisconsin Archeologist* 50, no. 2 (1969): 37–87.

2. Katherine P. Stevenson, Robert F. Boszhardt, Charles R. Moffat, Philip H. Salkin, Thomas C. Pleger, James L. Theler, and Constance M. Arzigian, "The Woodland Tradition," *Wisconsin Archeologist* 78, nos. 1–2 (1997): 250–297 [special issue: "Wisconsin Archaeology," edited by Robert A. Birmingham, Carol I. Mason, and James B. Stoltman].

3. Constance Arzigian, "The Emergence of Horticultural Economies in South-western Wisconsin," in *Emergent Horticultural Economies of the Eastern Woodlands,* edited by William F. Keegan, Occasional Paper, no. 7 (Carbondale: Southern Illinois University, Center for Archaeological Investigations, 1987), 217–242.

4. Stevenson et al., "Woodland Tradition."

5. Stevenson et al., "Woodland Tradition."

6. John T. Penman, "Late Woodland Sites in Southwestern Grant County, Wisconsin," *Journal of the Iowa Archeological Society* 32 (1985): 1–36. The presence of corn in the ancient diet is determined by carbon-isotope analysis of bone, measuring the relation of carbon 13 (C13) to carbon 12 (C12). For details, see Margaret M. Bender, David A. Baerreis, and Raymond L. Steventon, "Further Light on Carbon Isotopes and Hopewell Agriculture," *American Antiquity* 46 (1981): 346–353.

7. Chandler Rowe, *The Effigy Mound Culture of Wisconsin,* Milwaukee Public Museum Publications in Anthropology, no. 3 (Milwaukee: Milwaukee Public Museum, 1956).

8. William Green, "Prehistoric Woodland Peoples in the Upper Mississippi Valley," in *Prehistoric Mound Builders of the Mississippi Valley,* edited by James B. Stoltman (Davenport, Iowa: Putnam Museum, 1986), 17–25.

9. Norman C. Sullivan, "Tuberculosis in Late Woodland Effigy Mound Populations," *Wisconsin Archeologist* 66, no. 1 (1995): 71–76.

10. Norman Meinholz and Jennifer Kolb, *The Statz Site: A Late Woodland Community and Archaic Workshop in Dane County, Wisconsin,* Museum Archaeology Program, Archaeology Research Series, no. 5 (Madison: State Historical Society of Wisconsin, 1997).

11. Lynne Goldstein, "The Implications of Aztalan's Location," in *New Perspectives on Cahokia: Views from the Periphery,* edited by James B. Stoltman (Madison, Wis.: Prehistory Press, 1991), 209–226; John D. Richards, "Ceramics and Culture at Aztalan: A Late Prehistoric Village in Southeastern Wisconsin" (Ph.D. diss., Uni-

versity of Wisconsin–Milwaukee, 1992); Philip H. Salkin, "A Reevaluation of the Late Woodland Stage in Southwestern Wisconsin," *Wisconsin Academy Review* 33, no. 2 (1987): 75–79.

12. James B. Stoltman and George W. Christiansen, "The Late Woodland Stage in the Driftless Area of the Upper Mississippi Valley," in *Late Woodland Societies: Tradition and Transformation across the Mid-Continent,* edited by Thomas Emerson, Dale McElrath, and Andrew Fortier (Lincoln: University of Nebraska Press, in press).

13. David W. Benn, "The Woodland People and the Roots of Oneota," in *Oneota Archaeology: Past, Present, and Future,* edited by William Green, Report no. 20 (Iowa City: University of Iowa, Office of the State Archaeologist, 1995), 91–140; Kelvin W. Sampson, "Conventionalized Figures on Woodland Ceramics," *Wisconsin Archeologist* 69, no. 3 (1988): 163–188.

14. Victoria Dirst, "Stockbridge Harbor: A Late Woodland Village on Lake Winnebago," 1995, Wisconsin Department of Natural Resources, State Historical Society of Wisconsin, Madison.

15. Rodney E. Riggs, "Human Skeletal Remains from the Poor Man's Farrah (47-Gt-365) and the Bade (47-Gt-365) Sites in Southwestern Wisconsin," *Journal of the Iowa Archeological Society* 32 (1985): 37–74. Contrary to popular belief, the taking of trophy scalps (and sometimes whole heads) predates European contact and is well documented in the archaeological record. For a discussion of the archaeological evidence for scalping and precontact warfare, see George R. Milner, "An Osteological Perspective on Prehistoric Warfare," in *Regional Approaches to Mortuary Analysis,* edited by Lane Anderson Beck (New York: Plenum, 1995), 221–238, and Benn, "Woodland People and the Roots of Oneota," 125.

16. Milner, "Osteological Perspective on Prehistoric Warfare."

17. Sampson, "Conventionalized Figures on Woodland Ceramics."

18. Ruth Bliss Philips, "Dreams and Designs: Iconographic Problems in Great Lakes Twined Bags," in *Great Lakes Indian Art,* edited by David W. Penny (Detroit: Wayne State University Press and Detroit Institute of Arts, 1989), 52–68.

19. Benn, "Woodland People and the Roots of Oneota," 103.

20. R. Clark Mallam, "Ideology from the Earth: Effigy Mounds in the Midwest," *Archaeology* 35, no. 4 (1982): 60–64.

21. Cyrus Thomas, *Report on the Mound Explorations of the Bureau of Ethnology,* Twelfth Annual Report of the Bureau of American Ethnology, 1890–1891 (Washington, D.C.: Smithsonian Institution Press, 1985).

22. R. Clark Mallam, "The Mound Builders: An American Myth," *Journal of the Iowa Archeological Society* 23 (1976): 145–175.

23. R. Clark Mallam, *The Iowa Effigy Mound Manifestation: An Interpretative Model,* Report no. 9 (Iowa City: University of Iowa, Office of the State Archaeologist, 1979), 76.

24. Mallam, *Iowa Effigy Mound Manifestation.*

25. Lynne Goldstein, "Landscapes and Mortuary Practices: A Case for Regional Perspectives," in *Regional Approaches to Mortuary Analysis,* edited by Lane Anderson Beck (New York: Plenum, 1995), 101–120.

26. Rowe, *Effigy Mound Culture of Wisconsin.*

27. Mallam, "Birds, Bears, Panthers, 'Elephants,' and Archaeologists," *Wisconsin Archaeologist* 61, no. 3 (1980): 383.

28. Robert Hall, "Red Banks, Oneota, and the Winnebago: Views from a Distant Rock," *Wisconsin Archeologist* 74, nos. 1–4 (1993): 10–79 [special issue: "Exploring the Oneota–Winnebago Direct Historical Connection," ed. D. F. Overstreet].

29. Hall, "Red Banks, Oneota, and the Winnebago," 51.

30. George Christiansen III, "Burial Mound and Earthwork Research Project," 1998, Office of the State Archaeologist, State Historical Society of Wisconsin.

31. Mallam, *Iowa Effigy Mound Manifestation.*

32. Jane A. Hieb, ed., *Visions and Voices: Winnebago Elders Speak to the Children* (Trempealeau, Wis.: Western Dairyland Economic Opportunity Council, 1994), 18.

33. Rowe, *Effigy Mound Culture of Wisconsin.*

34. Hall, "Red Banks, Oneota, and the Winnebago," 42–43.

35. Paul Radin, *The Winnebago Tribe,* Thirty-seventh Annual Report of the Bureau of American Ethnology, 1923 (Lincoln: University of Nebraska Press, 1990), 137.

36. Radin, *Winnebago Tribe,* 239–240.

37. Charles E. Brown, "Water Spirit Legend, Told by Winnebago Indians," n.d., box 3, Charles E. Brown Papers, State Historical Society of Wisconsin.

38. Paul Radin, *The Road of Life and Death,* Bollingen Series, no. 5 (New York: Pantheon Books, 1945), 54–55.

39. Ronald J. Mason, "Archaeo-ethnicity and the Elusive Menominis." *Midcontinental Journal of Archaeology* 22, no. 1 (1997): 69–94; Louise S. Spindler, "Menominee," in *Handbook of North American Indians,* vol. 15, *Northeast,* edited by Bruce G. Trigger (Washington, D.C.: Smithsonian Institution Press, 1978), 708–724.

40. Robert J. Salzer, "Preliminary Report on the Gottschall Site," *Wisconsin Archeologist* 68, no. 4 (1987): 419–472; Hall, "Red Banks, Oneota, and the Winnebago."

41. Radin, *Winnebago Tribe,* 33.

42. James P. Scherz, "Eagle Mounds in Eagle Township (Richland County, Wisconsin)," January 1993, unpublished report in the files at the Office of the State Archaeologist, State Historical Society of Wisconsin.

43. C. K. Dean, *Mounds in Wisconsin,* Annual Report of the Board of Regents of the Smithsonian Institution, 1872 (Washington, D.C.: Smithsonian Institution, 1873), 415; Increase A. Lapham, "Man-Shaped Mounds in Wisconsin," in *Report and Collections of the State Historical Society of Wisconsin for the Years 1857 and 1858,* Fourth Annual Report (Madison: State Historical Society of Wisconsin, 1859), 365–368.

44. Benn, "Woodland People and the Roots of Oneota," 121.

45. Salzer, "Preliminary Report on the Gottschall Site."

46. Arlow B. Stout, "The Winnebago and the Mounds," *Wisconsin Archeologist,* o.s., 9, no. 4 (1910–1911): 101–103.

47. Charles E. Brown, "The Springs of Lake Wingra," *Wisconsin Magazine of History* 10, no. 3 (1927): 298–310.

48. Oliver La Mere to Charles E. Brown, 27 November 1926, box 3, Brown Papers.

49. Brown, "Springs of Lake Wingra."

50. Spindler, "Menominee."

51. Hall, "Red Banks, Oneota, and the Winnebago," 44.

52. David Lee Smith, "Winnebago History" (Speech delivered at the fiftieth anniversary celebration of Effigy Mounds National Monument, Marquette, Iowa, 14 August 1999).

53. Charles E. Brown, "The Intaglio Mounds of Wisconsin," *Wisconsin Archeologist,* o.s., 9, no. 1 (1910): 5–10.

54. James P. Scherz, "Pertinent Aspects of Geometry, Astronomy, Distance, and Time," *Journal of the Ancient Earthworks Society* 3 (1991): M-1–M-52. We are not convinced that the "ancient geometries" exist. Given the great variation in the orientation of the mounds throughout the effigy mound region, it is reasonable to suggest that examples of just about any angle can be found.

55. Anthony F. Aveni, ed., *Archaeoastronomy in the New World* (Cambridge: Cambridge University Press, 1982); E. C. Krupp, *Echoes of Ancient Skies: The Astronomy of Lost Civilizations* (New York: Harper & Row, 1983).

56. Brian Fagan, *Ancient North America: Archaeology of a Continent* (New York: Thames and Hudson, 1995), 394.

57. Warren L. Wittry, "Discovering and Interpreting the Cahokia Woodhenges," *Wisconsin Archeologist* 77, nos. 3–4 (1996): 26–35 [special issue, "The Ancient Sky Watchers of Cahokia: Woodhenges, Eclipses, and Cahokia Cosmology," edited by Melvin L. Fowler].

58. Scherz, "Pertinent Aspects."

59. E. C. Krupp to Robert A. Birmingham, 31 October 1991, Office of the State Archaeologist, State Historical Society of Wisconsin.

60. Frank D. Stekel, Larry A. Johns, and James P. Scherz, "Whitewater Effigy Mounds Park: The Maple Mounds Group," *Wisconsin Archeologist* 72, nos. 1–2 (1991): 118–126.

61. Gary Henschel, "Henschel Mounds (47 Sb 29) as Possible Solstice Markers: A Progress Report," *Wisconsin Archeologist* 77, nos. 1–2 (1996): 73–77.

62. William M. Hurley, *An Analysis of Effigy Mound Complexes in Wisconsin,* University of Michigan, Museum of Anthropology Anthropological Papers, no. 59 (Ann Arbor: University of Michigan, Museum of Anthropology, 1975).

63. W. C. McKern, *The Clam River Focus,* Milwaukee Public Museum Publications in Anthropology, no. 9 (Milwaukee: Milwaukee Public Museum, 1963).

64. Paul L. Beaubien, "Some Hopewellian Mounds at Effigy Mound National Monument, Iowa," *Wisconsin Archeologist* 34, no. 2 (1953): 125–138; Hurley, *Anal-*

ysis of Effigy Mound Complexes in Wisconsin; Warren L. Wittry, "The Kolterman Mound 18 Radiocarbon Date," *Wisconsin Archeologist* 37, no. 4 (1956): 133–134.

65. Hurley, *Analysis of Effigy Mound Complexes in Wisconsin.*

66. Stoltman and Christiansen, "Late Woodland Stage in the Driftless Area."

67. Hall, "Red Banks, Oneota, and the Winnebago," 51–52.

CHAPTER 6. TEMPLE MOUND BUILDERS: THE MISSISSIPPIAN TRADITION

1. Edward G. Bourne, *Narratives of the Career of Hernando de Soto,* 2 vols, (New York: Barnes); John R. Swanton, *Indian Tribes of the Lower Mississippi Valley and Adjacent Coast of the Gulf of Mexico,* Bureau of American Ethnology, Bulletin no. 43 (Washington, D.C.: Smithsonian Institution, 1911). For a highly readable account of the de Soto expedition, see David Ewing Duncan, *Hernando de Soto: A Savage Quest in the Americas* (New York: Crown, 1995).

2. Various descriptions of Cahokia are found in Thomas E. Emerson and R. Barry Lewis, eds., *Cahokia and the Hinterlands: Middle Mississippian Cultures of the Midwest* (Urbana: University of Illinois Press, 1991); Melvin L. Fowler, ed., *Explorations into Cahokia Archaeology,* Illinois Archaeological Survey, Bulletin no. 7 (Urbana: Illinois Archaeological Survey, 1969), and *The Cahokia Atlas: A Historical Atlas of Cahokia Archaeology,* Studies in Illinois Archaeology, no. 6 (Springfield, Ill.: Historic Preservation Agency, 1989); Claudia Gellman Mink, *Cahokia: City of the Sun* (Collinsville, Ill.: Cahokia Mounds Museum Society, 1995); and George R. Milner, *The Cahokia Chiefdom: The Archaeology of a Mississippian Society* (Washington, D.C.: Smithsonian Institution Press, 1998).

3. Robert Hall, *Archaeology of the Soul: North American Indian Belief and Ritual* (Urbana: University of Illinois Press, 1997), 145–146.

4. J. Witthoft, *Green Corn Ceremonialism in Eastern Wisconsin,* University of Michigan, Museum of Anthropology Occasional Contributions, no. 13 (Ann Arbor: University of Michigan, Museum of Anthropology, 1949).

5. For an overview of Mississippian sites in Wisconsin, see William Green, "Mississippian Peoples," *Wisconsin Archeologist* 78, nos. 1–2 (1997): 202–222 [special issue: "Wisconsin Archaeology," edited by Robert A. Birmingham, Carol I. Mason, and James B. Stoltman].

6. Robert J. Salzer, "Preliminary Report on the Gottschall Site," *Wisconsin Archeologist* 68, no. 4 (1987): 419–472.

7. Fred Finney and James B. Stoltman, "The Fred Edwards Site: A Case of Stirling Phase Culture Contact in Southwestern Wisconsin," in *New Perspectives on Cahokia: Views from the Periphery,* edited by James B. Stoltman (Madison, Wis.: Prehistory Press, 1991), 229–252.

8. William Green and Roland L. Rodell, "The Mississippian Presence and Cahokia Interaction at Trempealeau, Wisconsin," *American Antiquity* 59 (1994): 334–358.

9. Theodore H. Lewis, field notebook 16, 1884, Northwestern Archaeological Survey, Notebooks and Related Documents, Minnesota Historical Society, St. Paul;

George H. Squier, "Certain Archaeological Features of Western Wisconsin," *Wisconsin Archeologist*, o.s., 4, no. 2 (1914): 29–30.

10. Roland L. Rodell, "The Diamond Bluff Site Complex and Cahokia Influence in the Red Wing Locality," in *New Perspectives on Cahokia: Views from the Periphery*, edited by James B. Stoltman (Madison, Wis.: Prehistory Press, 1991), 253–279; Guy E. Gibbon and Clark A. Dobbs, "The Mississippian Presence in the Red Wing Area," in *New Perspectives on Cahokia: Views from the Periphery*, edited by James B. Stoltman (Madison, Wis.: Prehistory Press, 1991), 281–306.

11. James B. Stoltman and George W. Christiansen, "The Late Woodland Stage in the Driftless Area of the Upper Mississippi Valley," in *Late Woodland Societies: Tradition and Transformation across the Mid-Continent*, edited by Thomas Emerson, Dale McElrath, and Andrew Fortier (Lincoln: University of Nebraska Press, in press).

12. Rodell, "Diamond Bluff Site Complex."

13. Lynne Goldstein and Joan Freeman, "Aztalan—A Middle Mississippian Village," *Wisconsin Archeologist* 78, nos. 1–2 (1997): 223–249 [special issue: "Wisconsin Archaeology," edited by Robert A. Birmingham, Carol I. Mason, and James B. Stoltman]; Increase A. Lapham, *The Antiquities of Wisconsin, as Surveyed and Described*, Smithsonian Contributions to Knowledge, vol. 7 (Washington, D.C.: Smithsonian Institution, 1855); Robert Ritzenthaler, ed., "Aztalan: Exploration and Reconstruction" [special issue], *Wisconsin Archeologist* 39, no. 1 (1958); S. A. Barrett, "Ancient Aztalan," *Bulletin of the Public Museum of the City of Milwaukee* 13 (1933): 1–602; Lynne G. Goldstein and John D. Richards, "Ancient Aztalan: The Cultural and Ecological Context of a Late Prehistoric Site in the Midwest," in *Cahokia and the Hinterlands: Middle Mississippian Cultures of the Midwest*, edited by Thomas E. Emerson and R. Barry Lewis (Urbana: University of Illinois Press, 1991), 193–206; John D. Richards, "Ceramics and Culture at Aztalan: A Late Prehistoric Village in Southeastern Wisconsin" (Ph.D. diss., University of Wisconsin–Milwaukee, 1992).

14. William T. Sterling, "A Visit to Aztalan in 1838," *Wisconsin Archeologist* 19, no. 1 (1920): 18–19.

15. Witthoft, *Green Corn Ceremonialism;* Hall, *Archaeology of the Soul*, 167.

16. Goldstein and Freeman, "Aztalan," 223.

17. Barrett, "Ancient Aztalan," 232–233; Witthoft, *Green Corn Ceremonialism*, 62.

18. Richards, "Ceramics and Culture at Aztalan."

19. Goldstein and Richards, "Ancient Aztalan."

20. Goldstein and Freeman, "Aztalan."

21. Richards, "Ceramics and Culture at Aztalan."

CHAPTER 7. MOUND CONSTRUCTION AND USE IN LATER TIMES: ONEOTA,
NORTHERN WISCONSIN, AND THE HISTORIC PERIOD

1. David F. Overstreet, "Oneota Prehistory and History," *Wisconsin Archeologist* 78, nos. 1–2 (1997): 250–297 [special issue: "Wisconsin Archaeology," edited by Robert A. Birmingham, Carol I. Mason, and James B. Stoltman].

2. For various views on the origins of the Oneota, see Guy Gibbon, "Oneota Origins Revisited," in *Oneota Studies,* edited by Guy Gibbon, University of Minnesota Publications in Anthropology, no. 1 (Minneapolis: Department of Anthropology, University of Minnesota, 1982), 85–90; James B. Stoltman, "Ancient Peoples of the Upper Mississippi River Valley," in *Historic Lifestyles in the Upper Mississippi River Valley,* edited by John Wozniac (New York: University Press of America, 1983), 197–255, and "The Appearance of the Mississippian Cultural Tradition in the Upper Mississippi Valley," in *Prehistoric Mound Builders of the Mississippi Valley,* edited by James B. Stoltman (Davenport, Iowa: Putnam Museum, 1986), 26–34; and Overstreet, "Oneota Prehistory and History."

3. Stoltman, "Appearance of the Mississippian Cultural Tradition."

4. Mark E. Bruhy, Angie R. Teater, Cari S. Verplank, and Kim L. Potaracke, *Heritage Resources Management,* Cultural Resources Report, no. 7 (Rhinelander, Wis.: Nicolet National Forest, 1990); Mason, "Archaeo-ethnicity and the Elusive Menominis."

5. James Warren Springer and Stanley R. Witkowski, "Siouan Linguistics and Oneota Archaeology," in *Oneota Studies,* edited by Guy Gibbon, University of Minnesota Publications in Anthropology, no. 1 (Minneapolis: Department of Anthropology, University of Minnesota, 1982), 69–84.

6. Jody O'Gorman, *The Tremaine Complex: Oneota Occupation in the La Crosse Locality, Wisconsin,* Museum Archaeology Program, Archaeology Research Series, no. 3 (Madison: State Historical Society of Wisconsin, 1994); R. Eric Hollinger, "Residence Patterns and Oneota Social Dynamics," in *Oneota Archaeology: Past, Present, and Future,* edited by William Green, Report no. 20 (Iowa City: University of Iowa, Office of the State Archaeologist, 1995), 141–174.

7. Overstreet, "Oneota Prehistory and History."

8. Dale Henning, "Managing Oneota," *Wisconsin Archeologist* 79, no. 1 (1998): 122–130.

9. William Green, "Examining Protohistoric Depopulation in the Upper Midwest," *Wisconsin Archeologist* 74, nos. 1–4 (1993): 290–393 [special issue: "Exploring the Oneota–Winnebago Direct Historical Connection," edited by David F. Overstreet].

10. Paul Radin, *The Winnebago Tribe,* Thirty-seventh Annual Report of the Bureau of American Ethnology, 1923 (Lincoln: University of Nebraska Press, 1990), 5–10.

11. Thomas E. Emerson, "Water, Serpents, and the Underworld: An Exploration into Cahokian Symbolism," in *The Southeastern Ceremonial Complex,* edited by Patricia Galloway (Lincoln: University of Nebraska Press, 1989), 45–92.

12. David W. Benn, "Hawks, Serpents, and Birdmen: Emergence of the Oneota Mode of Production," *Plains Anthropologist* 34, no. 125 (1989): 233–260.

13. Benn, "Hawks, Serpents, and Birdmen"; Nancy O. Lurie, "Winnebago," in *Handbook of North American Indians,* vol. 15, *Northeast,* edited by Bruce G. Trigger (Washington, D.C.: Smithsonian Institution Press, 1978), 690–707.

14. Victoria Dirst, "Reconsidering the Prehistory of Northeastern Wisconsin," *Wisconsin Archeologist* 79, no. 1 (1998): 119 [special issue, "From the Northern Tier: Papers in Honor of Ronald J. Mason," edited by Charles E. Cleland and Robert A. Birmingham]; Overstreet, "Oneota Prehistory and History."

15. John A. Jeske, "The Grand River Mound Group and Camp Site," *Bulletin of the Public Museum of the City of Milwaukee* 3, no. 2 (1927): 139–214; Overstreet, "Oneota Prehistory and History." Enhanced knoll cemeteries are also documented for Oneota who lived in the Chicago area in James Brown, "Oneota Mortuary Contexts" (Paper presented at the Midwest Archaeological Conference, Milwaukee, October 1993).

16. David F. Overstreet, *Oneota Tradition Culture History—New Data from the Old Spring Site (47Wn350),* Great Lakes Archaeological Research Center, Reports of Investigations, no. 219 (Milwaukee: Great Lakes Archaeological Research Center, 1989).

17. Robert Hall, *Archaeology of the Soul: North American Indian Belief and Ritual* (Urbana: University of Illinois Press, 1997), 155–168.

18. W. C. McKern, *The Clam River Focus,* Milwaukee Public Museum Publications in Anthropology, no. 9 (Milwaukee: Milwaukee Public Museum, 1963).

19. Leland Cooper, *Indian Mounds Park, Archaeological Site, Rice Lake, Wisconsin,* Science Museum of the St. Paul Institute, Science Bulletin, no. 6 (St. Paul, Minn.: Science Museum of the St. Paul Institute, 1959).

20. Douglas A. Birk and Elden Johnson, "The Mdewakanton Dakota and Initial French Contact," in *Calumet and Fleur-de-Lys: Archaeology of Indian and French Contact in the Midcontinent,* edited by John A. Walthall and Thomas E. Emerson (Washington, D.C.: Smithsonian Institution Press, 1992), 205. A relatively large quantity of Ogechie Ware, which appears to date to the 1660s, has also been found at a large village site, the Cadotte site, in northwestern Wisconsin, on Madeline Island in Lake Superior, as reported in Robert A. Birmingham, "Historic Indian Archaeology at La Pointe," *Wisconsin Archeologist* 73, nos. 3–4 (1992): 177–198. A low conical mound is part of the site complex.

21. Carol I. Mason, "Historic Identification and the Oneota," in *Cultural Change and Continuity: Essays in Honor of James Bennet Griffin,* edited by Charles E. Cleland (New York: Academic Press, 1976), 335–348.

22. Carol I. Mason, *Introduction to Wisconsin Indians: Prehistory to Statehood* (Salem, Wis.: Sheffield, 1988).

23. The first documented European contact with the Ho-Chunk was in 1634, when Jean Nicolet visited a village on the shores of Lake Michigan. Most historians assert that this meeting took place on the lower Door Peninsula, near an area called Red Banks. In a review of historic documents, Robert Hall suggests that it occurred

in the Chicago area and concludes that Ho-Chunk territory covered much of eastern Wisconsin and northern Illinois, as discussed in "Relating the Big Fish and the Big Stone: Reconsidering the Archaeological Identity and Habitat of the Winnebago in 1634," in *Oneota Archaeology: Past, Present, and Future,* edited by William Green, Report no. 20 (Iowa City: University of Iowa, Office of the State Archaeologist, 1995), 19–32. The meeting with Nicolet probably preceded the decimating war with the Illinois.

24. John Blackhawk, "The Winnebago Indians and the Mounds," *Wisconsin Archeologist* 8, no. 3 (1928): 106–107.

25. Increase A. Lapham, *The Antiquities of Wisconsin, as Surveyed and Described,* Smithsonian Contributions to Knowledge, vol. 7 (Washington, D.C.: Smithsonian Institution, 1855).

26. Richard C. Taylor, "Notes Respecting Certain Indian Mounds and Earthworks in the Form of Animal Effigies, Chiefly in Wisconsin Territory, U.S.," *American Journal of Science and Art* 34 (1838): 88–104; Stephen Taylor, "Description of Ancient Remains, Animal Mounds and Embankments, Principally in the Counties of Grant, Iowa and Richland, in Wisconsin Territory," *American Journal of Science and Art* 44 (1843): 21–40; Lapham, *Antiquities of Wisconsin,* 27, 30, 59.

27. Taylor, "Notes Respecting Certain Indian Mounds and Earthworks," 98.

28. Archaeological Site Inventory, Office of the State Archaeologist, State Historical Society of Wisconsin, Madison.

29. Mason, *Introduction to Wisconsin Indians.*

30. Lapham, *Antiquities of Wisconsin,* 27, 30, 59.

CHAPTER 8. INDIAN MOUNDS IN THE MODERN WORLD

1. The burial ground, called the Marina Site, is located on Madeline Island in Lake Superior. It was saved when the owners of adjacent land bought the property and donated it to the town of La Pointe.

2. Robert A. Birmingham, "Charles E. Brown and the Mounds of Madison," *Historic Madison: A Journal of the Four Lakes Region* 13 (1996): 17–29.

Bibliography

Arzigian, Constance. "The Emergence of Horticultural Economies in Southwestern Wisconsin." In *Emergent Horticultural Economies of the Eastern Woodlands,* edited by William F. Keegan, 217–242. Occasional Paper, no. 7. Carbondale: Southern Illinois University, Center for Archaeological Investigations, 1987.

Atwater, Caleb. *Descriptions of the Antiquities Discovered in the State of Ohio and Other Western States.* Transactions and Collections of the American Antiquarian Society, vol. 1. Worcester, Mass.: American Antiquarian Society, 1820.

Aveni, Anthony F., ed. *Archaeoastronomy in the New World.* Cambridge: Cambridge University Press, 1982.

Barrett, S. A. "Ancient Aztalan." *Bulletin of the Public Museum of the City of Milwaukee* 13 (1933): 1–602.

Barrett, S. A., and E. W. Hawkes. "The Katz Creek Mound Group." *Bulletin of the Public Museum of the City of Milwaukee* 3, no. 1 (1919): 1–138.

Barrett, S. A., and Alanson Skinner. "Certain Mounds and Village Sites of Shawano and Oconto Counties, Wisconsin." *Bulletin of the Public Museum of the City of Milwaukee* 10, no. 5 (1932): 401–552.

Barton, David F. "Skare Site Projectile Points." *Wisconsin Archeologist* 77, nos. 1–2 (1996): 82–83.

Beaubien, Paul L. "Some Hopewellian Mounds at Effigy Mound National Monument, Iowa." *Wisconsin Archeologist* 34, no. 2 (1953): 125–138.

Bender, Margaret M., David A. Baerreis, and Raymond L. Steventon. "Further Light on Carbon Isotopes and Hopewell Agriculture." *American Antiquity* 46 (1981): 346–353.

Benn, David W. "Hawks, Serpents, and Birdmen: Emergence of the Oneota Mode of Production." *Plains Anthropologist* 34, no. 125 (1989): 233–260.

Benn, David W. "The Woodland People and the Roots of Oneota." In *Oneota Archaeology: Past, Present, and Future,* edited by William Green, 91–140. Report no. 20. Iowa City: University of Iowa, Office of the State Archaeologist, 1995.

Benn, David W., E. Arthur Bettis III, and R. Clark Mallam. "Cultural Transformations in the Keller and Bluff Top Mounds." *Plains Anthropologist* 38, no. 145, memoir 27 (1993): 52–73.

Birk, Douglas A., and Elden Johnson. "The Mdewakanton Dakota and Initial French Contact." In *Calumet and Fleur-de-Lys: Archaeology of Indian and French Contact in the Midcontinent,* edited by John A. Walthall and Thomas E. Emerson, 203–240. Washington, D.C.: Smithsonian Institution Press, 1992.

Birmingham, Robert A. "Charles E. Brown and the Mounds of Madison." *Historic Madison: A Journal of the Four Lakes Region* 13 (1996): 17–29.

Birmingham, Robert A. "Historic Indian Archaeology at La Pointe." *Wisconsin Archeologist* 73, nos. 3–4 (1992): 177–198.

Blackhawk, John. "The Winnebago Indians and the Mounds." *Wisconsin Archeologist* 8, no. 3 (1928): 106–107.

Bourne, Edward G. *Narratives of the Career of Hernando de Soto.* 2 vols. New York: Barnes.

Brown, Charles E. "The Arboretum: Notes and Reminiscences by Charles E. Brown." 1935. Charles E. Brown Papers. State Historical Society of Wisconsin, Madison.

Brown, Charles E. "Archaeological Items." *Wisconsin Archeologist,* o.s., 10, no. 3 (1911): 136–137

Brown, Charles E. "The Intaglio Mounds of Wisconsin." *Wisconsin Archeologist,* o.s., 9, no. 1 (1910): 5–10.

Brown, Charles E. "Lake Wingra." *Wisconsin Archeologist,* o.s., 14, no. 3 (1915): 75–117.

Brown, Charles E. "The Monona Mound." *Wisconsin Archeologist* 24, no. 4 (1943): 78.

Brown, Charles E. "The Preservation of the Man Mound." *Wisconsin Archeologist,* o.s., 7, no. 4 (1908): 140–154.

Brown, Charles E. "The Springs of Lake Wingra." *Wisconsin Magazine of History* 10, no. 3 (1927): 298–310.

Brown, Charles E. "The State Field Assembly at Madison." *Wisconsin Archeologist,* o.s., 9, no. 3 (1910): 57–78.

Brown, Charles E. "Superstitions about Indian Mounds." 1931. Charles E. Brown Papers. State Historical Society of Wisconsin, Madison.

Brown, Charles E. "Water Spirit Legend, Told by Winnebago Indians." N.d. Charles E. Brown Papers. State Historical Society of Wisconsin, Madison.

Brown, Charles E. "The Winnebago as Builders of Wisconsin Earthworks." *Wisconsin Archeologist,* o.s., 10, no. 3 (1911): 124–129.

Brown, James. "Oneota Mortuary Contexts." Paper presented at the Midwest Archaeological Conference, Milwaukee, October 1993.

Bruhy, Mark E., Angie R. Teater, Cari S. Verplank, and Kim L. Potaracke. *Heritage Resources Management.* Cultural Resources Report, no. 7. Rhinelander, Wis.: Nicolet National Forest.

Christiansen, George, III. "Burial Mound and Earthwork Research Project." 1998. Office of the State Archaeologist, State Historical Society of Wisconsin, Madison.

Bibliography

Clifton, James A. "Potawatomi." In *Handbook of North American Indians*. Vol. 15, *Northeast,* edited by Bruce G. Trigger, 725–742. Washington, D.C.: Smithsonian Institution Press, 1978.

Cooper, Leland. *Indian Mounds Park, Archaeological Site, Rice Lake, Wisconsin.* Science Museum of the St. Paul Institute, Science Bulletin, no. 6. St. Paul, Minn.: Science Museum of the St. Paul Institute, 1959.

Cooper, Leland. "A Preliminary Report on the Excavation of Two Late Middle Woodland Mounds in Northwestern Wisconsin." *Journal of the Minnesota Academy of Science* 32, no. 1 (1964): 17–23.

Cooper, Leland. "The Red Cedar River Variant of the Wisconsin Hopewell Culture." *Bulletin of the Public Museum of the City of Milwaukee* 16, no. 2 (1932): 47–108.

Deák, Gloria. *Discovering America's Southeast: A Sixteenth Century View Based on the Mannerist Engravings of Theodore de Bry.* Birmingham, Ala.: Public Library Press, 1992.

Dean, C. K. *Mounds in Wisconsin.* Annual Report of the Board of Regents of the Smithsonian Institution, 1872. Washington, D.C.: Smithsonian Institution, 1873.

Delcourt, P. A., and H. R. Delcourt. "Vegetation Maps for Eastern North America." *Geobotany* 11 (1981): 123–165.

Dillehay, T. D. *Monte Verde: A Late Pleistocene Settlement in Chile.* Vol.1, *Paleoenvironment and Site Context.* Washington, D.C.: Smithsonian Institution Press, 1989.

Dirst, Victoria. "Reconsidering the Prehistory of Northeastern Wisconsin." *Wisconsin Archeologist* 79, no. 1 (1998): 113–121. [Special issue, "From the Northern Tier: Papers in Honor of Ronald J. Mason," edited by Charles E. Cleland and Robert A. Birmingham]

Dirst, Victoria. "Stockbridge Harbor: A Late Woodland Village on Lake Winnebago." 1995. Wisconsin Department of Natural Resources. State Historical Society of Wisconsin, Madison.

Duncan, David Ewing. *Hernando de Soto: A Savage Quest in the Americas.* New York: Crown, 1995.

Emerson, Thomas E. "Water, Serpents, and the Underworld: An Exploration into Cahokian Symbolism." In *The Southeastern Ceremonial Complex,* edited by Patricia Galloway, 45–92. Lincoln: University of Nebraska Press, 1989.

Emerson, Thomas E., and R. Barry Lewis, eds. *Cahokia and the Hinterlands: Middle Mississippian Cultures of the Midwest.* Urbana: University of Illinois Press, 1991.

Fagan, Brian. *Ancient North America: Archaeology of a Continent.* New York: Thames and Hudson, 1995.

Fell, Barry. *America B.C.: Ancient Settlers in the New World.* New York, Quadrangle, 1976.

Finney, Fred, and James B. Stoltman. "The Fred Edwards Site: A Case of Stirling Phase Culture Contact in Southwestern Wisconsin." In *New Perspectives on Cahokia: Views from the Periphery,* edited by James B. Stoltman, 229–252. Madison, Wis.: Prehistory Press, 1991.

Bibliography

Fowler, Melvin L. *The Cahokia Atlas: A Historical Atlas of Cahokia Archaeology.* Studies in Illinois Archaeology, no. 6. Springfield, Ill.: Historic Preservation Agency, 1989.

Fowler, Melvin L., ed. *Explorations into Cahokia Archaeology.* Illinois Archaeological Survey, Bulletin no. 7. Urbana: Illinois Archaeological Survey, 1969.

Freeman, Joan. "The Millville Site: A Middle Woodland Village in Grant County, Wisconsin." *Wisconsin Archeologist* 50, no. 2 (1969): 37–87.

Gerend, Alphonse. "Sheboygan County." *Wisconsin Archeologist* 19, no. 3 (1920): 121–192.

Gibbon, Guy. "Oneota Origins Revisited." In *Oneota Studies,* edited by Guy Gibbon, 85–90. University of Minnesota Publications in Anthropology, no. 1. Minneapolis: Department of Anthropology, University of Minnesota, 1982.

Gibbon, Guy E., and Clark A. Dobbs. "The Mississippian Presence in the Red Wing Area." In *New Perspectives on Cahokia: Views from the Periphery,* edited by James B. Stoltman, 281–305. Madison, Wis.: Prehistory Press, 1991.

Gibson, Jon L. *Poverty Point: A Terminal Archaic Culture of the Lower Mississippi Valley.* Anthropological Study Series, no. 7. Baton Rouge: Louisiana Archaeological Survey and Antiquities Commission, Department of Culture, Recreation and Tourism, 1996.

Goldstein, Lynne. "The Implications of Aztalan's Location." In *New Perspectives on Cahokia: Views from the Periphery,* edited by James B. Stoltman, 209–226. Madison, Wis.: Prehistory Press, 1991.

Goldstein, Lynne. "Landscapes and Mortuary Practices: A Case for Regional Perspectives." In *Regional Approaches to Mortuary Analysis,* edited by Lane Anderson Beck, 101–120. New York: Plenum, 1995.

Goldstein, Lynne, and Joan Freeman. "Aztalan—A Middle Mississippian Village." *Wisconsin Archeologist* 78, nos. 1–2 (1997): 223–249. [Special issue: "Wisconsin Archaeology," edited by Robert A. Birmingham, Carol I. Mason, and James B. Stoltman]

Goldstein, Lynne G., and John D. Richards. "Ancient Aztalan: The Cultural and Ecological Context of a Late Prehistoric Site in the Midwest." In *Cahokia and the Hinterlands: Middle Mississippian Cultures of the Midwest,* edited by Thomas E. Emerson and R. Barry Lewis, 193–206. Urbana: University of Illinois Press, 1991.

Green, William. "Examining Protohistoric Depopulation in the Upper Midwest." *Wisconsin Archeologist* 74, nos. 1–4 (1993): 290–393. [Special issue: "Exploring the Oneota–Winnebago Direct Historical Connection," edited by David F. Overstreet]

Green, William. "Mississippian Peoples." *Wisconsin Archeologist* 78, nos. 1–2 (1997): 202–222. [Special issue: "Wisconsin Archaeology," edited by Robert A. Birmingham, Carol I. Mason, and James B. Stoltman]

Green, William. "Prehistoric Woodland Peoples in the Upper Mississippi Valley." In *Prehistoric Mound Builders of the Mississippi Valley,* edited by James B. Stoltman, 17–25. Davenport, Iowa: Putnam Museum, 1986.

Green, William, and Roland L. Rodell. "The Mississippian Presence and Cahokia Interaction at Trempealeau, Wisconsin." *American Antiquity* 59 (1994): 334–358.

Hackenberger, Steven, He Ping, and Larry A. Johns. "Final Report of the Rock County Indian Mounds Project." 1993. Division of Historic Preservation, State Historical Society of Wisconsin, Madison.

Hall, Robert. *Archaeology of the Soul: North American Indian Belief and Ritual.* Urbana: University of Illinois Press, 1997.

Hall, Robert. "Ghosts, Water Barriers, Corn, and Sacred Enclosures in the Eastern Woodlands." *American Antiquity* 41 (1976): 360–364.

Hall, Robert. "In Search of the Ideology of the Adena–Hopewell Climax." In *Hopewell Ideology: The Chillicothe Conference,* edited by D. W. Brose and N. Greber, 258–265. Kent, Ohio: Kent State University Press, 1979.

Hall, Robert. "Red Banks, Oneota, and the Winnebago: Views from a Distant Rock." *Wisconsin Archeologist* 74, nos. 1–4 (1993): 10–79. [Special issue: "Exploring the Oneota–Winnebago Direct Historical Connection," edited by David F. Overstreet]

Hall, Robert. "Relating the Big Fish and the Big Stone: Reconsidering the Archaeological Identity and Habitat of the Winnebago in 1634." In *Oneota Archaeology: Past, Present, and Future,* edited by William Green, 19–32. Report no. 20. Iowa City: University of Iowa, Office of the State Archaeologist, 1995.

Haskins, R. W. "The Legend of the Winnebagos." *Wisconsin Historical Collections* 1 (1903): 86–92.

Henning, Dale. "Managing Oneota." *Wisconsin Archeologist* 79, no. 1 (1998): 122–130.

Henschel, Gary. "Henschel Mounds (47 Sb 29) as Possible Solstice Markers: A Progress Report." *Wisconsin Archeologist* 77, nos. 1–2 (1996): 73–77.

Hickerson, Harold. "The Feast of the Dead among the Seventeenth Century Algonkians of the Upper Great Lakes." *American Anthropologist* 62 (1960): 81–107.

Hieb, Jane A., ed. *Visions and Voices: Winnebago Elders Speak to the Children.* Trempealeau, Wis.: Western Dairyland Economic Opportunity Council, 1994.

Highsmith, Hugh. *The Mounds of Koshkonong and Rock River: A History of Ancient Indian Earthworks in Wisconsin.* Fort Atkinson, Wis.: Fort Atkinson Historical Society and Highsmith Press, 1997.

Hoffman, Walter. *The Menominee Indians.* Fourteenth Annual Report of the Bureau of American Ethnology, 1892–1893. Washington, D.C.: Smithsonian Institution, 1896.

Hollinger, R. Eric. "Residence Patterns and Oneota Cultural Dynamics." In *Oneota Archaeology: Past, Present, and Future,* edited by William Green, 141–174. Report no. 20. Iowa City: University of Iowa, Office of the State Archaeologist, 1995.

Hruska, Robert. "The Riverside Site: A Late Archaic Manifestation in Michigan." *Wisconsin Archeologist* 48, no. 3 (1967): 145–260.

Hurley, William M. *An Analysis of Effigy Mound Complexes in Wisconsin.* University of

Bibliography

Michigan, Museum of Anthropology Anthropological Papers, no. 59, Ann Arbor: University of Michigan, Museum of Anthropology, 1975.

Hurley, William M. "The Late Woodland Stage: Effigy Mound Culture." *Wisconsin Archeologist* 67, nos. 3–4 (1986): 283–301. [Special issue, "Introduction to Wisconsin Archeology," edited by William Green, James B. Stoltman, and Alice B. Kehoe]

Hyer, Nathaniel F. "Ruins of the Ancient City of Aztalan." *Milwaukee Advertiser,* 25 February 1837, n.p.

"Indian Mounds Tell History and Folklore." *McFarland Community Life,* 15 March 1995, 7.

Jeske, John A. "The Grand River Mound Group and Camp Site." *Bulletin of the Public Museum of the City of Milwaukee* 3, no. 2 (1927): 139–214.

Kane, Lucille M., June D. Holmquist, and Carolyn Gilman, eds. *The Northern Expeditions of Stephen H. Long: The Journals of 1817 and 1823 and Related Documents.* St. Paul: Minnesota Historical Society Press, 1978.

Kehoe, Alice. "The History of Wisconsin Archaeology." *Wisconsin Archeologist* 78, nos. 1–2 (1997): 11–21. [Special issue: "Wisconsin Archaeology," edited by Robert A. Birmingham, Carol I. Mason, and James B. Stoltman]

Kennedy, Roger G. *Hidden Cities: The Discovery and Loss of Ancient North American Civilization.* New York: Free Press, 1994.

Keyes, Charles R. "The Hill–Lewis Survey." *Minnesota History* 9, no. 2 (1928): 96–108.

Kolb, Jennifer L. "The Archaeological Resources of Northwestern Wisconsin: Region 1 Archaeology Program, 1987–1988." 1988. Burnett County Historical Society, Siren, Wisconsin.

Krupp, E. C. *Echoes of Ancient Skies: The Astronomy of Lost Civilizations.* New York: Harper & Row, 1983.

Lange, Frederick. "The Bigelow Site (47-Bt-29)." *Wisconsin Archeologist* 50, no. 4 (1969): 215–255.

[Lapham, Increase A.] "Antiquities of Wisconsin." *Milwaukee Advertiser,* 24 November 1836, 2.

Lapham, Increase A. *The Antiquities of Wisconsin, as Surveyed and Described.* Smithsonian Contributions to Knowledge, vol. 7. Washington, D.C.: Smithsonian Institution, 1855.

Lapham, Increase A. "Man-Shaped Mounds in Wisconsin." In *Report and Collections of the State Historical Society of Wisconsin for the Years 1857 and 1858,* Fourth Annual Report, 365–368. Madison: State Historical Society of Wisconsin, 1859.

Lapham, Increase A. *Wisconsin: Its Geography, Topography, History, Minerology: Together with Brief Sketches of Its Antiquities, Natural History, Soil, Productions, Population and Government.* Milwaukee: Hopkins, 1846.

Leonard, William Ellery. *The Locomotive God.* New York: Century, 1927.

Lewis, Theodore H. "The 'Monumental' Tortoise Mounds of De-coo-dah." *American Journal of Archaeology and History of the Fine Arts* 2 (1886): 65–69.

Bibliography

Lewis, Theodore H. *The Northwestern Archaeological Survey*. St. Paul, Minn.: Pioneer Press, 1898.

Link, Adolph W. "Symbolism of Certain Oneota Designs and Use of Lifeform Decoration on Mississippi Ceramics." *Wisconsin Archeologist* 76, nos. 1–2 (1995): 2–26.

Lurie, Nancy O. "Winnebago." In *Handbook of North American Indians*. Vol. 15, *Northeast*, edited by Bruce G. Trigger, 690–707. Washington, D.C.: Smithsonian Institution Press, 1978.

Lurie, Nancy O. "Winnebago Protohistory." In *Culture in History: Essays in Honor of Paul Radin*, edited by Stanley Diamond, 791–808. New York: Columbia University Press, 1960.

Mallam, R. Clark. "Birds, Bears, Panthers, 'Elephants,' and Archaeologists." *Wisconsin Archeologist* 61, no. 3 (1980): 375–384.

Mallam, R. Clark. "Ideology from the Earth: Effigy Mounds in the Midwest." *Archaeology* 35, no. 4 (1982): 60–64.

Mallam, R. Clark. *The Iowa Effigy Mound Manifestation: An Interpretative Model*. Report no. 9. Iowa City: University of Iowa, Office of the State Archaeologist, 1976.

Mallam, R. Clark. "The Mound Builders: An American Myth." *Journal of the Iowa Archeological Society* 23 (1976): 145–175.

Martin, T. B., and Richard Flavin. "Twisting History: The Lies of the Ancient American." *News from Indian Country*, January 1995, 6–7.

Mason, Carol I. "Archaeological Analogy and Ethnographic Example: A Case from the Winnebago." In "Indians, Colonists, and Slaves: Essays in Memory of Charles H. Fairbanks," *Florida Journal of Anthropology Special Publication*, no. 4 (1985), edited by Kenneth W. Johnson, Jonathan M. Leader, and Robert C. Wilson, 95–104.

Mason, Carol I. "Historic Identification and the Oneota." In *Cultural Change and Continuity: Essays in Honor of James Bennet Griffin*, edited by Charles E. Cleland, 335–348. New York: Academic Press, 1976.

Mason, Carol I. *Introduction to Wisconsin Indians: Prehistory to Statehood*. Salem, Wis.: Sheffield, 1988.

Mason, Ronald J. "Archaeo-ethnicity and the Elusive Menominis." *Midcontinental Journal of Archaeology* 22, no. 1 (1997): 69–94.

Mason, Ronald J. "Oneota and Winnebago Ethnogenesis: An Overview." *Wisconsin Archeologist* 74, nos. 1–4 (1993): 400–421.

Mason, Ronald J. "The Paleo-Indian Tradition." *Wisconsin Archeologist* 78, nos. 1–2 (1997): 78–111. [Special issue: "Wisconsin Archaeology," edited by Robert A. Birmingham, Carol I. Mason, and James B. Stoltman]

Mason, Ronald J., and Carol Irwin. "An Eden–Scottsbluff Burial in Northeastern Wisconsin." *American Antiquity* 26 (1960): 43–57.

McKern, W. C. *The Clam River Focus*. Milwaukee Public Museum Publications in Anthropology, no. 9. Milwaukee: Milwaukee Public Museum, 1963.

McKern, W. C. "The Kletzien and Nitschke Mound Groups." *Bulletin of the Public Museum of the City of Milwaukee* 3, no. 4 (1930): 417–572.

McKern, W. C. "The Midwest Taxonomic as an Aid to Archaeological Study." *American Antiquity* 4 (1939): 301–313.

McKern, W. C. "The Neale and McCaughry Mound Groups." *Bulletin of the Public Museum of the City of Milwaukee* 3, no. 3 (1928): 213–416.

McKern, W. C. "Preliminary Report on the Upper Mississippi Phase in Wisconsin." *Bulletin of the Public Museum of the City of Milwaukee* 16, no. 3 (1945): 109–235.

McKern, W. C. "A Wisconsin Variant of the Hopewell Culture." *Bulletin of the Public Museum of the City of Milwaukee* 10, no. 2 (1931): 185–328.

McKusick, Marshal. *The Davenport Conspiracy.* Iowa City: University of Iowa Press, 1970.

McKusick, Marshal. "A Disturbed Bear that Bears Watching and Other Remarks on an Iowa Effigy Mound Interpretive Model." *Wisconsin Archeologist* 61, no. 3 (1980): 352–358.

Mead, Barbara. "The Rehbein I Site (47-Ri-81)." *Wisconsin Archeologist* 60, no. 2 (1979): 91–182.

Meinholz, Norman, and Jennifer Kolb. *The Statz Site: A Late Woodland Community and Archaic Workshop in Dane County, Wisconsin.* Museum Archaeology Program, Archaeology Research Series, no. 5. Madison: State Historical Society of Wisconsin, 1997.

Meinholz, Norman M., and Steven Kuehn. *The Deadman Slough Site.* Museum Archaeology Program, Archaeology Research Series, no. 4. Madison: State Historical Society of Wisconsin, 1996.

Milner, George R. *The Cahokia Chiefdom: The Archaeology of a Mississippian Society.* Washington, D.C.: Smithsonian Institution Press, 1998.

Milner, George R. "An Osteological Perspective on Prehistoric Warfare." In *Regional Approaches to Mortuary Analysis,* edited by Lane Anderson Beck, 221–238. New York: Plenum, 1995.

Mink, Claudia Gellman. *Cahokia: City of the Sun.* Collinsville, Ill.: Cahokia Mounds Museum Society, 1995.

Mires, Peter, Jennifer L. Kolb, and Edgar S. Oerichbauer. "The Archaeological Resources of Northwestern Wisconsin: Region 1 Program, 1988–1989." 1989. Division of Historic Preservation, State Historical Society of Wisconsin, Madison.

O'Gorman, Jody. *The Tremaine Complex: Oneota Occupation in the La Crosse Locality, Wisconsin.* Museum Archaeology Program, Archaeology Research Series, no. 3. 3 vols. Madison: State Historical Society of Wisconsin, 1994.

Overstreet, David F. "The Convent Knoll Site (47Wk327): A Red Ocher Cemetery in Waukesha, Wisconsin." *Wisconsin Archeologist* 61, no. 1 (1980): 34–90.

Overstreet, David F. "Oneota Prehistory and History." *Wisconsin Archeologist* 78, nos. 1–2 (1997): 250–297. [Special issue: "Wisconsin Archaeology," edited by Robert A. Birmingham, Carol I. Mason, and James B. Stoltman]

Overstreet, David F. *Oneota Tradition Culture History—New Data from the Old Spring*

Bibliography

Site (47Wn350). Great Lakes Archaeological Research Center, Reports of Investigations, no. 219. Milwaukee: Great Lakes Archaeological Research Center, 1989.

Overstreet, David F., Larry Doebert, Gary W. Henschel, Phil Sander, and David Wasion. "Two Red Ocher Mortuary Contexts form Southeastern Wisconsin—the Henschel Site (47 Sb 29), Sheboygan County and the Barnes Creek Site (47 Kn 41) Kenosha County." *Wisconsin Archeologist* 77, nos. 1–2 (1996): 36–62.

Overstreet, David F., with Daniel J. Joyce, Ruth Blazina-Joyce, David Wasion, and Keith A. Sverdrup. *FY 1992 Historic Preservation Survey and Planning Grant: Early Holocene Megafaunal Exploitation, Kenosha County, Wisconsin*. Great Lakes Archaeological Research Center, Reports of Investigations, no. 325. Milwaukee: Great Lakes Archaeological Research Center, 1993.

Overstreet, David F., with David Wasion, Keith A. Sverdrup, and Michael Kolb. *FY 1993 Historic Preservation Survey and Planning Grant: Ice Age Landscapes of Southeastern Wisconsin*. Great Lakes Archaeological Research Center, Reports of Investigations, no. 366. Milwaukee: Great Lakes Archaeological Research Center, 1994.

Peet, Stephen D. *Emblematic Mounds and Animal Effigies*. Vol. 2 of *Prehistoric America*. Chicago: American Antiquarian Office, 1898.

Peet, Stephen D. "The Mound Builders." *American Antiquarian* 2, no. 3 (1880): 185–199.

Penman, John T. "Late Woodland Sites in Southwestern Grant County, Wisconsin." *Journal of the Iowa Archeological Society* 32 (1985): 1–36.

Philips, Ruth Bliss. "Dreams and Designs: Iconographic Problems in Great Lakes Twined Bags." In *Great Lakes Indian Art*, edited by David W. Penny, 52–68. Detroit: Wayne State University Press and the Detroit Institute of Arts, 1989.

Pidgeon, William. *Traditions of De-coo-dah and Antiquarian Researches: Comprising Extensive Explorations, Surveys, and Excavations of the Wonderful and Mysterious Earthen Remains of the Mound-Builders in America; the Traditions of the Last Prophet of the Elk Nation Relative to Their Origin and Use; and the Evidences of an Ancient Population More Numerous Than the Present Aborigines*. New York: Thayer, Bridgman, and Fanning, 1853.

Radin, Paul. *The Road of Life and Death*. Bollingen Series, no. 5. New York: Pantheon Books, 1945.

Radin, Paul. "Some Aspects of Winnebago Archaeology." *American Anthropologist* 13 (1911): 517–538.

Radin, Paul. *The Winnebago Tribe*. Thirty-seventh Annual Report of the Bureau of American Ethnology, 1923. Lincoln: University of Nebraska Press, 1990.

Richards, John D. "Ceramics and Culture at Aztalan: A Late Prehistoric Village in Southeastern Wisconsin." Ph.D. diss., University of Wisconsin–Milwaukee, 1992.

Riggs, Rodney E. "Human Skeletal Remains from the Poor Man's Farrah (47-Gt-365) and the Bade (47-Gt-365) Sites in Southwestern Wisconsin." *Journal of the Iowa Archeological Society* 32 (1985): 37–74.

Bibliography

Ritzenthaler, Robert. "The Osceola Site: An 'Old Copper' Site near Potosi, Wisconsin." *Wisconsin Archeologist* 38, no. 4 (1957): 186–203. [Special issue: "The Old Copper Culture in Wisconsin," edited by Robert Ritzenthaler]

Ritzenthaler, Robert. "Radiocarbon Dates for the Clam River Focus." *Wisconsin Archeologist* 47, no. 4 (1966): 219–220.

Ritzenthaler, Robert. "The Riddle of the Spencer Lake Horse Skull." *Wisconsin Archeologist* 45, no. 2 (1964): 115–123.

Ritzenthaler, Robert, ed. "Aztalan: Exploration and Reconstruction" [special issue]. *Wisconsin Archeologist* 39, no. 1 (1958).

Ritzenthaler, Robert, ed. "The Old Copper Culture in Wisconsin" [special issue]. *Wisconsin Archeologist* 38, no. 4 (1957).

Rodell, Roland L. "The Diamond Bluff Site Complex and Cahokia Influence in the Red Wing Locality." In *Perspectives on Cahokia: Views from the Periphery,* edited by James B. Stoltman, 253–279. Madison, Wis.: Prehistory Press, 1991.

Rowe, Chandler. *The Effigy Mound Culture of Wisconsin.* Milwaukee Public Museum Publications in Anthropology, no. 3. Milwaukee: Milwaukee Public Museum, 1956.

Rusch, Lynn A. "The Early and Late Woodland Occupations at the Bachman Site in East Central Wisconsin." 1988. State Historical Society of Wisconsin, Madison.

Sagan, Carl. *The Demon Haunted World: Science as a Candle in the Dark.* New York: Random, House, 1995.

Salkin, Philip H. "The Lake Farms Phase: The Early Woodland Stage in South Central Wisconsin as Seen from the Lake Farms Archaeological District." In *Early Woodland Archaeology,* edited by Kenneth B. Farnsworth and Thomas E. Emerson, 92–120. Kampsville Seminars in Archaeology, vol. 2. Kampsville, Ill.: Center for American Archaeology Press, 1986.

Salkin, Philip H. "A Reevaluation of the Late Woodland Stage in Southeastern Wisconsin." *Wisconsin Academy Review* 33, no. 2 (1987): 75–79.

Salzer, Robert J. "Oral Literature and Archaeology." *Wisconsin Archeologist* 74, nos. 1–4 (1993): 80–119.

Salzer, Robert J. "Preliminary Report on the Gottschall Site (47Ia80)." *Wisconsin Archeologist* 68, no. 4 (1987): 419–472.

Salzer, Robert J. "The Wisconsin North Lakes Project: A Preliminary Report." In *Aspects of Upper Great Lakes Anthropology,* edited by Elden Johnson, 40–54. Minnesota Prehistoric Archaeology Series, no. 11. St. Paul: Minnesota Historical Society, 1974.

Salzer, Robert J. "The Woodland Tradition: An Introduction." *Wisconsin Archeologist* 67, nos. 3–4 (1986): 239–243. [Special issue, "Introduction to Wisconsin Archeology," edited by William Green, James B. Stoltman, and Alice B. Kehoe]

Salzer, Robert J., and Larry A. Johns. "Final Report of the Dane County Indian Mounds Identification Project." 1992. Division of Historic Preservation, State Historical Society of Wisconsin, Madison.

Sampson, Kelvin W. "Conventionalized Figures on Woodland Ceramics." *Wisconsin Archeologist* 69, no. 3 (1988): 163–188.

Bibliography

Scherz, James P. "Pertinent Aspects of Geometry, Astronomy, Distance, and Time." *Journal of the Ancient Earthworks Society* 3 (1991): M-1–M-52.

Silverberg, Robert. *The Mound Builders of Ancient America.* New York: New York Graphic Society, 1968.

Smith, Bruce D. Introduction to *Report on the Mound Explorations of the Bureau of Ethnology,* by Cyrus Thomas. Washington, D.C.: Smithsonian Institution Press, 1985.

Smith, David Lee. "History of the Winnebago and Relationship to the Mounds." Speech delivered at the fiftieth anniversary celebration of Effigy Mounds National Monument, Marquette, Iowa, 14 August 1999.

Spindler, Louise S. "Menominee." In *Handbook of North American Indians.* Vol. 15, *Northeast,* edited by Bruce G. Trigger, 708–724. Washington, D.C.: Smithsonian Institution Press, 1978.

Springer, James Warren, and Stanley R. Witkowski. "Siouan Linguistics and Oneota Archaeology." In *Oneota Studies,* edited by Guy Gibbon, 69–84. University of Minnesota Publications in Anthropology, no. 1. Minneapolis: Department of Anthropology, University of Minnesota, 1982.

Squier, Ephraim G., and Edgar H. Davis. *Ancient Monuments of the Mississippi Valley.* Smithsonian Contributions to Knowledge, vol. 1. Washington, D.C.: Smithsonian Institution, 1848.

Squier, George H. "Certain Archaeological Features of Western Wisconsin." *Wisconsin Archeologist,* o.s., 4, no. 2 (1914): 29–30.

Stekel, Frank D., Larry A. Johns, and James P. Scherz. "Whitewater Effigy Mounds Park: The Maples Mound Group." *Wisconsin Archeologist* 72, nos. 1–2 (1991): 118–126.

Sterling, William T. "A Visit to Aztalan in 1838." *Wisconsin Archeologist* 19, no. 1 (1920): 18–19.

Stevenson, Katherine P., Robert F. Boszhardt, Charles R. Moffat, Philip H. Salkin, Thomas C. Pleger, James L. Theler, and Constance M. Arzigian. "The Woodland Tradition." *Wisconsin Archeologist* 78, nos. 1–2 (1997): 250–297. [Special issue: "Wisconsin Archaeology," edited by Robert A. Birmingham, Carol I. Mason, and James B. Stoltman]

Steward, Julian H. *Theory of Cultural Change.* Urbana: University of Illinois Press, 1955.

Stoltman, James B. "Ancient Peoples of the Upper Mississippi River Valley." In *Historic Lifestyles in the Upper Mississippi River Valley,* edited by John Wozniac, 197–255. New York: University Press of America, 1983.

Stoltman, James B. "The Appearance of the Mississippian Cultural Tradition in the Upper Mississippi Valley." In *Prehistoric Mound Builders of the Mississippi Valley,* edited by James B. Stoltman, 26–34. Davenport, Iowa: Putnam Museum, 1986.

Stoltman, James B. "The Archaic Tradition." *Wisconsin Archeologist* 78, nos. 1–2 (1997): 112–139. [Special issue, "Wisconsin Archaeology," edited by Robert A. Birmingham, Carol I. Mason, and James B. Stoltman]

Stoltman, James B., and George W. Christiansen. "The Late Woodland Stage in the

Bibliography

Driftless Area of the Upper Mississippi Valley." In *Late Woodland Societies: Tradition and Transformation across the Mid-Continent,* edited by Thomas Emerson, Dale McElrath, and Andrew Fortier. Lincoln: University of Nebraska Press, in press.

Stout, Arlow B. "Prehistoric Earthworks in Wisconsin." *Ohio Archaeological and Historical Quarterly* 20, no 1 (1911): 1–30.

Stout, Arlow B. "The Winnebago and the Mounds." *Wisconsin Archeologist,* o.s., 9, no 4 (1910–1911): 101–103.

Struever, Stuart. "Woodland Subsistence-Settlement Systems in the Lower Illinois River Valley." In *New Perspectives in Archeology,* edited by S. R. Binford and L. Binford, 285–312. Chicago: Aldine, 1968.

Sullivan, Norman C. "Tuberculosis in a Late Woodland Effigy Mound Population." *Wisconsin Archeologist* 66, no. 1 (1995): 71–76.

Swanton, John R. *Indian Tribes of the Lower Mississippi Valley and Adjacent Coast of the Gulf of Mexico.* Bureau of American Ethnology, Bulletin no. 43. Washington, D.C.: Smithsonian Institution, 1911.

Taylor, Richard C. "Notes Respecting Certain Indian Mounds and Earthworks in the Form of Animal Effigies, Chiefly in Wisconsin Territory, U.S." *American Journal of Science and Art* 34 (1838): 88–104.

Taylor, Stephen. "Description of Ancient Remains, Animal Mounds and Embankments, Principally in the Counties of Grant, Iowa and Richland, in Wisconsin Territory." *American Journal of Science and Art* 44 (1843): 21–40.

Theler, James L. "The Early Woodland Component at the Mill Pond Site, Wisconsin." In *Early Woodland Archaeology,* edited by Kenneth B. Farnsworth and Thomas E. Emerson, 137–158. Kampsville Seminars in Archaeology, vol. 2. Kampsville, Ill.: Center for American Archaeology Press, 1986.

Thomas, Cyrus. *Report on the Mound Explorations of the Bureau of Ethnology.* Twelfth Annual Report of the Bureau of American Ethnology, 1890–1891. Washington, D.C.: Smithsonian Institution Press, 1985.

Trigger, Bruce. *The Children of Aataentsic: A History of the Huron People to 1660.* 2 vols. Montreal and Kingston: McGill–Queen's University Press, 1976.

Van Langen, Howard, and Thomas F. Kehoe. "Hilgen Spring Park Mound." *Wisconsin Archeologist* 52, no. 1 (1971): 1–19.

Warriner, Pliny. "Legend of the Winnebagos." *Wisconsin Historical Collections* 1 (1903): 86–93.

West, George A. "The Indian Authorship of Wisconsin Antiquities." *Wisconsin Archeologist,* o.s., 6, no. 4 (1907): 167–256.

Willey, Gordon R., and Jeremy A. Sabloff. *A History of American Archaeology.* San Francisco: Freeman, 1968.

Williams, Stephen. *Fantastic Archaeology: The Wild Side of North American Prehistory.* Philadelphia: University of Pennsylvania Press, 1991.

Witthoft, J. *Green Corn Ceremonialism in the Eastern Woodlands.* University of Michigan, Museum of Anthropology, Occasional Contributions, no. 13, Ann Arbor: University of Michigan, Museum of Anthropology, 1949.

Bibliography

Wittry, Warren L. "Archaeological Studies of Four Wisconsin Rockshelters." *Wisconsin Archeologist* 40, no. 4 (1959): 137–267.

Wittry, Warren L. "Discovering and Interpreting the Cahokia in Woodhenges." *Wisconsin Archeologist* 77, nos. 3–4 (1996): 26–35. [Special issue, "The Ancient Sky Watchers of Cahokia: Woodhenges, Eclipses, and Cahokia Cosmology," edited by Melvin L. Fowler]

Wittry, Warren L. "The Kolterman Mound 18 Radiocarbon Date." *Wisconsin Archeologist* 37, no. 4 (1956): 133–134.

Index

Adams site, 148, 171
Adena Complex, 83–84, 96–97
Algonquian-speaking peoples, 20, 38, 49, 118, 134, 165, 174
American Antiquarian Society, 5, 23
American Ethnological Society, 14, 18
Ancient Earthworks Society, 62
Antiquarians, 18, 39
Archaic tradition, 74–81, 86
Armstrong site, 171
Ashland County, 137
Astronomical observations, 62, 128–133, 145, 159
Atwater, Caleb, 18
Avoca Mound Group, 202
Aztalan, 8, 21, 23, 41, 45, 47, 51, 105, 124, 148, 152–162, 164, 175, 202

Bachman Site, 87
Bade Mound Group, 59
Baraboo, 41, 45, 111, 121, 125, 205
Barrett, Samuel, 36, 46, 66, 155, 158, 159
Barron County, 32, 96, 193
Baum Mound Group, 195
Bayfield County, 137
Beach Site, 87
Bear ceremonialism, 95, 96, 124
Beloit, 27
Benn, David, 67, 88, 104, 121
Bennett, H. H., 195
Bettis, Arthur, 67
Bigelow Site, 53–54, 138
Black Earth, 121
Blackhawk, John, 45, 174
Black River, 95

Black River Falls, 45, 174
Blue Mounds, 5, 22
Bone bundles. *See* Burial customs
Brown, Charles E., 9, 11, 35, 37, 39–45, 47, 52, 66, 116, 118, 122, 174, 186, 195, 197, 199, 200, 201
Brown County, 73
Bureau of Ethnology, 31–32, 37, 38, 201
Burial customs, 3, 32, 47, 73, 77, 78, 79, 85, 91, 93–95, 127, 138, 141, 155–156, 158, 171, 174, 177, 201
Burial Sites Preservation Law, 10, 60, 95, 181–184
Burial Sites Preservation Program, 30
Burnett County, 50, 172
Burnett County Historical Society, 58
Burrows Park, 195

Caciques, 143, 145, 151, 155
Cahokia. *See* Mississippian culture
Calumet ceremony, 171–172
Calumet County Park, 40, 194
Canfield, W. H., 205
Cannibalism, 161
Cedarburg, 90
Ceremonial centers. *See* Mounds, function
Chain (compound) mounds, 113. *See also* Mounds
Charnel houses. *See* Burial customs
Cherokee, 16
Chetek, 45
Chief Winneshiek. *See* Winneshiek, Chief
Chillicothe, Ohio, 18–19
Chippewa, 13, 20, 36, 38, 52, 59, 60, 172, 173, 174, 177, 178, 181

Index

Choctaw, 17
Christiansen, George, 152
Clam Lake Mound, 50, 137–138, 139, 140, 172
Clans, 21–23, 36–37, 52, 66, 92, 116–118, 119, 124, 125, 128–129, 141, 167, 171
Climate change, 98, 101, 103, 162
Collared ware. *See* Pottery
Columbia County, 195
Conical mounds, 5–6, 32, 50, 83–84, 90–91, 92–96, 125, 137–138, 152, 158–159, 171, 172–173. *See also* Mounds
Cooper, Leland, 172
Cooper Mound Site, Minnesota, 173
Copper. *See* Old Copper Complex/culture
Cranberry Creek Mound Group, 6, 110
Crawfish River, 21, 124, 148, 152, 159, 202
Crawford County, 32
Creek, 17, 142, 161
Cremation. *See* Burial customs
Cutler Park, 41, 45, 207
Cyrus Thomas Mound Group, 96, 201

Dakota, 36, 38, 50, 51, 53, 116, 138, 172, 173, 174, 181
Dane County, 21, 32, 116, 120, 130, 163, 183, 184, 195–200
Dane County Parks Department, 59
Daughters of the American Revolution, 41, 203
Davenport, Iowa, 32
Davis, Edgar H., 18, 62
Delaware. *See* Leni-Lenape
De Soto, Hernando, 17, 142, 155, 159
Devil's Lake State Park, 120, 205
Diamond Bluff Site, 6, 148, 152–153, 171
Dick, Fred, 122
Diffusionist theories, 9, 61–64
Disease, 17, 57, 103, 167–168, 173–174
Division of Mound Exploration. *See* Bureau of Ethnology
DNA testing, 58, 185
Dobbs, Clark, 153
Dodge County, 53, 124, 138, 177
Door Peninsula, 167, 169
Douglas County, 137
Drexel, Reverend, 201
Dunn County, 201

Eagle Township, Richland County, 25, 110, 120, 121
Early Woodland stage, 82–83, 86–91

Earth-Diver, Earth-Maker. *See* Native American cosmology
Edgewood Mound Group, 196
Edna Taylor Conservancy, 196
Effigy mounds, 5, 6–7, 22, 29, 37, 53–54, 109–136, 138–141, 152. *See also* Late Woodland stage; Mounds
Effigy Mounds National Monument, Iowa, 138, 208
Elm Grove, 79
Elmside Park, 186–187, 196
Enclosures, 7, 66, 84, 96–97, 98, 109, 135, 160, 207
Equinoxes. *See* Astronomical observations
Ethnocentrism, 9, 61–62

Fagan, Brian, 79
Farwell's Point Mound Group, 197
Feast of the Dead, 77–78, 137, 138
Federated Women's Clubs of Wisconsin, 41
Fell, Barry, 61
Fish Lake, 207
Forest Hill Cemetery, 182, 197
Fort Atkinson, 125, 127, 203
Fort Atkinson Historical Society, 203
Four Lakes, 5, 37, 42, 116, 130, 136, 163, 195. *See also* Madison
Fox, 33, 36, 38, 52, 147, 174
Fox Bluff Mound Group, 42
Fox River, 4, 96, 112, 167, 174
Freckman, Kermit, 207
Fred Edwards Site, 148, 150, 161

Gallatin, Albert, 14, 18
General Atkinson Mound Group, 203
Gerend, Alphonse, 90
Gilmore, Reverend P. M., 43
Glendale, 126
Glenn, Robert, 201
Glottochronology, 165
Goldstein, Lynne, 112, 160
Goodland County Park, 195
Gottschall Rockshelter, 55, 67, 119, 121, 148, 149–150
Governor Nelson State Park, 3, 198
Grand Medicine Society, 134
Grand Village, 171
Grant County, 32, 52, 59, 77, 102, 201
Grant River, 150
Great Lakes Intertribal Council, 59
Green Bay, 20, 110, 167, 169
Green Corn Ceremony, 145, 157, 159, 160

Green Lake County, 171
Greenwood Mound Group, 158, 160

Hall, Robert L., 11, 66–67, 86, 91, 113,
    115–116, 119, 122, 125, 141, 171
Hancock, 207
Harbor Springs Mound Group, 124
Harper's Ferry Great Mound Group, Iowa,
    110
Heckewelder, John, 16
Henschel, Gary, 133
Henschel Mound Group, 90, 91, 93, 124,
    133
High Cliff State Park, 3, 194
Highsmith, Hugh, 203
Hilgen Spring Mound Group, 90, 91, 93
Hill, Alfred J., 27
Hixton Silicified Sandstone, 71, 73, 95,
    143, 147, 151
Hoaxes, 32, 50
Ho-Chunk (Winnebago), 11, 13, 20,
    36–38, 44–45, 49, 50, 51, 52, 59,
    66–67, 91, 107, 116–118, 119, 121,
    122, 125, 132, 141, 165, 167, 169–171,
    174–175, 177, 178, 179, 181, 185, 186,
    187, 198, 199, 200, 205
Hoffman, Walter, 36
Hopewell, 7, 51, 84–86, 92–98
Hornung Mound Group, 200
Hudson Park, 196
Hurley, William, 53–54, 64, 136, 138
Huron, 77, 161
Hyer, Nathaniel, 21

Indian Mound Park, Chetek, 45
Indian Mound Park, McFarland, 198
Indian Mounds Campground, 204
Indian Mounds Park, New Lisbon, 204
Indian Mounds Park, Rice Lake, 193
Intaglios, 46, 125–127, 203, 206
Iowa County, 21, 119, 121, 141, 174,
    202
Ioway, 51, 67, 121, 165, 167, 174,
    181
Iron County, 137

Jackson County, 73
Jefferson, Thomas, 15
Jefferson County, 8, 21, 148, 163, 202–203
Jefferson County Indian Mounds and Trail
    Park, 203
Johns, Larry, 59, 133
Juneau County, 6, 204

Kenosha County, 71
Key-hole structures, 103, 157
Kickapoo, 174
Kickapoo River, 59
Kingsley Bend Mound Group, 195
Kletzien Mound Group, 206
Kolterman Effigy Mound Site, 53, 138
Kratz Creek Mound Group, 46, 66
Krupp, E. C., 132–133

La Crosse, 45, 59, 110, 167, 170
Lake Buffalo, 46
Lake Butte des Morts, 33
Lake Koshkonong, 37, 96, 112, 161, 162,
    167
Lake Mendota, 43, 44, 96, 110, 118, 124,
    129, 130, 188, 195, 197, 198
Lake Menomin, 201
Lake Michigan, 49, 174
Lake Michigan ware. See Pottery
Lake Mills, 45, 124, 152, 202
Lake Monona, 60, 96, 111, 124, 181,
    186–187, 196, 199, 201
Lake Park, 45, 204
Lake Side Park, 202
Lake Superior, 174
Lake Tomahawk, 204
Lake Waubesa, 87, 195, 198
Lake Wingra, 44, 122
Lake Winnebago, 20, 40, 167, 194
La Mere, Oliver, 37, 45, 122
Lapham, Increase, 5, 7, 8, 14, 21, 23–24,
    42, 97, 155, 175, 176, 177, 194, 203,
    205, 207
La Pointe, 20
Late Woodland stage, 100–142, 159–
    160, 161, 164–165. See also Effigy
    mounds
La Valle Man Mound, 120
Lemonweir River, 204
Lemonweir Rock Art Site, 108
Leni-Lenape (Delaware), 16
Leonard, William Ellery, 42–43
Lewis, Theodore H., 26–29, 42, 64, 121,
    135, 136, 151
Lewis Mound Group, 198
Libby, Willard, 53
Linear mounds, 6, 22, 29, 37, 109, 125,
    137. See also Mounds
Lizard Mounds County Park, 62–63,
    122–123, 132–133, 206–207
Long, Stephen H., 4
Longhouses, 37, 59, 167

Index

"Lost Race" myth, 8–9, 14–20, 21, 24, 33–34, 35, 36, 61–62, 84
Lowerworld. *See* Native American cosmology
Lurie, Nancy, 39

Madison, 3, 9, 37, 42, 44, 45, 71, 72, 87, 110, 111, 112, 122, 136, 182, 186–187, 195–198, 200
Madison ware. *See* Pottery
Mallam, R. Clark, 33, 57, 67, 109, 110, 112, 113, 115, 129
Man Mound County Park, 41, 45, 110–111, 120, 121, 205
Maples Mills Mound Group, 133
Marquette, Iowa, 208
Marquette County, 46
Mason, Carol I., 173
Mason, Ronald, 67, 118
Mauston, 108
McFarland, 9, 198
McKern, William C., 38–39, 48–51, 52, 67, 137–138, 172
Mendota State Hospital Mound Group, 7, 110, 112, 118, 197
Menominee, 13, 20, 36, 38, 47, 49, 51, 52, 107, 116, 118, 124, 141, 165, 171, 174, 175, 177, 178, 181
Menominee County, 53, 137
Menominee River, 79
Menomonie, 201
Mero Complex, 6, 153
Miami, 174
Middle Mississippian culture. *See* Mississippian culture
Middle Woodland stage, 84–86, 92–99, 160
Mill Pond Site, 87
Millville Site, 96, 100
Milwaukee, 5, 23, 45, 79, 125, 126, 177, 204
Milwaukee County, 163, 204
Milwaukee River, 90, 124
Minnesota Historical Society, 27
Mississippian culture, 47, 49, 119, 121, 132, 141, 142–162, 164, 167, 169
Mississippi River, 20, 25, 27, 32, 48, 77, 87, 92, 102, 110, 112, 119, 142–147, 150, 152, 167, 171, 201, 208
Monona, 6, 93, 181, 186, 199
Monona Landmarks Commission, 186
"Mound Builder Myth," 8
Mound Cemetery, 45
Mounds: chronology, 5–6, 33, 49, 50–51,

53–54, 138; construction, 46, 47, 85, 91–95, 125–138, 155–157; distribution, 6, 57, 92, 110, 111–112, 115–124, 136–137; excavation, 32, 46–48, 50, 53, 90–95, 96, 172; function, 32, 37, 47, 54, 57, 67, 84–86, 98–99, 109, 121, 127–134, 140–141, 155–159, 186; historic use, 21, 172–175, 177, 200; preservation, 41–45, 59, 60, 106; reconstruction, 43, 44, 59, 67, 155, 195; symbolism, 21–23, 36, 37, 52, 66–67, 86, 91, 93, 109, 113–125, 129. *See also* Chain mounds; Conical mounds; Effigy mounds; Linear mounds; Platform mounds
Mount Horeb, 120
Muscoda, 5, 7, 25
Myrick Park, 45

Natchez, 17, 142, 143
National Historic Preservation Act of 1966, 58, 60
National Register of Historic Places, 58
Native American cosmology, 37, 66, 82, 88, 91, 104–108, 113–125, 129, 152, 160, 169, 194
Native American Graves and Repatriation Act, 60, 183–184
Necedah, 110
Nelson Dewey State Park, 3
New Lisbon, 204
News from Indian Country, 64
Nicholls Mound, 92, 93, 94, 95
Nine Springs Mound Group, 124
Nitschke Mound Group, 124, 138
Northern Highlands/American Legion State Forest, 204
Northwestern Archaeological Survey, 27

Observatory Hill Mounds, 198
Office of the State Archaeologist, 30, 41, 115
Olbrich Park, 196
Old Copper Complex/culture, 51, 75–77, 79
Oneida County, 204
Oneota, 49, 51, 101, 102, 119, 141, 152, 161, 162, 163–170, 171, 185
Oral tradition, 11, 32, 37–39, 67–68, 167, 173–175, 181
Osceola Site, 77
Ossuary. *See* Burial customs
Outlet Mound Group, 93, 186, 199, 201

Paleo-Indian tradition, 69–73
Panther intaglio, 203
Papal Edict of 1537, 15
Peet, Reverend Stephen, 16, 27
Perrot State Park, 3
Pheasant Branch Mound Group, 124
Picnic Point Mounds, 199
Pidgeon, William, 24–27
Pierce County, 6, 152
Platform mounds, 8, 17, 21, 47, 143,
    150–152, 155–157. *See also* Aztalan; Mis-
    sissippian culture; Mounds
Poor Man's Farrah, 102, 103
Portage County, 138
Potawatomi, 13, 20, 38, 49, 52, 126, 174,
    175, 176, 177, 178
Pottery, 49, 88–89, 104–108, 150, 152,
    160, 161, 168–170, 173, 195
Poverty Point, Louisiana, 82, 132
Powell, John Wesley, 30, 31
Prairie du Chien, 4, 20, 25, 45, 92, 95, 177,
    201
"Princess" Burial. *See* Aztalan
Pseudoscience, 25–26, 60–61
Public Museum of the City of Milwaukee,
    35, 36, 46, 48, 50, 91, 92–93, 96, 137,
    155, 206

Racine, 45
Radin, Paul, 37–38, 48–49, 66, 67,
    116–118, 119, 168, 174–175
Radiocarbon dating, 51, 53, 55
Raisbeck Mound Group, 52, 102, 128
Rave, John, 37
Red Cedar River, 201
Red Horn, 67, 119, 121, 149
Red ocher, 79, 82, 90, 138–139
Red Ocher Complex, 79–82, 86, 89–90
Red Wing, Minnesota, 152
Rehbain I Mound Group, 59
Renier Site, 73
Rice Lake, 96, 172, 193, 201
Rice Lake Mound Group, 172, 193
Richards, John, 160
Richland County, 29, 59, 110, 118, 120, 184
Ritzenthaler, Robert, 50
Riverside Site, Michigan, 79
Rock River, 96, 112, 127, 203
Rowe, Chandler, 52, 57, 66, 113, 116
Roxbury Creek, 200

Salzer, Robert, 67, 119, 121
Sampson, Kelvin, 104, 107

Sanders Site, 53–54, 136, 138
Santee Sioux. *See* Dakota
Satterlee, John, 47
Sauk, 36, 38, 52, 120, 174
Sauk City, 200
Sauk County, 120, 205
Sauk County Historical Society, 41, 205
Scaffold burials. *See* Burial customs
Scherz, James, 7, 62–63, 64,ß 121, 132–133
Schwert Mound Group, 48, 93
Sheboygan, 87, 206
Sheboygan County, 32, 90, 133, 206
Sheboygan Indian Mound County Park, 206
Sheboygan Marsh, 90, 124, 133
Sherwood, 194
Signal Hill Mound Group, 201
Silverberg, Robert, 14–15, 16, 17, 25
Silver Mound, 73, 95, 143, 151
Siouan-speaking peoples, 20, 38, 49, 52,
    134, 149, 165
Skare Site, 71, 72
Skinner, Alanson, 36, 47
Smithsonian Institution, 5, 14, 18, 23, 26,
    31, 33, 34, 35, 92, 172, 193, 201
Social status, 76–77, 79, 84, 85–86, 95–96,
    98–99, 100, 128, 143–145, 159
Society of American Indians, 44
Solstices. *See* Astronomical observations
Spanish *entrada,* 17
Spencer Lake Mound, 50, 138, 172
Springer, James, 165
Springs, 90, 91, 112, 122–133, 199
Squier, Ephraim G., 18, 62
Squier, George, 151
State Fair Park, 45
State Historical Society of Wisconsin, 3, 36,
    37, 40, 41, 42, 58, 59, 115, 122, 136,
    174, 183
State Historic Preservation Offices, 58
Statz Site, 103, 104, 134
Stekel, Frank, 133
Stevens Point, 53
Stockbridge, 194
Stoltman, James B., 152
Stout, Arlow B., 37, 42, 52, 66, 116, 122

Taylor, Richard C., 5, 21, 36, 175
Temple mounds. *See* Platform mounds
Ten Lost Tribes of Israel, 8, 15
Territorial markers, 77, 79, 133
Theresa, 177
Thomas, Cyrus, 31–33, 35, 36, 110, 172,
    201–202

Index

Tollackson Mound Group, 131
Trade, 73, 75–77, 79, 84, 86, 95, 96, 97,
    98, 99, 145–149, 150–151, 160, 161
Transoceanic contact. *See* Diffusionist theo-
    ries
Trempealeau, 93, 95
Trempealeau County, 48, 92, 135, 171
Trempealeau Mounds, 148, 150
Trempealeau River, 92, 95
Tuberculosis, 57, 103

University of Wisconsin–Madison, 43, 44,
    155, 198, 199
University of Wisconsin–Milwaukee, 58,
    155, 157, 159
Upper Mississippian culture. *See* Oneota
Upper Wakanda Park Mound Group, 201
Upperworld. *See* Native American cos-
    mology
Utley, 138

Vernon County, 32, 131
Vilas Park, 200
Vilas Park Circle, 200
Von Däniken, Erich, 61

Wa-con-jaz-gah. *See* Yellow Thunder
Wakanda Park, 53, 201
Warfare, 6, 16, 17, 79, 98, 103, 107, 140,
    145, 147, 161–162, 167, 173–174
Washington County, 123, 206–207
Water spirits. *See* Native American cos-
    mology

Waukesha, 21, 41, 45, 176
Waukesha County, 163, 177, 207
Waunakee, 103, 198
Waupaca County, 138
Waushara County, 207
West, George A., 36
West Allis, 45
West Bend, 122, 206–207
Whistler Mound Group and Enclosure, 207
White, Joseph, 45
Whitehorse, Harry, 186–187, 196
Whitewater Indian Mound Park, 133
Winnebago. *See* Ho-Chunk
Winneshiek, Chief, 45
Wisconsin Archeological Society, 35, 40,
    41, 42, 44, 45, 122, 186, 199, 200, 201,
    205
Wisconsin Archeological Survey, 155
Wisconsin Dells, 37, 45, 122, 179, 195
Wisconsin Natural History Survey, 40
Wisconsin River, 4, 5, 7, 25, 29, 92, 96,
    100, 108, 112, 118, 119–121, 136, 163,
    175, 200, 201, 202
Witkowski, Stanley, 165
Wittry, Warren, 55
Woodward Shores Mound Group, 130
Works Progress Administration, 195
Wyalusing State Park, 3, 45, 201

Yahara River, 72, 103, 196
Yellow River, 110
Yellow Thunder, 45, 179
Yellow Thunder, Albert, 45